NEW YORK TIMES BESTSELLER

M. WILLIAM PHELPS

TARGETED

A DEPUTY, HER LOVE AFFAIRS, A BRUTAL MURDER

WILDBLUE
PRESS

WildBluePress.com

TARGETED *published by:*
WILDBLUE PRESS
P.O. Box 102440
Denver, Colorado 80250

Copyright 2017 by M. William Phelps

ISBN 978-1-947290-09-9 Trade Paperback
ISBN 978-1-947290-08-2 eBook

Interior Formatting/Book Cover Design by Elijah Toten www.totencreative.com

All photos in this book are courtesy of the author.

TARGETED

"For the heart, life is simple: it beats for as long as it can. Then it stops."

—**Karl Ove Knausgaard,** *My Struggle*

TABLE OF CONTENTS

AUTHOR'S NOTE

THE PROCESS OF WRITING is what keeps the blood pumping feverishly through my veins. I don't feel right in the world unless I wake up, put some sentences together on the page and wrestle with the words until I get them into the right place. Publishing, on the other hand, is what dampens that excitement at times, pilfering much of the vigor and passion out of it. I'm coming up on what is my 20th year writing books, most within the true-crime space. It is a genre I have seen change from an ignored category the literary establishment turned its nose to—denying any interest in—to a genre split into subclasses, where some will gather together in support of, and award, those "true crime" books with long, cerebral titles and even longer subtitles. You know what I'm talking about: those true-crime books purporting to be bigger, smarter, more important and, certainly, far more intelligent than (God forbid!) those ugly, nasty, mendacious mass-market, red-and-black-covered paperbacks made popular in the Seventies, Eighties and Nineties, with *deadly* and *evil* in every other title. Truthfully, the alienation and snubbing is a facet of publishing that stokes the flames of fire within me. The notion that a writer is judged, literally, by the cover of the book he or she has written is unnerving, ignorant and, coming from the mouths of what are alleged to be intelligent and literary people, small-minded. It's insulting and hurtful. We—those of us in the true-crime trenches, writing year after year—work just as hard as any prize winner and/or celebrated writer. And despite what title or the type of cover a true-crime book is given (generally never by the author, by the way, but the marketing and publicity machines instead), what matters is the reporting and writing between the cardboard.

Nothing else.

You can shine up a shitty book, put some sort of subtitle on it beckoning the reading public to believe the book somehow "changed the world" by broaching all sorts of social issues we are told to take note of; you can compare it to that often-conjured, popular piece of fiction forever referred to as having birthed the genre, *In Cold Blood* (some of which was falsified and frankly made up), a book topping just about every All-Time Top Ten True-Crime Books list; but in the end, a solid, well-reported and -researched book in which a murder or some nefarious crime occurs stands on its own merits. A literary prize, or even a nomination, a place on a list, a flashy blurb by some Pulitzer-winner does not make it any better, worse or more important than a book you'd find in a rack at the drugstore or supermarket (back in the day when those establishments actually carried true crime).

Look, are there tawdry and pulpy true-crime books in the marketplace not worth your time or money? Of course. Is there trash in every genre, including true crime? Absolutely. But come on now, let us not be judged by the clothes we wear or the house we live in. Step back and at least consider the work before handing down your insults and conclusions.

When I started, I didn't view writing true crime as writing true crime. When I wrote my first book, *Perfect Poison*, I had no idea I was writing a "true-crime book." I looked at it as telling the incredible true story of a contemporary female serial killer, a narrative populated with interesting people, exposing the injustices and victories of some of those involved. It wasn't until somebody told me it was a true-crime book that I understood I was now pigeonholed into the red-headed stepchild genre of literature and quarantined to the dusty bottom shelf, somewhere in the back of the bookstore, in the corner, far away from civilization, generally near the restrooms or janitor's closet.

It's been 34 books and quite a ride. I've seen the genre go from books flying off shelves at a rate writers could barely keep up with to the space to sell those same books chiseled down to a few sleeves in the few bookstores left—Kmart, Target, Walmart and the drugstores cutting their space to a third of what it used to be—while adult coloring books (really!) and young adult novels, in which the same futuristic dystopian tale is told (nauseatingly) over and over—erotica, gift items and coffee shops taking up much of the space once dedicated to shelving and selling books.

I could continue to stand high atop my soapbox and wax frustratingly about the industry and all that is wrong with it, or display my irritation for the gluttony of self-published garbage saturating the marketplace and confusing the book buyer today, but that is speech for another time. I will say, however, that having a publisher such as WildBlue Press, and others like it, emerge from the hard-knock slog of selling books over the past 10 years has been, for me, a godsend. To be able to bring my readers—old and new—the stories I feel are worthy of their time and money, without those industry people totally out of touch with the zeitgeist telling me the story is "not quite right" or "needs a stronger female lead" or "readers want high-profile 'Making a Murderer' type of narratives today with recognizable criminal names" is, without a doubt, one of many benefits of publishing with a press such as WildBlue, run by people who understand the genre and, most importantly, what readers want within a contemporary context.

All of which brings me to the book you have purchased.

THE WOMAN AT THE center, Tracy Fortson, will not like everything she reads about herself and her case.

Moreover, Tracy's supporters will find fault in some of my reporting. This is inevitable. I cannot stop it. Yet I do want to acknowledge it, adding that within this story—seeing how at its core lies the challenge of believing that overwhelming circumstantial evidence and questionable forensic evidence is enough to convict and the idea that a cover-up took place seems more and more likely as you begin to dig in—is the first time I have encountered a murder victim's parent siding with the person convicted of his murder. That, alone, is something we need to take note of and keep in mind as we go through this case and try to understand what happened.

I could not—and would not—have written this book without Tracy Fortson's input. I promised Tracy a voice in this book and entirely delivered on that.

As I began to wind down my interviews and finish the manuscript, I began to see that there are additional questions to be answered. The more I dug in, the more I began to agree that this case needs an objective investigation, from an outside official source, separated from the bounds of the good ol' boys' Southern Justice League in the Deep South. I have issues with certain aspects of this investigation and the players involved. I am certain most readers will, too.

There were several people involved in this case I chose not to speak to—and they know why. I don't apologize for that. Just want to point it out.

Lastly, this book, save for the interviews I conducted, is based on thousands of pages of primary documents connected to the case and those I dug up myself. The public record for this case is immense.

Finally, I want to thank Donna Dudeck and Jupiter Entertainment for once again introducing me to an incredible true-crime story.

PART I

"When dealing with people, remember you are not dealing with creatures of logic, but with creatures bristling with prejudice and motivated by pride and vanity."

— **Dale Carnegie**

1.

SHERIFF TOM LUTZ had a terrible cough. He didn't know it yet, but the Persian Gulf War veteran was on the verge of being diagnosed with interstitial pneumonitis, a rare but powerful lung disease from being exposed to chemical weapons. As a sergeant with the Madison County Sheriff's Department (MCSD) in Danielsville, Georgia, an exceptionally small county north of Athens, Lutz considered the morning of June 17, 2000, an average day thus far. A lazy, hot-as-hell, Saturday morning in the South, nothing too spectacular happening in the office or around town. No urgent calls of break-ins or domestic issues. No drunks from the previous night waking up in the tank, sitting in their own piss and puke. No cops scraping somebody off the interstate with a shovel after a terrible accident. It was, in the scope of a Saturday morning, your typical start to your typical weekend in north central Georgia, the local sheriff watching the clock until he could head home to his family.

In law enforcement, however, all you have to do is be patient long enough and your day will take a turn you *never* saw coming. For Lutz and the MCSD, that abrupt, full-circle pivot began just after 9 a.m. As Lutz finished his second cup of coffee of the morning, a rather interesting call came in. A man in Colbert, a shanty little county town of fewer than 500 residents, just over 200 households, less than a square mile in size, reported several dead birds he and his girlfriend had stumbled upon across the street from his house.

Birds?

Not crows, blue jays, chicken hawks or robins, as if some sort of celestial, horror event out of Stephen King novel had occurred. Or perhaps a random and unexplained environmental event that Steven Spielberg might open one of his films with. The birds this man referred to were pastel-colored, exotic fowls you might encounter in the rainforest, Asia, or perhaps locales such as Australia and New Zealand.

"Name's Larry Bridges," the man said before explaining what he'd found, giving dispatch his address.

Near 9:40 a.m., Sheriff Lutz found himself driving into Colbert, meeting Larry Bridges in the driveway of his home. Larry explained to Lutz that he was "concerned" about a neighbor, a man he had not seen in close to two weeks. Larry Bridges further clarified that it was the neighbor's exotic birds, actually, that he and his girlfriend had found dead.

Standing in front of Larry Bridges, listening to this strange tale, Lutz adjusted his Stetson, put a hand on his duty belt and then glanced across the street.

"You say birds?" Lutz said.

"Yeah," Larry said. "Come with me. I'll show you."

John Sharpe Road, where Lutz was now walking across after leaving Larry Bridge's driveway en route to the alleged missing neighbor's property, could not have been any more off the beaten path. Jack Sharpe Road met Tom Sharpe Road at a fork that connected to John Sharpe Road, a dead end in the shape of a tuning fork. When someone out here said "everybody knows everybody," they weren't speaking in clichéd, general terms; everyone on this street was on a first-name basis. Just so happened that Larry Bridges and Doug Benton, the 38-year-old alleged missing neighbor, had been good friends. Larry was worried about his buddy. It was unlike Doug not to care for his birds.

Lutz was a cautious man and ardent investigator who did not jump to conclusions. Having been a medic with the 2nd Battalion 7th Infantry, awarded his first Bronze Star with "V" for valor and a second Bronze Star while serving in Bosnia from 1996–97, Lutz was well-schooled in the art of dealing with people under duress. What's more, having been a volunteer soccer coach with the Madison County Recreation Department—not to mention a public servant all these years—the sheriff knew how to talk to people, understanding what motivated their needs and concerns. Listening to Larry, feeling a true sense of dread the man projected, Lutz knew it had taken Larry Bridges a lot to make the call and wouldn't have done so unless he truly believed something was wrong. Larry's gut was speaking to him. And if there was one thing a cop knew to trust more than perhaps most everything else, it was that intuitive, internal instinct all human beings possess.

Sheriff Lutz knocked on the front door.

No answer.

After checking each door (all were locked) and cupping his hands near his temples to block the sun while looking in all the windows, Larry Bridges pointed out something.

"Look at this."

Scattered around the property, out back of the house, inside the garage and there on the front porch, Doug Benton kept a dozen or so birdcages. Doug was a collector of exotic birds, Larry explained, which he had been breeding with the hopes of selling. Doug loved his birds. He took great pride in caring for them.

"It's so unlike Doug to leave, be gone for so long, and not make arrangements for someone to take care of his birds," Larry told Lutz.

This baffled Doug's neighbor. Why would Doug take off and leave the birds to fend for themselves?

Didn't make any sense.

How did Larry know, however, that Doug had not set someone up with the task of watching the birds?

Because 11 of them, Larry and the sheriff soon realized, were dead.

"Do you have any idea where Mr. Benton might be?" Sheriff Lutz asked.

"Have no idea. But I *know* those birds are worth about $35,000."

"Do you remember the last time you saw him?"

"Oh, geez, must have been somewhere between June 1st and the 4th, about two weeks ago. He had a fight with his girlfriend. He left."

"You know his girlfriend?"

"Yeah … yeah … name's ah… um … Tracy … Tracy Fortson. She's an Oglethorpe County [deputy]."

Larry Bridges then explained how it was he remembered Doug leaving on Sunday, June 4, 2000. He recalled the day specifically because Doug rode a Harley-Davidson motorcycle and Larry heard the roar of the tailpipes close to 10 a.m. on that day. So he looked out and watched as Doug drove away. He recalled Doug returning later that evening about 5 p.m. His girlfriend, Tracy Fortson, had shown up looking for Doug around 3 p.m., Larry claimed. He never actually saw Tracy, however—but had only noticed her truck parked in the driveway. Tracy Fortson's truck was not hard to miss. A 1998 Ford F-150 4X4, with an extended cab and tinted windows, for starters. It also had a black grill guard on the front and dark black bars snaked along the bottom of the vehicle (like a step rail). Tracy had a black tag on the front of the truck, with a "thin blue line" running through it to represent her dedication to, and support of, law enforcement. The license plate tag, Larry said, was also unforgettable: "2TUFF2."

"Like the Ford commercials say, 'Built Ford tough,' " Tracy later told me as we began discussing her missing boyfriend, Doug Benton. " '1TUFF1' was already taken when I applied for a tag, so I had to settle for '2TUFF2.' It was about the truck," she concluded, speaking of her tag.

"Not me."

Tracy was not a tepid, passive woman, afraid of her own shadow. Nor was she ever known *not* to speak her mind. She was rugged. "Tomboyish," some later said. Hard. A tough chick who didn't take shit from anyone. Being the first female sheriff of the county, she'd worked in a sometime tough, male-dominated, prickly atmosphere, at least for a woman.

Consequentially, however, this made Tracy one hell of a sheriff.

Doug had a truck, too. A white and beige 2000 Ford F-250 he'd just recently purchased. The entire bed of Doug's truck was filled with welding equipment. Doug ran his business, Benton Welding Company, out of the truck, which had magnetic signs on both doors. Thus, in that respect, Doug's truck was also hard to miss.

Doug and Tracy, Larry went on to explain, weren't getting along lately. They fought a lot. Tracy might have left—he couldn't recall the exact time—somewhere right before Doug got home that Sunday, June 4.

As the days (and soon a week) went by, Larry Bridges explained, he didn't think much of Doug not being home. Doug generally worked construction welding jobs; with times being as tough as they were, work was hard to come by. So Doug followed the job wherever it took him. He would sometimes head out of town, even out of state, to chase work.

"The first week I didn't think nothing about it," Larry recalled. "The next weekend went by and I didn't see (Doug) come home, which he normally did."

Doug weighed 250 pounds. He went about 5 feet 9 inches tall, a stocky, brute of a build. He was powerful and could be, some later insisted, explosive—especially when he got himself going on something. He had a passion for lifting weights. In fact, Doug and Tracy often worked out together in Doug's home gym.

AS THEY STOOD OUTSIDE Doug's house, Larry Bridges told Sheriff Lutz he had asked the neighbors, many of whom were home during the day while Larry was gone at work, if they had seen Doug.

Larry heard a resounding no from everyone, he told Lutz. Nobody had seen Doug for quite some time.

Larry also worked construction. He and Doug would sometimes hang out together. After not hearing from Doug for several days, Larry started paging him. But Doug failed to respond to any of Larry's pages, which was also very much unlike Doug's usual behavior.

Larry's said his job had called on that Saturday morning before he phoned the MCSD to let him know he didn't need to come into work. So he and his girlfriend decided to take a walk over to Doug's and have a look around. By now, Larry was growing increasingly concerned about his neighbor and friend.

"Let's look in the windows to see what's going on," Larry told his girlfriend.

As soon as they got across the street and Larry noticed many of Doug's birds dead inside their cages, he decided to call the sheriff. There was no way, Larry felt, Doug would ever allow his birds—an investment—to starve, wither and die. Moreover, Doug being the type of person he was, there wasn't a chance that had one of the birds died, he would have left the thing to rot in its cage.

Several birds, Lutz noticed, were still alive, but they looked "poorly from lack of food and water." This told Lutz nobody had been over to the house in quite some time.

The entire situation had a strange feel to it.

Lutz made arrangements with Larry Bridges to care for

the birds that remained alive—until, that is, Doug could be located. Lutz didn't share it with Larry Bridges, but he was going to make a call and get someone out here to do a wellness check on the inside of the house. The MCSD certainly had probable cause to force their way in.

2.

WHEN SHERIFF TOM LUTZ returned to the MCSD, he called the Oglethorpe County Sheriff's Department (OCSD). If Doug's girlfriend were a fellow sheriff, she'd want to help. Maybe she knew where Doug had run off to. If not, she was likely going to be more than willing to give Lutz a list of names he could call to begin trying to hunt Doug Benton down.

"Was looking for Tracy Fortson, a deputy," Lutz said to a deputy who answered the phone.

"She no longer works here," the deputy said.

"Oh?"

It was a long story, the deputy mentioned. "But I can reach out to her and let her know you're looking for her."

It was clear that the deputy had some sort of personal connection with Tracy. Maybe she'd gotten herself a promotion and moved on?

"Appreciate that, deputy."

Lutz hung up and figured Doug was probably with his girlfriend and they had taken off somewhere. The guy lived by himself for the most part, according to the neighbors Lutz had spoken to while walking around the vicinity of Doug's house. Doug had kids and they spent time with him once in a while, but he lived alone. He didn't need to answer to anyone and could come and go as he pleased.

Still, as Lutz thought about it, there was a missing piece of the puzzle. The entire scenario did not feel right. Those dead birds spoke to the situation. Their deaths *meant* something.

3.

TWICE DIVORCED, TRACY Fortson was a pretty woman, however rough and rugged she might have come across. As some would later say, "Either you liked Tracy and understood her, or you didn't." There was no gray area with Tracy. She told you how it was in her own manner of speaking. You accepted her personality and put up with it, or you stayed the hell away. On those terms alone, one could say, Tracy and Doug were the perfect match.

At 36, with dark brown, curly and shoulder-length hair, bangs cut like ribbon across her forehead and around her ears, Tracy was not your typical girly-girl who did her nails on Saturday mornings and baked cookies on Sundays. She was 5 feet 6 inches tall and a solid and healthy 150 pounds. No slouch at the gym, Tracy and Doug dead-lifted heavy weight, a sport they shared an equal adoration for. She hunted. Fished. A crack shot with a pistol, Tracy once dreamed of becoming a game warden, but gave up on the dream to pursue a career in law enforcement. Although Tracy had been jaded by a major incident that had recently happened to her within the sheriff's department, she adored what the job had offered and had personally given her.

"That 'good ole boy system' that has always been associated with Southern Justice is alive and well," Tracy told me, bitter and cynical about her dealings with the OCSD during her final days behind the badge. "The police don't always make arrests based on probable cause or evidence."

Doug and Tracy met in September 1997. Not in the least bit attracted to him on that day, if you ask Tracy, Doug was not the type of man she ever envisioned herself being with— at least not then.

"Although he was nice looking, he just didn't seem like the type of guy I would be interested in."

Doug wore an earring and tight-fitting, Spandex workout pants "that guys shouldn't wear!" Tracy commented, a bit of haughty amusement in her tone. Doug had an attitude back then, Tracy recalled. He came across as having this "I-know-I'm-good-looking" swagger and it turned her off. Tracy was thinking of getting into the sheriff's department at the time, while earning a living behind the counter of Ultimate Tan in Athens. Doug worked out next door at Gold's Gym.

"It was common for some of the guys that worked out at the gym to come in to tan," Tracy said. "Doug happened to be one of them—although, I had never seen him in the salon until this particular day. I had only caught brief glimpses of him cruising by in his blue Corvette convertible."

Checking him out on that day, Tracy figured Doug was a "power lifter," as opposed to a body-builder. He didn't have the "cut" look: gaunt facial, starving-himself-to-make-a-weight-class stare and withdrawn eyes the guys who train for competitions generally display. Doug's thick mane of black hair was styled in a mullet, the look of the day, and he sported somewhat of a "beer belly," Tracy recalled.

"Hey," Doug said to Tracy after walking into the tanning salon. She stood behind the counter checking him in. Doug had an appointment for that afternoon.

"How are you?" Tracy said, business-like, uninterested.

"Was wondering," Doug came out with, "you want to go out some night?"

Tracy was taken aback. She thought: *In your dreams, buddy. Not a chance.*

Something, however, then made Tracy lean over the counter to see if Doug was wearing a wedding ring. So she bent her body over the partition separating the two of them to look down toward Doug's hand, which happened to be positioned over his crotch.

"And he thought I was checking out his package," Tracy said later.

In doing this, Tracy had embarrassed Doug, she realized. He thought one thing while she another.

"The look on his face was priceless."

Feeling sorry for Doug in that situation, Tracy took out a piece of paper and wrote down her pager number, still thinking there wasn't a chance she'd ever go out with him.

4.

TRACY FORTSON CALLED Sheriff Lutz at some point. It's unclear when, exactly. Lutz never noted the date or time in his report. Yet, Tracy told me during a series of interviews, there was no way the OCSD could have called her to let her know Lutz was looking for her because she had changed her telephone number to "unlisted" after the "incident" that had made her leave the sheriff's office.

"Nowhere in (Lutz's) report does it mention that Oglethorpe Deputy Walt Williams came to my house and told me that Madison County was trying to get hold of me and would I call them, which I did," Tracy later explained.

According to Lutz's version of that phone call, it was fairly standard. Tracy recalled Deputy Walt Williams coming by her house at about 10 a.m. She said she called MCSD not long after that. In fact, she said, she had to actually leave a call-back number for Lutz because he wasn't there.

"We're looking for Doug Benton—his neighbors have reported him missing—and wanted to know if you've seen him?"[1]

Tracy said Lutz told her here that "some of Doug's birds had died."

---

1   The following conversation is based on a combination of my interviews with Tracy, Lutz's report and trial testimony. Of note, much of what Tracy later recalls saying to the sheriff is not in his report.

"We are broken up," Tracy explained. "I haven't seen him for the past couple of weeks."

"Where might he have gone?" Lutz asked in a conversational tone.

Tracy claimed she gave Lutz contact info for Jerry Alexander and Jeff Bennett, because both were Doug's closest friends.

"Doug's mother lives in Michigan," Tracy told Lutz. "Not long ago, he talked about going up there. He has a brother living there, too. But they don't get along too well."

"When was the last time you saw him?"

"June 4th.[2] You should call Jeff Bennett, Doug's good friend. He will probably know where Doug is."

As Lutz thought about it, June 4 seemed to be the last time anyone could place Doug in Oglethorpe County.

---

2   Tracy would later say "June 5."

5.

SHE'D FORGOTTEN ABOUT Doug Benton after they met that afternoon in 1997 at the tanning salon. Tracy had viewed Doug, in a way, as a stuck-up weightlifter with a hubristic chip on his shoulder. Meeting him while manning the tanning salon counter spoke of something to Tracy: Doug's vanity. She wanted nothing to do with a man like that.

She had given Doug her pager number, however. After waiting the new relationship grace period of two days, Doug paged Tracy.

So she called him. Would it hurt to have a phone conversation with the guy?

Tracy thought not.

While Doug awkwardly began speaking, Tracy could hear a small child in the background.

He's married, she thought. *Sonofabitch. He's one of* those *guys.*

"That's my son," Doug said. "I have him while my ex-wife is at work."

Yeah, right.

Tracy considered that Doug was lying, that he was married and had called while his wife was at work. So she cautiously went about the conversation, having no interest in taking things any farther than this one call.

As they spoke, Tracy was turned off by the fact that Doug, she said, "Talked about himself a lot and didn't seem interested in what I had to say."

Tracy pressed him on being married. Doug "assured" her he was divorced.

She considered it.

"So," Doug said at one point, "you want to go out?"

Thinking seriously about turning him down, "Um, I guess," Tracy said. Even though she wasn't interested, Tracy didn't have the nerve to tell him no.

"This Friday?"

"Yeah, sounds good."

As the days passed and the weekend approached, the more she thought about dating a divorced father, a guy who liked to talk about himself more than anything else, Tracy decided Doug was not the type of man she wanted to be with. There was nothing Doug had that Tracy wanted. She'd been down this road with married men before. So she decided to turn him down.

"I didn't want to get involved with someone who was all about self and was divorced and had a small child," Tracy recalled. "Plus, I had this nagging feeling that things were not as they seemed."

By then, Tracy had pulled herself out from underneath a second divorce, healed, was on the road toward bettering her life and was not about step back into a serious relationship. Two failures were enough—at least for the moment. A divorced guy with kids just didn't sound tempting. Too much baggage. Too much drama.

"Hey, listen," Tracy said, calling Doug back a day later, "you're a nice guy, but I need to cancel our date."

Doug didn't seem to care much. "OK," he said. Then hung up.

"And Doug Benton," Tracy said later, "never called me again."

6.

SHERIFF TOM LUTZ had a sense that foul play was involved in Doug's sudden disappearance. A guy like Doug Benton—Lutz understood from talking to Doug's friends, neighbors and even Tracy Fortson—didn't just step off the grid without any sign. It wasn't in Doug's character to leave and not say anything to anyone about where he was going. Whenever he left on an extended trip, Doug usually told someone where he was going and when he was coming back. Lutz had called Jeff Bennett, as Tracy suggested. Jeff and Doug had known each other for years. Jeff told Lutz to phone Jerry Alexander, another mutual friend. Jerry might know where Doug went off to.

"I saw Doug's truck at Jerry's house," Jeff Bennett explained to Lutz. It was just recently, he added, within the past week.

But when he took a drive by Jerry's again just a day or so ago, the truck was gone.

Had Doug come by and picked up his truck?

"Listen," Lutz asked, "do you know of any problems between Doug and Tracy?" Lutz gave no prologue as to why he wanted this information, or what made him ask. There had been no indication from anyone thus far that Tracy would have any reason to want Doug gone. There was no reason to suspect animosity between Doug and his girlfriend, other than maybe Larry Bridges saying they fought from time to time. If you read Lutz's report, it seems as if the question came out of the blue. Yet, in the totality of the investigation, Lutz was more or less being thorough. Trying to cover every base. By all accounts, Doug Benton had not been seen or heard from in two weeks. That is significant. Add the dead birds to the equation and here you have a cop simply doing his job, following his gut, asking questions, and digging for information.

"They had a really bad fight," Jeff Bennett explained, but gave no specific date as to when—though the impression was recently. "Tracy pulled a gun, pointed it at herself, then at Doug, and a physical fight occurred." Jeff then made a point to say they "had fought many other times," explaining how he had, in fact, stopped hanging out with Doug and stopped working out with him because he couldn't stand to be around Tracy Fortson anymore. She was belligerent and loud and always butting into Doug's business. She wouldn't leave the guy alone. She pestered him about everything. "I told him, 'You get rid of Tracy,' " Jeff Bennett concluded, " 'because I'm tired of it … and we'll hang out again.' "

That day never came.

Lutz wondered about family.

Jeff said Doug's immediate family lived in Michigan. He gave Lutz Doug's mother's phone number.

Lutz told Jeff he'd be back in touch. He wanted to call Doug's family and see if maybe Doug had taken off north to get away from Tracy. Maybe he was staying in Michigan for a while for a change of pace. Let things back home cool down.

Doug's brother was home when Lutz called. Doug's mother, Carol Benton, was out. Doug's brother said they had not heard from Doug "in a while, and that was not like him." Meaning, he always called and said hello and stayed in touch.

So Doug had not gone to Michigan, after all. That would

have been the most obvious answer. More than that, he had not even called home during any part of the two weeks he'd been gone.

Lutz asked where else Doug could have gone off to and his brother explained that he had been out of touch with Doug's friends in Georgia. He couldn't really help much there.

Lutz said he'd be calling back at some point.

Armed with this new information, Lutz felt he needed to speak with Tracy again. In his report, Lutz said, "I then called Tracy and asked her about the fight. Tracy avoided all questions about the fight, but said Doug called her and told her to stay away from him and his home."

And so she did.

"Lutz talks to me via phone," Tracy explained in one of our 2016 email exchanges. "Lutz claims I avoid all questions about a fight. There was no fight. I am the one who told him we had an argument on Saturday night that led to (a) message left by Doug on June sixth."

June 6 would have been two days after Doug had last been seen.

"The argument Doug and I had on Saturday night," Tracy continued, "June third, was during the movie 'An Officer and a Gentleman.' We were arguing over the part where the girl told the guy she was pregnant, trying to get him to marry her. Doug got angry because (he claimed a woman had once done that to him) … Doug was paying a considerable amount of child support and attorney fees connected (to this)."

Tracy went on to explain that this "argument" was blown way out of proportion later on in these reports. Doug and Tracy had disagreements all the time, as couples often do.

"That argument was not a 'fight.' I was not avoiding questions (from Lutz) pertaining to a fight. And, that argument was not serious enough to keep Doug angry from Saturday until Tuesday, when I last heard from him."

7.

IT WAS SEPTEMBER 1999, one month after Doug had been officially divorced for a second time. Nearly two years to the day when Tracy had last spoken to Doug, or, for that matter, had even thought about him. Tracy sat inside Ryan's Steakhouse in Athens having lunch with her father. This was something they did "faithfully" every Friday afternoon, Tracy said. A daughter and her dad catching up.

As Tracy was finishing her meal, listening to her father talk, she happened to look toward the entrance into the restaurant.

"And in walks this *gorgeous* guy," she said later.

He wore jeans and a "tight, white V-neck T-shirt and work boots."

Unable to take her eyes off the dude, Tracy immediately thought that something about the man looked familiar. She kept staring at him, trying to figure out where she had seen him before.

"But also because he looked so good."

"Excuse me, Dad," Tracy said. She picked up her plate and walked over to the salad bar to get a better look at the guy.

As Tracy piled lettuce on her plate, she could hear another guy talking. He was sitting with the man she was infatuated with. He said: "She's checking you out, dude."

As Tracy turned and saw the man closer up, she was pleasantly shocked and surprised when she realized it was Doug Benton.

"What a difference. His hair was cut short. He had a neatly trimmed moustache." Doug looked "very clean-cut." Yet, Tracy recalled, "It was his body; he had lost weight and he was ripped. Muscles everywhere. Chest. Biceps. Gone were the earring, the long hair and the beer belly. He looked like a totally different person. I was certainly interested this time."

After the check came and Tracy and her father got up to pay and leave, she "took a detour" over to Doug's table.

"Don't I know you?" she said, standing, staring at him. "Aren't you Doug ... Benton?"

He laughed. "Yes, I am. Good to see you!" He seemed to recognize Tracy from the tanning salon.

"You look so different," Tracy said. She was beaming. Totally smitten. Doug could easily tell she was into him. "I'll see you around."

Doug smiled as he watched Tracy and her dad leave the restaurant.

As Tracy walked out, "I remember thinking: *Man, I'd like to see him again!*"

Leaving the parking lot, Tracy drove to a pub she hung out in once in a while, sat and chatted with several friends. About a half hour into the conversation, she felt her hip buzz, looked down and saw that her pager was going off.

She did not recognize the phone number.

It was Doug. He'd gone home that afternoon, searched hell and high water for her phone number from two years before, found it and called. Doug had felt a connection, apparently. He was calling to see if Tracy wanted to hook up, ending the message with, "Give me a call when you get home."

Tracy didn't waste any time. As soon as she got home, she called.

"And this time we *really* talked. He seemed so different from the person he was before, not just physically, but he even talked different. It wasn't 'all about me' this time. He was genuinely interested in what I had to say. And this time, when he asked me to go out, I didn't hesitate. We decided that we would meet somewhere for dinner that Saturday night."

The closer it got to Saturday, however, Tracy changed her mind again.

"Indeed. I had another idea. I called Doug that morning, and told him, 'If you want to go out with me, then come and pick me up like a real gentlemen and take me to lunch today.' And that's what he did. At noon, on the dot, Doug came driving up in my yard in a red Dodge dually, a far cry from the Corvette convertible I had seen him in before. This guy had totally changed his image. I love trucks! Big trucks. So this was just one more thing to like about him. Again, he was wearing jeans, a tight shirt and boots. I just couldn't get over the difference."

Both Doug and Tracy were, as she put it, "Into watching what we ate." Both were trying to stay as physically fit as possible. The first restaurant they stopped at didn't have any type of "healthy" seafood, so they left. After they found a nice spot with healthier choices, they drove to a park, held hands and walked around. They soon found a bench seat near a lake and sat.

"We found that we had so much to talk about," Tracy continued. "We shared our entire life experiences that day. Conversation was easy. I found out that he was a welder and he found out that I was a deputy. It was like talking to an old friend, someone I could really relate to, and it was wonderful. It was as if we had waited our entire lives for that moment. Doug told me about his childhood, what it was like to grow up in Michigan and then move to Georgia. It was a total culture shock. He had been picked on a lot as a boy because he was small and that was what had given him the incentive to lift weights. He wanted to get 'big' so people would stop picking on him. Not only was Doug big, he was strong. He had won a few bench-press competitions and could bench 500 pounds. Nobody messed with Doug anymore ... nobody."

Cupid had speared them both on that day. Tracy and Doug had found each other two years after first meeting. Both were primed and ready for a relationship. Yet, as Doug began telling Tracy about his past, the "more I realized what that nagging feeling had been the first time I had talked to him."

Doug had secrets, Tracy claimed. And here he was, sitting, hours into their first official date, spilling many of them.

8.

THE PHONE WAS RINGING. Sheriff Tom Lutz waited for someone to pick up. He was hoping Doug's good friend, Jerry Alexander, would answer. It had been Doug's other friend, Jeff Bennett, who'd said Doug's truck had been parked at Jerry's house one day, gone the next.

"Have you seen Doug lately?" Lutz asked after introducing himself.

"I have not," Jerry said.

"Is Doug's truck parked at your house?"

"It is. Yes."

"How come you have Doug's truck if you have not seen him?" This didn't make much sense to Lutz. But then, thinking about it, maybe Doug and Larry had some sort of deal between them whereby Doug could drop off his truck anytime he wanted and Larry would keep an eye on it. It was well documented that Doug loved that vehicle. He took care of it like one of his birds. He wouldn't just leave it where it could be stolen or vandalized, especially without explanation.

"The truck had been dropped off in the middle of the night last Sunday … with a note."

By "last Sunday" Jerry meant the weekend Doug had last been seen.

"A note?"

"Yeah."

"What did the note say?"

"Well, let me get it."

Lutz waited.

Jerry came back on the line and read it word for word: " 'Jerry, I trust you to take care of my truck. Don't try to contact me. I'll contact you later.' "

"That it?"

"Just about."

"You mind if I stop by and have a look at the truck?"

"No, not at all. Come on over."

They hung up.

Jerry lived in Lexington, Georgia. He had known Doug for about 10 years, having worked with him most of that time.

"We got to know Doug," Jerry said later in court, referring to him and his wife, "and (brought) him to church at Corinth back (in 1990). We were real close and he got saved back then."

As he thought about it, Jerry was certain Doug's truck had been dropped off at his house on that Sunday night, June 4, the weekend Doug went missing. Jerry was sure of this "because we never heard anything, but that Monday morning (June 5, 2000), when I went outside, the truck was parked on the side of my yard right there ... backwards."

At an angle, in other words. Hastily parked, as if Doug was in some sort of hurry to ditch the vehicle and take off.

When he spotted the truck that morning, Jerry thought Doug was probably inside his house sleeping. That he had come over in the middle of the night, didn't want to wake anyone up, found a place inside to crash and went to sleep. So Jerry walked back into his house, looked upstairs and down, all over the house, "hollering" Doug's name.

But he came up empty. Doug was nowhere to be found.

"And I said to myself, he's got to be around here somewhere. He never brings his truck and just leaves it."

Jerry went back out and looked inside the truck. He found the keys in the ignition. He considered this "kind of weird" on Doug's part. Again, something Doug would never do.

Not only did he find the keys, but that note he'd read to Lutz. It was "attached right there on the side, taped right there on the side of the window," Jerry explained.

So Jerry pulled the note off the window and stared at it.

"It looked just like Doug's handwriting. It looked identical. He always wrote scribbly like I do most of the time. We both always kidded around, said we had Japanese handwriting."

What worried Jerry most about finding the truck and the note was that he felt Doug had "a lot of problems with depression." That this was a sign, telling Larry that Doug had gone and done something to himself.

Could Doug, Jerry considered, have taken his own life?

JERRY ALEXANDER LIVED IN a white house with black shutters. The front of the place was hidden behind overgrown tree limbs and brush. When Lutz and another deputy arrived later that day, June 17, 2000, to "secure the vehicle," Jerry met them outside in the driveway.

Lutz asked (again) how Jerry had come across Doug's truck.

Jerry changed his story up just a little here. He said he at first didn't recognize it as being anybody's truck he knew, so he searched through the glove box and found documents that told him it was Doug's. He did not mention the note.

So Lutz asked: "What about that note?"

"It's in the house."

Lutz didn't see the truck. "Where is it now?"

"In back."

Jerry said he'd moved it, but couldn't recall exactly when. Perhaps a few days after he found it parked. He couldn't remember exactly when.

"Listen, Doug had a lot of problems with depression,"

Jerry stated next, according to Lutz's report and Jerry's later testimony. "I don't think he left the property. He might have hung himself in that building back there." There was an abandoned barn behind Jerry's house.

Lutz and the deputy walked back to the barn. Pushed the door open. Shined a flashlight inside. Nothing.

Doug's truck was parked nearby. They searched it. Nothing.

Lutz decided to call his lieutenant to see what he wanted to do from this point. They had Doug's truck, this strange note and several people now saying they had not heard from Doug in nearly two weeks. Every sign pointed to Doug not coming back.

"We've secured the vehicle, sir," Lutz reported.

"Have it towed in."

Lutz explained to Jerry that they were going to have Doug's truck towed into the sheriff's office. Standard police business. A wrecker was on the way.

This didn't sit so well with Jerry. "He became outraged," Lutz later reported.

"I want to see a warrant!" Jerry snapped.

"Please calm down, sir," Lutz said. "We do not need a warrant. The truck is part of an investigation of a friend of yours who is missing."

"I already contacted a lawyer and you need a warrant to take his truck away," Jerry stated for a second time.

"Once again, sir, I do not need a warrant, I assure you. This truck is part of an investigation."

Jerry looked toward the truck, back at the sheriff. Then at the truck. He was thinking.

"I guess," he said, rubbing his chin.

Just then, Jerry's wife walked out of the back door toward them. She was obviously upset at what was going on.

"I spoke to Tracy," she said of Doug's girlfriend, blurting it out without being asked, "at about 10:30 this morning. She called to ask if we had seen Doug because the sheriff's office was looking for him."

"What else can you tell us about Tracy?" Lutz wondered.

"Well, I can tell you that she has caused severe marital problems between my husband and I and I do not like that woman."

They talked a bit more. Nothing much came out of it. As they were discussing Doug, the tow truck arrived.

Jerry Alexander thought of one more thing. He pulled Lutz off to the side.

"What is it?" the sheriff asked.

"Well, I know Doug, Sheriff. And Doug would *never* have left his house and let his birds die—this is *really* serious."

"Thanks," Lutz said.

9.

AFTER THAT FIRST DATE, which ended in the park with Tracy and Doug sharing their life stories, Tracy later said, "We became inseparable." As Tracy got to know her new man more personally, she added, Doug revealed the secrets of his life. For one, he'd suffered from a drug and alcohol problem, Tracy alleged, but had since went to war with those demons and won. Doug was clean now. Sober, enjoying his new life.

The underlying substance abuse, however, was only part of a larger problem. According to Tracy, Doug also struggled with "anger issues," which she called "just a dreadful mix. Not to mention the steroid use, which caused a great deal of frustration and irritability," more commonly known as " 'Roid Rage."

Tracy said Doug had been through tough times in life. During his younger days, he had unresolved issues of which he had no outlet to channel, which ultimately led him into a line of work he wasn't proud of later on.

"He was an angry person and wanted to take it out on others," Tracy told me. "So it was his work as an enforcer for a local drug dealer known as (Painkiller, a pseudonym) that gave him the reason he was looking for to beat up someone or break a bone or two. He also worked as a bouncer in the local strip bars, which also gave him an excuse to do the same. He went to work hoping a fight would break out. Doug enjoyed inflicting pain on his adversaries. He was making up for all those times he had been bullied as a boy."

Doug had a habit, Tracy said, of sitting in public places with his back to the wall, facing the entrance and/or exits.

"As a police officer, I know why I do it," Tracy told her man after the first few times Doug sat like this and she noticed. "But why do you do it, Doug?"

"You never know who is out to get you," he said. "I have a lot of enemies."

As their relationship continued into 2000, Tracy and Doug routinely lifted weights together. Whenever they weren't working their jobs, they spent time together. Doug opened up even more.

Apparently, Doug had not only worked for Painkiller, but also wound up becoming an influential force in helping to convict the guy in the years after he got off Painkiller's payroll. Which, as one might imagine, caused Doug some problems on the street.

"I helped put (Painkiller) in prison," Doug explained to Tracy one night. "He will kill me when he gets out."

Isn't that good enough reason by itself, Tracy wondered, *to keep your back to the wall and watch the door?*

Certainly is.

"Doug also told me he had been responsible for cleaning up the Madison County Sheriff's Department and he had lots of friends there he helped out. He also allowed them to use his property to set up surveillance on a nearby meth house. According to Doug," Tracy concluded, "he was a C.I."

Confidential informant.

All reasons—err, motives—Tracy insisted, without coming out and saying as much, for someone maybe wanting to kill Doug.

At this time, Tracy worked a 12-hour shift at the sheriff's department, 7 to 7. When she got out of work, Doug was there, waiting to take Tracy and her daughter, Elise, out to dinner or just hang out. It seemed to Tracy, as their relationship blossomed into a serious affair throughout the winter of 2000, that Doug's past was behind him. He was a working man now. A welder. Owned his own business. He lifted weights and still took steroids, according to Tracy, but he was out of all the nonsense associated with being a tough guy, drug dealer's enforcer and C.I.

Tracy and Doug yearned for a more peaceful, predictable, routine life. Work, dinner, weekend getaways, birthdays and holidays with family and friends. Settle down. Maybe even live together someday.

"As a matter of fact, Doug didn't know that I could cook for the first two months of our relationship. On my days off, he took us out to eat breakfast, lunch and dinner. My truck didn't move from its parking spot in my yard for almost as long. I never had to drive anywhere because Doug was always willing to take me wherever I needed to go."

One day, Tracy and Doug got to talking about hobbies. How each passed the time when not working. Tracy told her lover she adored hunting, fishing, horseback riding and weightlifting, of course—but also, as a kid, Tracy was totally taken in by riding motorcycles.

Tracy had begun riding a steel horse at 6 years old, the same age she started riding a real horse.

"I had my first motorcycle before I got my first horse."

Tracy was fascinated with Harley-Davidson motorcycles. She told Doug one day she'd always dreamed of owning a chopper.

Well, when Doug found out, he explained that he had a Harley, but had loaned it to a friend after the friend had expressed interest in buying it.

"Oh, no, Doug," Tracy said, "*don't* you sell it."

Doug got the bike back soon after.

Doug then went out and bought himself a Fatboy Harley and gifted his other bike to Tracy. Now they could ride together. Two lovers, on bikes, chugging around town.

Tracy was living the dream.

Here it was, not five months before Doug Benton would turn up missing, and Tracy and Doug were in love, riding, lifting weights side-by-side, dining out with her daughter and taking walks in the park hand-in-hand. It seemed as if they'd carved out a piece of life's bliss. Doug had been married and divorced twice. Tracy had come from a few tumultuous relationships and marriages herself. Neither had given up on romance, Tracy said, and they'd finally found it again: a second chance at love.

10.

AMORY "BUCK" SCOGGINS, an investigator with the MCSD, had been involved on the fringes of the Doug Benton missing person case as Sheriff Lutz made strides in gathering information over that weekend Doug went missing. Now with Doug's truck sitting for two weeks or so at a friend's house, a note left on the window, Doug nowhere in sight, Scoggins was interested in the case as he walked into the office on Sunday morning, June 18, 2000, for his weekend shift. The plan was for the MCSD to dig in heel-deep, call some of those people back they'd already had spoken to. These types of investigations, in the early stages, relied on having conversations with people the person knew.

One was Jeff Bennett. Scoggins got hold Jeff first thing Sunday morning, after picking up the case from where Lutz left off.

Agreeing to come back into the station, Jeff Bennett said that after leaving the MCSD the previous day, having come in to speak with Lutz, he thought of something that might be relevant.

Scoggins was all ears.

"Doug told me that after one of their arguments, Tracy took his wallet, cell phone and pager back to her house."

"OK ... ?"

"So he called her and demanded she return them. That he

needed his money so he could eat. She told him that she was going to work the next morning and that he could come to her house and pick up the items."

What was the significance of the story, Scoggins wondered. It displayed a bit of Tracy's character, sure. But couples played these sorts of games on each other sometimes when they fought. So Doug and Tracy were not getting along? What was the big deal? Couples quarreled. They took back gifts and other things they'd given each other. They hid wallets and keys and yelled and screamed.

They also made up.

"She told him that the items would be on her coffee table. She wouldn't be home. Doug went by and grabbed the items."

"When was this?"

Jeff Bennett thought about it.

"Not sure."

Big help that was.

"Was there anything else?" Scoggins asked.

Bennett said he had plenty.

"Let's hear it."

Scoggins had Jeff sit down in one of the conference rooms so he could take a more formal statement from him.

Jeff agreed.

Doug Benton's friend began with how he had known Doug for 16 years. They met as welders in Barrow County, Jeff explained, while working for a company called Base Manufacturing. "The past seven years we've become close," Jeff added. "We started working out together and competing together in bench-press competitions. We always stayed in constant contact—that is, until last year, when Doug began dating Tracy."

"Why is that?" Scoggins asked.

Jeff Bennett rubbed his chin, took a deep breath. "Tracy is a dominating person ... and is basically a possessive tomboy type of person. She demanded that Doug show her constant attention. She is manipulative and has violent tendencies. She demanded to know all of his affairs and she consumed all of his time. She always wanted to know who he was with and where he was."

This sounded dramatic and perhaps even dangerous. As Bennett talked, Scoggins took notes and detailed the interview in his reports. In the grand scope of the MCSD's investigation, however, what did it actually mean? So Tracy Fortson was a pain in the ass? She wanted to know Doug's every move. She lifted weights like a man. She acted tough and nasty, even. But what the hell did it have to do with Doug having gone missing?

Jeff indicated he had more.

"Go right head, Mr. Bennett."

"I do not like her. She does not like me," Jeff added. He took a sip from a bottle of water the sheriff had given him. "Doug told me many times that she would get violent toward him and when they had trouble she would threaten to shoot herself or would take things from the house and threaten to turn him in. He was not sure what she was referring to."

Scoggins listened intently. If Jeff Bennett was being honest and not just sour at Tracy for coming in between him and his bestie, the relationship between Doug and Tracy was a bit more volatile than everyday boyfriend-girlfriend arguments, kissing and making up. There was possibly more to it than that.

"Doug told me Tracy had explained to him how she had beat up both of her ex-husbands and that one of them she hit in the head with a pipe while drunk, telling police a burglar had done it. She also told Doug that she once set their trailer on fire, trying to burn it with him (the ex-husband) inside of it, but the fire went out. She had threatened to shoot herself once, holding a gun to her head to get (Doug) back. Whenever they had an argument, she would go home and then call him incessantly until he would let her come back over. She would not leave him alone."

"Was he afraid of her?"

"No. He was not afraid and did not believe she could hurt him."

"Is there anything else?" Was all of this leading somewhere? There seemed to be a buildup. If what Jeff said was true, Doug and Tracy's relationship was a powder keg. If nothing else, Tracy Fortson had some explaining to do.

"Tracy worked for Doug. She did work on the computer for him. Filing. Bills and documents. Doug told me they once got into an argument and she went into his house and started deleting items off the computer."

She was vengeful.

Not a good sign.

When Doug realized what she was doing, Jeff added, Doug grabbed her and pulled her away.

Tracy then went outside and tried to kick over one of his Harleys.

She turned as he stopped her and threw a punch at him.

Doug blocked it. Grabbing her by the throat and holding her against the wall inside the garage, he warned: "Don't you *ever* try to hit me again."

Doug let her go.

Tracy walked toward her truck. She said: "I will kill your ass!"

As Tracy reached inside, Doug looked on, knowing she kept a pistol there. He walked over and picked up his rifle. Pointed the barrel in her face: "I will shoot you if you get out of that truck with your pistol."

Tracy stared at him. Started her truck and tore out of the driveway.

It was a hell of a story. If true, it showed how deceitful, maybe even violent not only Tracy could be under certain duress, but also Doug. It appeared they got each other going.

"When was the last time you saw Doug?" Scoggins asked Jeff Bennett.

"On May 22nd and 23rd, I went over to his house and

lifted (weights) with him."

"Was Tracy there?"

"Yes, she was."

"What happened?"

"Well, I was supposed to go back over on May 25th and work out, but I called and told him I wasn't coming over if Tracy was going to be there."

Jeff went on to explain how he called Doug on that day but got no answer. Doug called back later on and said he was outside feeding his birds.

"Did you go over?"

"No, I went to Gold's Gym."

"When did you next see or speak with Doug?"

"I never saw him again."

AFTER JEFF BENNETT LEFT the MCSD, Scoggins sat back and thought about the interview. The stakes had changed. There was much more rigidity and bitterness within the Doug and Tracy relationship, more than the MCSD had been first led to believe by what they'd uncovered. There was a violent thread woven through the fabric of Tracy and Doug's life together. They could both become angry and turn to violent means. Doug himself had admitted to Jeff—if true—that he once grabbed his girlfriend by the throat and pointed a gun in her face. You add dangerous behaviors into the mix of love, most good cops knew, and anything became possible.

Scoggins needed to get Tracy in for a more formal chat. Also, according to his report and later testimony, something that bothered Scoggins here was Doug's mental state at the time he went missing. They had reports from close friends indicating Doug suffered from depression. If he and Tracy had broken up, Doug was likely upset. Could he have been suicidal?

Scoggins called Tracy.

"Sure," she said. "I can come in."

"Six o'clock?" Scoggins asked.

Tracy agreed.

11.

THERE WERE OTHER SECRETS, Tracy Fortson insisted, Doug kept from her. For one, she explained to me in 2016, "I didn't find out that Doug had a second son ... until several months" into the relationship. Doug's other child had blurted out one night, as we were going out to eat, that he had a brother.

This shocked Tracy.

"I was confused at the time because Doug had never mentioned a second marriage or second child."

There came a point in their relationship when Doug said, "I want you to meet my best friend, Jeff (Bennett), and his wife."

It was decided they'd meet for dinner at the local Red Lobster. As they pulled in, Jeff and his wife were waiting in the parking lot.

"That's him," Doug said of Jeff. "Over there, standing with his wife."

Tracy recognized the guy right away, she later said.

After Doug made formal introductions, Tracy and Jeff looked at each other and said: "I know you."

Jeff had been a customer at the tanning salon for many years and Tracy knew him by sight alone.

Doug had a "funny reaction" to this. An odd look crossed his face. "But he didn't say anything at the time."

They sat down to dinner.

The talk was a bit much for Tracy. Jeff liked to constantly dig at Doug, according to Tracy.

As they finished dinner, Tracy later claimed to have gotten the feeling Jeff didn't like it that the two of them (Doug and Tracy) were together as a couple.

"Jeff made a big production of how Doug had told him all about meeting me and that Doug had been really excited about it. I could tell they were very close, but I could also tell Jeff wasn't as happy about our newfound relationship as he wanted us to believe. There was underlying sarcasm in everything he said."

Could this have simply been Jeff Bennett's way of acting? Could it have been his normal jabbing at a friend?

Tracy takes the leap later that it was directed at her and Doug's relationship, but she didn't know this for certain. She speculated.

As the days ticked off the calendar of their relationship, Doug and Tracy got to talking about Jeff Bennett a lot. Doug's friendship with the man came up all the time. Doug's explanation concerning Jeff was always that they were "really close friends and were in touch with each other daily." They had also been workout partners for years and had a set schedule for 4 p.m. each day at Doug's home gym.

"The (home) gym was Doug and Jeff's remedy to prevent paying gym fees."

When Doug explained all of this to Tracy, she said (according to her), "OK, that's cool. I'm a member at Ladies 1st Fitness." She claimed to have "worked out there every day and went to the tanning salon afterward."

Tracy felt their lives were gelling like Southern biscuits and gravy as the spring of 2000 came. She and Doug did everything together.

However, according to Tracy's later recollection, Jeff Bennett was becoming "quite irritable because Doug was missing workouts." She believed Jeff blamed her for the lapse in their friendship and less and less time they spent together.

"Rather than being at home at 4 for their routine, Doug was most often with me," Tracy said. "That caused Jeff to have to miss working out or go to a gym. … Doug's idea was that he and I could work out together and I wouldn't have to go to a gym, either. That was OK, if it was just me and Doug," Tracy insisted. "But when Jeff came over, it was a lot of work. They worked out with 200 pounds and went up. I started out with 50 pounds and went up to 100. Imagine how many (weight) plates had to be removed then added back between sets when I was in the mix. Not good."

Tracy began to feel like she was in the way.

Tracy said Jeff didn't like it when she was there, Jeff later admitting as much in court. She was coming in between what had been a routine the men had been accustomed to for years before she was ever even in the picture. Now she was causing the workout to be longer and more difficult. Jeff Bennett had a hard time focusing. And lifting heavy weight, anyone involved in the practice would agree, is all about focus.

Body. Mind. Soul.

Funny what love can do? How it can change a man.

"Jeff's attitude got worse by the minute," Tracy insisted. "If Doug didn't make a workout, Jeff got mad. He called two and three times a day asking Doug where he was at and if he was with me. Once, when Doug and I were going to breakfast, Jeff called and asked Doug what he was doing. When Doug said, 'Going to breakfast,' Jeff came back with, 'Are you with that bitch?' "

"What's Jeff's problem?" Tracy began asking Doug.

Why couldn't Jeff understand they were in love, Tracy wondered. Give them the space the relationship required.

"He's just mad," Doug said.

"But why?" Tracy countered. She couldn't figure out why Jeff was getting so angry when she was with Doug.

They were in love. Shouldn't he be happy that his best friend had found love?

"I remember the time Jeff had said that he was glad Doug had finally found someone he could be happy with. The fact that he was mad didn't sound like the same person to me that Doug had been describing."

One day, Tracy was with Doug as he was out working a welding job. Doug was underneath a trailer, welding the axle. His cell phone rang.

"Get that, would you, babe?" Doug told Tracy.

"Hello?" Tracy said into the phone. She looked at the screen and knew it was Jeff calling.

All Tracy could hear was static. Bad connection.

"Hello … I cannot hear you … hello," she kept repeating.

Jeff continued to talk, not hearing Tracy. Soon, she hung up because she could not hear anything.

"Who was it?" Doug asked.

She told him what happened.

"He'll call back."

Later that night, Jeff called while Tracy and Doug were at Doug's house enjoying dinner. Jeff, according to Tracy, started in on Doug and yelled so loudly, Tracy claimed, "I could hear him (through the phone while) standing next to Doug."

Jeff was convinced Tracy could hear him when he called earlier that day and blew him off, was rude and—worst of all—intentionally hung up on him.

12.

TRACY SHOWED UP AT the MCSD as promised at 6 p.m. on Sunday, June 18, 2000, sheriff Amory Scoggins' report of the interview noted. What's important about this meeting is that the MCSD was still in the information-gathering stage of looking for a missing person. Nothing more. MCSD was looking to discover information from everyone Doug knew, including Tracy. This was a voluntary interview. Tracy was there to help. Not to be interrogated.

Scoggins and Tracy sat, shook hands and smiled. Two cops, at least fundamentally speaking, after the same answer. Tracy, undoubtedly, one would think, was wondering where in the hell her ex-boyfriend had run off to. Although Tracy wasn't with the sheriff's department any longer, having initiated a lawsuit against the department, she still held the look of the law in her eyes. In the way she walked and spoke, Tracy carried herself like a cop.

"When was the last time you saw Mr. Benton?" Scoggins asked after they exchanged pleasantries.

"On Monday," she said, "June 5th."

"When?"

"Oh, between 6 and 8 p.m. It was at his house. I had been in court and traveled out to see him afterward."

"How was your relationship then?"

"Rocky," Tracy said, taking a breath. "Doug had become

jealous, wanting to know my whereabouts at all times and more specifically, on that Monday in particular, he was in a foul mood."

Tracy had stopped by Doug's to talk, she further explained. She started to help him as he tended to the birds, as she normally would. But Doug snapped at her: "I don't need any help!"

"I stayed there until around 10:30," Tracy told Scoggins. "Then I went back to my house."

That would have been between two and four-and-a-half hours, depending on what time Tracy had arrived.

"Did you two make plans to see each other again?"

"I also received a voicemail from him. He said not to come over, not to call him anymore and, basically, that the relationship was finished."

What was she supposed to do? She'd tried to mend fences. Doug wasn't interested. So she began to let go.

That was about all Tracy had for the MCSD. What else could she offer? She'd seen the guy. He was bitter. He wanted nothing to do with her anymore. It was over. Now he was gone.

Where in the hell was Doug Benton?

13.

TRACY FORTSON AND Doug Benton, if we are to believe what Tracy later said about their relationship, were madly in love during the spring of 2000. She believed they shared a deep connection and had many things in common. Tracy had explained to her mother one day after meeting Doug that she thought they were meant to be together—that Doug was "the one." Tracy's mother, on the other hand, knew Tracy's relationships with men "never lasted very long."

"I had been married twice," Tracy explained to me, "and neither marriage lasted more than 18 months. I just didn't do well with relationships."

Tracy said the "underlying reason" for the dissolution of most relationships she'd been involved in, after being in love with her daughter's father, was simple: "I compared every man I ever met with (him—Elise's dad), and no one ever came close. I had it in my brain that no one would ever measure up, and they didn't. As a result, my relationships never went anywhere. The men I became involved with were not as good-looking … not as passionate, not as tall, not as built, just not (him) and never would be. He had been perfect, in my 18-year-old eyes. Doug was the first man I had ever met that I did not compare to (him). Doug was the 'total package.' He had it all."

There was one night when Doug and Tracy sat at the

kitchen table inside her mother's house. Tracy's mother was cooking dinner. The smells of childhood wafting up from the pot on the stove. Her mother standing, apron on, preparing a meal. It was not only nostalgic, but comforting in a way that only being back home can be. Although Tracy would later talk about many bad memories associated with her childhood, this was one image she treasured.

Tracy stared at Doug.

This is nice, she thought. *It feels so right.*

"I want to tell you how we met, Mother," Tracy began.

Tracy's mother said she couldn't wait to hear.

After Tracy concluded the story, Doug spoke: "I had said a prayer and asked God to send a woman who would love me and care for me, someone I could love in return. Two days later, there you go, I met Tracy."

"Isn't that the sweetest thing you ever heard?" Tracy said.

Her mother smiled.

"Doug was right," Tracy later recalled, "it was a God thing."

If there was one characteristic about Doug she adored, Tracy later explained, it was that he never tired of being around her. They saw each other every day. He brought her flowers at work. Took her shopping. They rode those steel horses together whenever weather permitted.

"I will even learn to ride a horse," Doug said one day, kissing Tracy, speaking softly. "Just to be able to ride with you."

Doug seemed to be interested in anything Tracy wanted to do.

When Tracy worked at the sheriff's department, Doug liked to pop in to say hello or take her out to lunch. On one afternoon, as they often did, Doug and Tracy met at Papa's Pizza in Crawford, just a few miles from the OCSD on Athens Road where Tracy worked. Most of the deputies ate at the restaurant. It was one of those local joints in the area law enforcement frequented.

Tracy waited inside her patrol car. Doug had said he'd meet her in the parking lot. He gave specific instructions to wait there in her car until he arrived. As she stared out the window, Doug not anywhere in sight, on the driver's side, in the window, Doug popped up. He had a dozen red roses in his hand. A smile on his face.

According to Tracy, it was somewhere "along this timeframe when some of my coworkers started making comments about Doug coming around so much."

This bothered Tracy. For one, there were other employees whose spouses and boyfriends were periodically stopping by the department. One in particular had her boyfriend there most of the day. But Tracy thought since the woman was in her 60s, it was never an issue.

There had always been "talk," as Tracy termed it, within the workplace, as there is in any corporate or private office environment. She expected as much. She especially pointed out how if someone came around the department and wasn't "one of us" (not a cop, in other words), "smart remarks" were made by some. In one example, Tracy explained how a Georgia Bureau of Investigation (GBI) agent came in one day. Two of her colleagues and Tracy were looking out the window as he walked up to the front door. Turned out the deputy he was looking for was in the office next door, so they sent the agent across the parking lot to the other building. As he left and walked out of earshot, according to Tracy, one of the men she was with said, "Well, that sawed-off son of a bitch is so short he'd have to have a stepstool just to take a piss in the toilet."

They all laughed—including Tracy.

"That was just how (things were)," Tracy added. "Everyone was short compared to (this guy). He stood about 6 feet 2 inches. It was funny."

But then the comments turned toward Doug, which were, of course, not as funny to Tracy.

After the first time Doug came into the office for a visit, Tracy explained, one of her coworkers said, "Well ... damn ... Squirrely (Tracy's OCSD nickname), he's so short, you'd lose him in the grass."

When Tracy told Doug about it, something she later reckoned she should have never done, he became angry. He couldn't see it for what it was: a joke. A way cops like to rip each other and make fun of people and certain situations. Humor, however insulting to others, is part of being on the job and dealing with the horrors cops see every day. Their sense of humor is generally twisted and arcane to the average person—and can sometimes hurt others.

Still, Doug was livid. He had a look in his eyes. He wasn't going to take it again, Tracy knew.

DOUG GOT INTO A pretty bad bike accident one day and spent some time in the hospital. He decided, after talking it over with Tracy, that maybe they should ditch the bikes. It was dangerous, after all.

"Doug had a fractured ankle and a severely bruised arm and shoulder, along with his bruised ego," Tracy said.

Tracy was the one who brought Doug into the hospital because the accident had occurred not far from the department after Doug visited one day. Even this—an accident—Tracy said had caused problems between her and Jeff Bennett—a situation she thought had resolved itself after she and Doug talked about it and Doug decided that Jeff would have to understand he was in love with Tracy. That *she* came first now.

Jeff showed up at the accident.

"You need to go to the hospital," Tracy told Doug. She had arrived in her patrol car, along with several EMTs. Doug had called Jeff and told him what happened.

"I'll take him," Jeff said.

"No. He can go in an ambulance or I'll take him in my patrol car. I'm his girlfriend," Tracy said. "I want to be with him."

Why the hell is he even here? Tracy thought, looking at Jeff.

"I wasn't sure who to call," Doug said. He was pretty banged up. "So I called you both."

Not long after, they decided they weren't going to ride on the highways any longer. They couldn't, in the end, give the bikes up all together.

Those comments about Doug bouncing around the OCSD, however, continued, Tracy claimed. Getting worse with time.

"Although I should have known better," Tracy explained, "I made the mistake of telling Doug about the comments being made, and not only those about him, but also those that had been made to me the entire time I had worked there."

This was something Tracy said she overlooked for a long time. Being a woman in a male-dominated environment, she expected some talk that would be uncomfortable and maybe even sexist. It was the way of the world, she came to understand and even accept to some extent.

"Doug was furious," Tracy recalled. "It pissed him off to learn that my coworkers were talking about him, but he felt disrespected when he found out what they had said about me, as well as, *to* me."

There was one morning, according to Tracy, while she was at the OCSD and someone in the office happened to answer the phone. An elderly couple in a nearby town was calling, worried about a cat that had been perched on top of their barn for several days. They believed the cat might be hurt and called to see what kind of help the OCSD could offer.

"I'll send someone right over to have a look," the man said.

He hung up the phone. Tracy was standing nearby. Then he stood, walked over to her and said, "Come on, Squirrely, let's go get a little pussy."

"Now, we all know that his statement had a little double meaning to it. But I didn't let it faze me at all. So, I grabbed the keys to his car and drove him right up to the address given. The couple was glad to see us and while (he) chatted with them, getting a little politicking in for good measure, I had the not-so-glamorous duty of climbing on top of the barn, where said cat was curled up asleep. Well, that is, until I got within 10 feet of him, at which point he went airborne off the rooftop. Nothing wrong with that cat! The little old couple were quite happy and the (man) and I went on back to the office. Nothing else was said about the cat or the comment."

That was the beginning of it, Tracy claimed. Another deputy got in on the commenting next. For whatever reason, this deputy wanted the guys in the department "to believe that I had been a stripper prior to becoming a deputy."

Which was not true, Tracy said.

He would wait until there were at least three or four other deputies in the office and then he would make an announcement.

"Ya'll know (Tracy here) used to be a stripper, don't ya? Yeah, I got a picture of her with two men."

From there, the conversation took on a more direct tone, pointed at Tracy. All with sexual undertones.

"Well, what color is your thong?" that same deputy asked one afternoon while several officers stood around.

Tracy turned red. She could tell him to fuck off, but she was more hurt than anything by it. It was insulting. It went back to her comment that if she were older, maybe less attractive, would they still be making such sexist, sexually explosive comments?

"The funny thing is I have never been a stripper at all, anywhere, so I never understood what got him started saying that. The comment about a picture of me with two men? He never produced a photo of me at all."

14.

THE LAST TIME TRACY heard from Doug Benton, she later said, he left her a voicemail indicating he didn't want to speak to her anymore. In addition, Doug had said he didn't want to ever see her again. The tone of this message sounded final to Tracy.

As Tracy left the MCSD and thought about Doug being gone for so long, she went back to that voicemail. Doug had done this before, Tracy insisted. He'd get angry, snap and say don't call or talk to him ever again.

Tracy called Doug's mom, Carol Benton, the first time this happened. She asked about Doug. Told her what had happened.

"Just give him some space," Carol suggested.

Doug needed to cool off. He needed to figure things out on his own. He needed time.

"That's what I was doing," Tracy said later, referring to those days in June 2000 when Doug was reportedly missing. "And that's why I had not seen or heard from him since (that first weekend in June). I didn't *know* he was missing."

When she realized no one had seen Doug in so long, Tracy phoned his friend Jerry Alexander's wife and asked what was going on. If they knew anything.

Not much, Tracy said the Alexanders told her.

Tracy never mentioned that Jerry knew of a note left on

Doug's truck. Why wouldn't Jerry say anything to Tracy about this note?

Tracy phoned Doug's brother.

"Haven't heard from him," he said. "Mom hasn't, either."

Tracy "thought" about calling Jeff Bennett, but decided against it because of their history.

"I just didn't feel comfortable calling him."

Tracy phoned a sheriff friend of hers on or about "that Saturday," June 17, 2000. She knew him well. But then re-thinking it later, she couldn't recall if it was actually that Sunday, June 18, when she phoned her friend.

"Do you need me to go over and help with Doug's birds?" Tracy said she asked him.

"No, we've got someone doing that."

"OK."

Tracy explained to her sheriff friend how she had heard from Doug via voicemail. The sheriff said he already knew about the call.

"Listen, Tracy, if Doug told you not to go over to his house, it's probably better that you don't," her law enforcement friend recommended, according to Tracy.

"OK," she said and left it there.

15.

DURING THE WINTER OF 2000, as Doug Benton and Tracy Fortson's relationship seemed to be moving in a positive direction, Tracy's professional life in law enforcement began to unravel. The more time she spent around the OCSD, the more Tracy began to feel the banter around the officer was not something that made her feel at all comfortable or welcome.

As Tracy explained to Doug what was going on at work—those rude, potentially sexist comments, the put-downs and the highly sexually charged atmosphere—Tracy said Doug put pressure on her to leave the job.

Tracy had failed at becoming a game warden. She had joined the OCSD at 33 years of age in 1998. Here she was now, only 18 months into that job she so desperately saw as long-term career, and she was thinking about giving it up.

Sheriff Ray Sanders, in a published report, later commented on the accusations Tracy wound up lodging against the department: "(Tracy) said she always wanted to be in law enforcement, and thought she could add to the county, and she did. She was a good deputy."

Sanders went on to note that Tracy was doing a great job for the department. She was an asset to the team—that is, until about December 1999, or two months before she would ultimately walk away. That was about the time, Ray Sanders claimed in that public report, that Tracy's attitude took on a different tone.

"She changed her personality, her work and everything," Sanders was quoted as saying.

The feeling around the OCSD as 1999 gave way to the year 2000 was in stark contrast to what Tracy would later say about her relationship with Doug at the time. Tracy and Doug were fighting, many of the deputies and the sheriff believed, and that volatile atmosphere in which Tracy was involved at home had a detrimental effect on her work ethic and overall approach, mood and demeanor while on the job.

Sanders was further quoted saying that at first, Tracy started to "complain about working conditions within the department."

Then she told him "she needed more money."

Note that none of the deputies or the sheriff indicated Tracy was complaining about harassment of any type. It was money and "working conditions," which meant different things, realistically.

Then, without warning, one day in February 2000, Tracy walked out of the department "without working out a two-week notice" with the sheriff. She then went to work for Doug, making what Ray Sanders claimed was "$300 a week in cash helping with (Doug's) welding business and a side job raising exotic birds."

While Tracy worked for Doug during this period, she started to tell her boyfriend what had been going on in the office. After hearing about it all in more detail, Tracy claimed Doug spearheaded the idea of filing a lawsuit against the department.

"You're sitting on a gold mine," Doug said to her one day.

This comment got her thinking.

"I went along with this idea," Tracy told me in 2016. "It never crossed my mind (until then) that anything so extreme (as what was about to happen) would result from it. ... I never considered the consequences or repercussions of filing the claim. If I had thought that something like (what would take place next) would happen because of filing that claim, I never would have considered it."

In April 2000, Tracy went to the Department of Labor and applied for unemployment compensation. Her claim was that she had been sexually harassed while working at the OCSD. It was all that talk around the office she now was certain had been directed at her, along with inappropriate language used around her. According to Tracy, she had been "made to feel uncomfortable by rough language used by deputies and inappropriate joking in the office."

Ray Sanders vehemently denied the charges (as he does to this day) and appealed the unemployment claim.

"I filed a sexual harassment/discrimination case against Sheriff Ray Sanders and the Oglethorpe County Sheriff's Department," Tracy told me in 2016. "I went to the Equal Employment Opportunity Commission in Atlanta, Georgia, to file this claim. I hired Attorney Margaret Dyal to represent me. I had audiotapes of the sheriff making lewd, sexual comments to me on the job.[3] Doug notified the newspaper and made it public. This was highly embarrassing to the sheriff. He is a very proud man. He never took embarrassment well and he had a notorious temper."

According to Doug's mother, "There was ... a history between Doug and Ray Sanders. I believe it was (a friend of Doug's) who told (her) that Doug wanted retribution for something that had happened between them (Sanders and Doug) in the past. I never found out what that was and wasn't aware that Doug knew Sanders prior. Whatever happened between them is what caused Doug to want retribution. There are just too many gaps that haven't been filled. Too many unanswered questions."

Regardless what anyone thought—or if there ever was

---

3   I have never heard these tapes.

an issue between Doug and the sheriff—on June 12, a week after Doug went missing, Tracy and Ray Sanders met face-to-face at the Labor Department for a board hearing. The issue of compensation and whether Tracy was sexually harassed, of course, came up during this hearing, but it remained unresolved. The arbitrator determined then that it would take another hearing, maybe several more, with witnesses and possibly even evidence, before a resolution or judgment could be made.

So, as the search for Doug continued into Monday, June 19, 2000, Tracy was waiting to hear from the Department of Labor when she and Ray Sanders would square off again.

Neither could have known then, but that next hearing date would never take place. But maybe more than that: one aspect of the case the MCSD was interested in, as Doug Benton's whereabouts became a central focus of the investigative team, became that note Doug had supposedly left on his truck in Jerry Alexander's driveway. After a careful examination of Doug's handwriting, several investigators believed there was no way Doug Benton could have written the note. In fact, Madison County sheriff Clayton Lowe came out and said publicly: "Somebody else wrote it."

PART II

"I've crossed some kind of invisible line. I feel as if I've come to a place I never thought I'd have to come to. And I don't know how I got here. It's a strange place. It's a place where a little harmless dreaming and then some sleepy, early-morning talk has led me into considerations of death and annihilation."

— **Raymond Carver,** *Where I'm Calling From: New and Selected Stories*

16.

THERE'S AN UNRESTRAINED curiosity, or maybe it can be explained as, say, a rubberneck mentality, we all exhibit when coming into contact with an object or person in a place where neither belongs. Take, for example, a man walking across a freeway during rush hour, not paying any mind to oncoming traffic. He's not supposed to be there. Our brains take a moment to adjust to such an unusual image. Not that seeing the object—or the man on the freeway—sounds some sort of internal alarm system; quite contrarily, it's the *reason* behind the man or object being there that becomes the mystery—not the action of which he is engaged, or who he actually is. Why is the man walking across a busy freeway without a care in the world? He must be "crazy," right? Or certainly out of his mind? Maybe he's on drugs. Yes, that's it. Bath salts. THC. He does not know what the fuck he is doing.

Either way, whatever conclusion we come to internally, our curiosity sounds and we *need* an answer.

Which is what happened when Rob Poston and his wife were out among the 1,500 acres of cattle land Rob oversaw on that Sunday afternoon in June when everyone seemed to be looking for Doug Benton. Rob caught sight of an oblong, coffin-shaped metal container that, hitting just the right amount of sunlight at that particular hour, made him stop his

ATV, turn the bike around, go back and check it out. Rob's instincts told him to investigate. What's more, as Rob and his wife hopped off the four-wheeler and started walking toward the object, curiosity pumping through their veins, there was something else. Something much more profound and alarming than seeing the object.

An intense smell: putrid and potent.

Death.

This, mind you, in an area of the farm where you'd think the skunk cabbage—or maybe all of the horse and cow shit and a few dead raccoons and squirrels—would overpower any other aroma you might encounter.

But not on this day.

"What is it?" Rob said aloud, more to himself than his wife.

Rob's responsibilities on the Stephens, Georgia, farm he supervised ran the gamut. With a large herd of beef cattle, he was forever cruising the terrain, looking out for predators and problems. Spending his days and even sometimes nights roaming, plus living on the farm with his wife and daughter, Rob knew every one of the 1,000 acres—along with an additional 500 more the land owner rented out to farmers and ranchers.

"We kind of have a game preserve, too," Rob said later, "where people do a lot of hunting and whatnot."

So, outsiders, friends of the owner and others were familiar with the land (a fact you should store somewhere in your brain, because within the scope of Doug Benton's disappearance, that information will become important soon enough).

It was one of those daily life contingencies we deal with placing Rob and his wife on an ATV, four-wheeling over a stretch of terrain in the back part of the farm Rob would have otherwise not had reason to tend to. His daughter had been riding an ATV the previous day, Saturday. The bike got a flat. Rob had gone out to this section of the farm to find the bike and fix the tire. It is a piece of property, Rob said in court, that he normally never "went to," adding, "It was after turkey season, before deer season, so unless we just have a purpose to go back there, we normally don't go back there at this time of the year."

After fixing the flat, Rob headed through what he described as "the last cattle pasture ... across the last cattle guard." This area was a quarter-mile or so down and over that slight hill he'd come upon before seeing the object, sticking out just above the soil line, a death-like smell permeating the area around it.

So now, here Rob stood over it, looking down and wondering what in the name of Georgia peaches is this thing doing in the field.

17.

STANDING BY THE object, Rob's wife in back of him, that atrocious smell overcoming both of them, "A cattle trough?" Rob asked aloud, figuring out what it was.

Strange.

It made no sense for a cattle trough to be this far out, in the middle of nowhere, sort of hidden and partially buried.

Rob took a closer look.

The trough was full of something.

Stepping back, he thought the resemblance to a coffin was unmistakable.

Holding his breath, wondering what was causing the smell, Rob bent down. His first thought was maybe someone had filled the trough with garbage, drove it out here away from everything and tossed it. People could be ignorant of the land and dump whatever the hell they felt like: tires, mattresses, busted-up concrete and everyday garbage. But this trough, Rob realized, was brand new. Not only that, but somebody had crudely painted the outside of it in what they'd hoped to look like camouflage.

Rob tried to move it.

Thing wouldn't budge.

"I better take some pictures of it," Rob said to his wife. "Then head back and get the tractor and get it out of here."

An hour later, Rob was back at it with his tractor. He

hoisted the trough out of the ground. It had been buried only several inches, not entirely; one end of it actually was a bit deeper into the ground than the other. It appeared to be filled with fresh, hardened concrete. Newly painted on the outside was that rudimentary camouflage mish-mash of colors, spotted greens and browns and blacks. It was covered on the top with fresh soil—definitely not dirt from anywhere on the farm.

Looking closer, Rob said, "That's peat moss." The same stuff you'd sprinkle on a lawn or garden from a bag bought at the Home Depot or feed store.

The trough now sitting on top of the ground, Rob and his wife tried to flip it over.

Not a chance. Thing was as heavy as five tombstones.

Rob stared at it. He had a funny feeling.

Something was wrong.

Yes, very, very wrong.

"I better go back and call the sheriff," Rob said.

Rob's gut was talking to him.

The June heat was unbearable. Beating down on the dry land, the knee-high grass all around them. It was getting late. The sun just now doing its little amber twilight dance before hiding behind the horizon until the following morning.

OCSD Sheriff Mike Smith drove out to the farm after Rob called it in. With him was an investigator from the GBI, Special Agent Ben Williams, who had just happened to be at the office when Rob's call came in. Smith never mentioned why he brought Williams along.

Using the tractor, Rob Poston and Mike Smith managed to flip the trough on its side, while Ben Williams looked on.

The sheriff had a small chisel and screwdriver. Before he began, Smith made several notes about the trough: "It was covered with some kind of black material and looked like it was encased with cement and had a foul odor coming from it."

The more he thought about it, Smith decided to see if

Rob, using the forks on the front of his tractor, could pick the trough up off the ground and drop it, cracking it open.

Didn't work.

"There was a lot of black stuff," Rob said later. "It wasn't completely filled. And it had been drained."

With the smell, the size of the trough and now a black, muddy liquid draining from it, the sheriff, special agent and Rob looked at each other and realized there probably wasn't an animal buried in that concrete. So Smith decided he'd better call in EMS, adding, "I'm going to call out the coroner, too."

Just in case.

18.

ALTHOUGH THEY WERE "in back" of the farm, far away from most of the farming equipment and active farmland, this "cow part of the farm," as Rob later referred to it, was easily accessible from the main road. It was considered the "preserve" section of the farm, which one could access though a dirt road connected to the main street. A car or truck could turn off the main road and jump onto this access—or dirt—road and make its way out to where the cement-filled trough had been found—that is, if the driver could get through the locked gate or knew of another way onto the land.

This was a section of the farm the owner, Rodney Sturdivant, allowed friends and others to hunt. In fact, Tracy Fortson, considered by some to be an "expert hunter" who had "bagged several trophy deer" and even a wild turkey on this very spot of land, was someone Sturdivant had hunted with on occasion out here.

What about admittance to the area? GBI SA Ben Williams and OCSD Sheriff Mike Smith wondered as they waited for the coroner and EMS personnel to arrive.

The dirt road passed by "175 feet or so from where the container was found," Rob Poston explained.

There were two gates to get into the property near this same section of the farm. Rob had taken a ride over to both while law enforcement checked out the trough and, sure enough, one of the gates had been busted open.

The coroner and EMS arrived on scene, where Rob, Sheriff Smith and Agent Williams waited. The thought was that whatever they were about to uncover inside the trough, encased in fresh concrete, was going to require the services of a medical examiner. Smith had experience with the odor coming from the trough, as did Williams.

It smelled like the morgue. Using his chisel and screwdriver, after several tries, Smith created a crack in the concrete and stepped back as a putrid, multi-colored liquid pissed out.

Which was when the sheriff saw something.

An arm.

My God.

Staring at the arm, Smith later said, he had a "good idea" who the dead man encased in concrete was.

He knew that arm.

"I have seen it before," Smith commented, referring to the tattoo of a single rose visible on the arm.

Incredibly, it wasn't that Smith had recognized the victim as someone he knew personally, but he'd seen the guy on several occasions. Same as many of the other investigators and deputies and sheriffs.

"At the Oglethorpe County Sheriff's Department."

Smith knew his name: Doug Benton.

Then it all came together.

"Ain't there some missing person's report out on Doug Benton?" Smith asked Williams.

They needed to call it in and find out.

And so, as investigators got together to confirm the man buried in the concrete was, in fact, Doug Benton, it appeared Doug had not run away, after all. Nor had he gone into the woods to kill himself. But somebody had murdered the guy and buried him in a horse trough, covering Doug's corpse with concrete.

19.

GBI AGENT BEN WILLIAMS, Mike Smith and several other investigators were back at the OCSD brainstorming where to take the investigation next. They'd want an absolute confirmation, but by all accounts, the dead man in the concrete was Doug Benton. Smith had been told Doug's mother and brother were on their way south and would be in town soon. By then, they'd have Doug's body out of the trough and a positive ID could be made. Until that time, they were going under the assumption that Doug had been murdered and encased in concrete. Probably, the thought was, on or near June 4, 5 or 6, the last time anyone had reportedly seen or heard from him.

Before heading back to the sheriff's department, Smith and Williams stopped at Jerry Alexander's house. It was close to 6 o'clock on that same evening Doug's body had been found. Being a Monday, Jerry had just gotten home from work as they pulled in.

They asked Jerry if he would mind following them down to the OCSD so they could have a chat.

"What's going on?" Jerry wondered. They could tell he sensed something was up.

Once they were at the OCSD, Smith sat down with Jerry. Other investigators were present.

"Doug's dead," Smith told Jerry. Doug wasn't missing.

They'd found his remains.

"What?"

Smith didn't say how, where or what they found, but indicated that Doug's body had been recovered. It wasn't a suicide, either, as Jerry had thought.

Jerry "became emotional," Smith's report said.

After Jerry had some time to collect himself, he started talking about Tracy. Here was one of Doug's besties painting an interesting picture of Doug and Tracy's relationship, in the scope of what they had uncovered. Later, when recalling this interview in court, Jerry said he hadn't planned on pointing a finger at Tracy as a potential suspect in Doug's murder. But the thought was the first thing that came into his mind.

What spawned this sudden interest in Tracy?

"The only reason ... was that me and Jeff (Bennett) were the only ones that showed up Sunday"—which would have been the day before the police interview—"to go looking for Doug," Jerry had said in court.

This seemed odd to Doug's friend.

Jerry had made several calls after the sheriff and deputies were over to his house on that Saturday to impound Doug's truck and take the note. He firmly believed Doug had gone out into the woods and killed himself. He spoke to a few friends, a local sheriff he knew, and decided to get a group together and search the woods. One of the men Jerry got hold of wound up calling Tracy. But it seemed to him that she didn't care. Or, rather, she didn't see an urgent need to go out looking. Tracy never showed up to help—even though, according to the friend who had called her, she said she would.

"I talked to (a deputy I knew)," Jerry explained. "And he said Tracy was supposed to come and help us look. But she never showed up. That is the *only* reason it gave me suspicion."

Mike Smith asked Jerry about Doug and Tracy's relationship. Could he add anything? The pendulum, it seemed, was doubling back toward Tracy, law enforcement leaning in a direction of Tracy perhaps wanting Doug out of the picture. Tracy would later contend this focus on her as a suspect came out of left field. Why would law enforcement accuse her so quickly?

When you look at what investigators were being told, the urge is always to follow the evidence. How could they *not* begin to think Tracy might have had something to do with Doug's murder? If nothing more, they needed to run it down, separate truth from rumor. Eight out of 10 people murdered are killed by someone they knew. The odds were, Doug knew his murderer.

Jerry had plenty to say in regard to Tracy. He called Doug and Tracy's arguments "huge" spectacles. He said Doug had told him about a time when Tracy took a gun to herself and then pointed it at Doug.

"I told Doug on many occasions," Jerry added through tears, "that he needed to leave Tracy alone and get away from her."

Jerry then talked about how Jeff Bennett once told him Tracy hit her ex-husband with a pipe. Yet, in the same breath, Jerry also brought Ray Sanders, the sheriff, into the conversation, adding, "Doug told me he was going to get Ray Sanders because Ray ran his mouth. ... Doug really needed someone to talk to."

Smith asked about Tracy, specifically. Her demeanor around Doug. Her overall character.

"She's really insecure," Jerry said. Then he mentioned how Tracy had called the house one night and spoke to his wife. Jerry's wife had been the one to explain to Tracy that Doug's truck had been parked at the house since early June.

"I remember Tracy once coming over the house and telling my wife I didn't want her in the house and she told me that I should leave my wife alone because all she wanted was money. She caused a lot of marital problems for me."

They discussed the past few days. Went over information

the sheriff's office had collected and some of what GBI SA Williams had just learned. For one, the magnetic sign on Doug's truck—his business name and number—had been taken off the side doors. This felt odd. Also, the seat inside Doug's truck had been pushed back farther than its normal position for Doug to drive.

"Doug had gotten Tracy to file the sexual harassment (suit) against Ray Sanders because of something that had happened a long time ago," Jerry said.

Williams wrote as Jerry spoke, detailing this conversation in several reports.

"Chuck Haster," Jerry said, "he is someone you need to talk to." Chuck (a pseudonym) was a guy Tracy had once lived with. Jerry knew him. "Tracy pulled a gun on him when she used to live with him. He has not seen her in a long time, but might have something for you."

Later that same day, SA Williams got hold of Jeff Bennett and explained Doug was dead. It wasn't a suicide, Jeff was told.

Silence. Jeff said nothing for a few moments.

Then, "Tracy had something to do with (it)," Jeff Bennett blurted out.

20.

THE NEXT MORNING, TUESDAY, June 20, a multi-agency team secured the proper paperwork and gathered to head out and search Doug's house. There was a second crime scene somewhere. Doug obviously was not murdered on the grounds of that cattle ranch. Early word coming from the medical examiner's office was that Doug had been shot and, possibly, stabbed. The autopsy was going to take some extra time due to, mainly, the fact that Doug's body had been encased in concrete.

MCSD investigator Amory Scoggins was part of the team headed over to Doug's. Scoggins had gone into Doug's house on June 17, the day Doug had been reported missing by his neighbor, Larry Bridges. When Scoggins went in that first time, there were several "things," he later referred to them, that felt "unusual" as he walked through Doug's home.

"As far as entering the residence," Scoggins said of that earlier search on June 17, "nothing I guess you would say that would catch your nose. It looked like just a general residence." However, there was an odd piece of equipment that stood out to the investigator as he made his way through: a blower inside the house. "I don't know if the air conditioner was frozen up or what, but there was a blower at that particular time, which was circulating the air." Scoggins thought perhaps there was some sort of raunchy smell Doug had been trying to get rid of, adding, "But as far as any overt odors, I did not smell any."

Still, it seemed strange—save for maybe a flood of some sort, which there clearly hadn't been—for a blower to be left on inside the house of a man who had not been home for, all indicators pointed, about two weeks.

Walking in on June 20, three days later, there was a different feel—and an entirely different smell—to Doug's house. By now, the team knew Doug had been murdered. Here, they were looking to see if that crime had taken place inside his house and what, if any, evidence might have been left behind. Suddenly, with the discovery of his body and a period of time in between law enforcement visits, that blower Scoggins noticed several days before took on new significance.

"Our scope of looking for a missing person is a little bit different than after you have a homicide investigation started," Scoggins noted.

Alongside Scoggins were SA Ben Williams and OCSD deputy Mike Smith. Each jurisdiction, each law enforcement agency, was properly represented.

There had been some confusion about which side of the house was the back and which might be the front. There was a wooden deck—a "platform," Scoggins called it—built on what they soon figured out was the front entrance to the home. They called this the main entryway. Doug lived in a mobile/modular home and there were two ways he could enter, both of which could be considered a front door.

When they were out there on June 17, Scoggins had noticed a water hose lying on the ground. It had been left on, trickling and leaking water out of the nozzle.

Which, unbeknownst to them, was so Doug could provide water to his birds. Not necessarily, as a general opinion would later become, mix concrete.

When they arrived on June 20 and stood on Doug's wooden deck, Scoggins said, they had a good overall view of the yard from a slightly elevated viewpoint. Any cop worth his weight begins an investigation of a potential crime scene the moment he steps out of his vehicle. Looking around the yard from the deck, the three of them noticed impressions near a few bushes on the side of the deck. And that water hose (left on three days before) had been turned off.

"It appears that a vehicle of some type has been here," Scoggins said.

Smith and Williams agreed. You look down from the deck, there were faint tire impressions in the grass and the bushes had been crunched and pushed in where the vehicle had, they theorized, probably backed up to the deck.

"There was one limb broken off of a bush," Scoggins explained later, "… and an indentation … where the bush was broken right at the deck."

Interesting. Why would a vehicle back up to Doug's deck? Especially while he had been, presumably by then, dead? After all, Scoggins never reported seeing the indentation or broken branches when he and Doug's neighbor were out there poking around days ago.

The three investigators walked into Doug's home.

By this time, GBI special agent and crime scene specialist Terry Cooper had arrived. The feeling was that something had taken place here. Cooper was going to go through the home, inch by inch, inside and out, to see if there were any indication as to what might have happened to Doug Benton—and one better, who might have been responsible.

Cooper walked up and asked the three men if they had touched anything. Had they noticed anything out of the ordinary?

They had done nothing more than wait, walk in, take a cursory look around and call in the CSS. They had to go in, of course, and determine if the home was safe for a CSS investigation. But beyond that hasty, superficial walk-through, they hadn't touched anything. Several things looked out of whack, however, right from the get-go. The most distinguishable being the smell as soon as Scoggins, Williams and Smith entered Doug's house.

Fuel. Kerosene, diesel or gasoline. It was potent. Ubiquitous. Heavy. Thick in the air, like humidity.

"Damn," someone said.

Not only that, but Scoggins mentioned something significant: he had not recognized the smell as having been in the home three days prior, which could only mean somebody had come into the house within that three-day span.

Cooper took a walk around. He needed to find the source of the smell, which could pose a great danger just being in the house. As he entered the living room, immediately Cooper noticed a "discoloration" on what was a horseshoe-shaped couch. It was pink in color and that specific area of the couch cushion appeared to be more worn than anywhere else, as if it had been scrubbed.

Latex gloves snapped on, Cooper walked over to the couch and went in for a closer look.

Immediately, he noticed the discoloration was, in fact, where someone had rubbed and tried to clean the couch, wearing down the fabric. Then, near the armrest portion of the couch, in back of it on the carpet, lay a candle. Burned down to a green nub, with a "small scorch mark on the arm of the couch." To the right side of the couch lay a second candle, this one inside "a little flat holder," completely burned down.

Not something you see every day.

Cooper stepped back and, before doing anything else, photographed all of it. Then he bagged and tagged the candle, or, rather, what was left of it, literally having to cut it out of the carpet.

Next, Cooper took a knife and carefully sliced open a section of the couch where he'd spotted the discoloration. He needed to see inside the cushion. Maybe there was a clue behind the idea of someone vigorously scrubbing a couch.

Inside the cushion, Cooper spotted a "reddish brown

stain."

He knew that stain. Had seen it before.

Blood.

CSS Cooper then took out his phenolphthalein test kit—a "PT kit" checks for presumptive blood—and extracted a sample of the partially dried material, just to prove his hunch.

Indeed. A bloodstain.

Whoever had scrubbed the couch was trying to get rid of the blood.

After inspecting the entire couch, finding various areas saturated with blood—mainly confined to one end, Cooper had the couch moved out of his way. He wanted to get underneath the couch and see what secrets the carpet directly below might give up.

He bent over, cut a section of the carpeting and peeled it back.

More reddish-brown stains.

Lots of blood.

It was clear the blood had originated from the couch, by the armrest and to the right of it. A stream of blood had run down in between the cushion and the armrest, through the bottom of the couch and into the carpet, flowing through the carpet fibers and soaking into the padding. This could only mean one thing: a lot of blood had been spilled here. Someone cutting his or her finger, for example, would not produce as much blood as to drain through the couch cushion and into the carpet fibers and padding.

Doug was murdered right here.

Everyone worked under this theory.

Cooper studied the couch. It appeared that someone—presumably Doug—was lying on the couch, his head against the armrest. The injuries must have been traumatic—a massive head injury of some sort, Cooper surmised. The head bleeds profusely, much more than most other sections of the body.

Analyzing the situation, Cooper assumed that the person

whose head had made the injury—considering the massive cleanup that took place after blood was present—had to have been there, on the couch, "Anywhere from [a few] hours to a couple of days." More than that, the blood had dried. So it was also some time since the incident that had caused the injury had occurred.

Cooper noticed something else when he peeled the carpet back: a far more profound aroma of kerosene.

He followed it.

"It started underneath where the couch was located and it comes across the floor toward the location of the wood-burning heater," Cooper later said.

A scenario was taking shape. Someone, no doubt Doug's killer, had murdered him on the couch where he was, likely, asleep. Then tried to clean up the mess. Not having much luck, Doug's killer perhaps poured kerosene over the couch and the carpet, leaving a trail toward the wood-burning heater. Then he or she placed a candle on the carpet near the couch and lit it, hoping when the candle burned down and the flame ignited the kerosene, the entire house would go up in flames.

Only problem was the candle had burned out and failed to light the place on fire—leaving behind all of the forensic evidence CSS Cooper was uncovering and collecting.

So much accelerant had been poured over the inside of Doug's residence (actually a modular home, or double-wide trailer, he had put several additions on) that Cooper's latex gloves were wet from cutting and lifting the saturated carpet off the floor.

It had definitely not been there three days ago, either.

Looking around the dining area of the trailer, Cooper found something else. In the hallway leading to a bedroom was a "built-in type (set of) cabinets," Cooper called them. There were two cords inside one cabinet, an electrical and a white cord of some sort. But that wasn't what caught the CSS's attention, however; it was a stain on the doorknob.

Cooper popped off several more photographs and took a closer look at the stain.

Blood.

As he studied it, Cooper noticed different shaped "ridges" and curves, much like a fingerprint. Before Cooper swabbed the stain to preserve it, he lifted an impression, in case it could be later used to compare against other fingerprints, either found inside the trailer or elsewhere.

Taking the impression, however, Cooper realized there was no way a print was coming from it. Whoever had left the impression had worn, by Cooper's estimation, latex or rubber gloves. Now that he had a better look at it, he could see the impression was smooth, with no ridges.

Still, the stain told the CSS something about the crime scene. Whoever had come into Doug's house and murdered him, scrubbing the couch, cleaning up, trying to light it on fire, it seemed that same person (or persons) had done a careful job of trying to hide his or her identity—along with trying to cover up the murder scene.

21.

CAROL BENTON ARRIVED IN town to the news that her firstborn son had been murdered. It was devastating to hear, of course. Carol and Doug had been close. Even though she had moved north to Lansing, Michigan, Doug stayed in touch and visited Carol and his brother when he could. A Christmas baby, born on Dec. 25, Doug would have turned 39 that year. Carol was thinking about this as she pulled into the parking lot of the OCSD.

In a letter to the governor of Georgia six years after Doug's murder, Carol wrote that her son, for reasons neither she nor her late husband could fathom, "Was an alcoholic and drug user for many years." Distancing herself from her son's issues, Carol added how Doug, by her estimation, had been "brought up right and didn't learn his bad habits from us."

Still, that was the "Douglas" of yesteryear, Carol continued. Because, as his friend Jerry Alexander had told police already, Carol reiterated: "In 1992, Douglas became a Christian and turned his life over to Christ. At that time, I believe he experienced a miracle cure of all his addictions. I know for sure he never used addictive drugs or alcohol after that."

Carol was proud of her son. Beating an addiction was no easy task. Then again, Doug had always been a doer. He set his mind to something, he completed the job. Whatever it was.

As she began to consider the loss of her son, Carol talked about a moment years before Doug's murder when he experienced some sort of portend.

It was 1996. Carol and Doug's dad were at home. A package arrived.

"What's that?" Carol asked.

"Let's open it and find out."

It was from Doug. A videotape. Carol popped it into the VCR. A message from their son. How nice. How special. How personal.

Doug stared down the barrel of the camera and began talking: "*God doesn't promise us tomorrow*," Doug had said on that video, "*and all that any of us has is ... right now.*"

Thinking about this taped message later, Carol reflected that she believed Doug "had made a strange statement about his possible early death." Almost like he had a feeling he would not live a long life. It was two years later, in 1998, when Doug's father passed. Death seemed to be on Doug's mind. For Carol, when she looked back, she saw a different scenario.

"Doug never mentioned to either of us that he was involved in any undercover work fighting drugs. I found this out after his death and (it) may explain the strange video from all those years before."

What was Carol talking about? That the things Doug had been involved in scared him so much and were so serious that Doug thought he might be one day killed over it all?

Carol believed Doug had kept this from his parents so as not to worry them.

"He may have been very ashamed of his association and knowledge of the drug world in a three-county area, but was using this to help the FBI."

Was Doug Benton a confidential informant for law enforcement?

22.

BACK INSIDE DOUG'S TRAILER, something interesting was taking place. GBI special agent Ben Williams, along with two colleagues, searched Doug's house after the crime scene team finished collecting fingerprint and blood evidence, fibers and candle fragments, along with other items they deemed important in the search for Doug's killer. GBI had just inventoried a curtain sash—the curtain itself missing—and some papers titled "To Whom It May Concern," along with a Remington Speed master rifle, Model 552, and a piece of paper with 35 names on it.

"What do you suppose that list is?" one of investigators wondered.

"Not sure," another responded.

Far as they could tell, all of the names on the list were male.

23.

THINGS WERE STARTING TO look suspicious to me," Tracy said later in a letter to the media explaining what was going on in her mind at this time of the investigation, oddly adding next, "and I was definitely upset over Doug's disappearance."

Tracy had been staying at her mother's house with her daughter, Elise. She received a call from her cousin, Cindy Farmer (a pseudonym), while there during the time the investigation into Doug's murder was pumping full steam ahead.

"They found Doug's body in a lake at Roddy's (that farm) and they think you did it," Tracy later said her cousin told her over the phone.

"I felt a roaring in my ears and I could not speak," Tracy recalled feeling in that moment.

How could they think she'd had anything to do with Doug's disappearance or his death? Where was this accusation coming from? It seemed too early to even make a statement like that.

"Someone I know at the Oglethorpe County Sheriff's Office called me and told me," Cindy said.

"It was then," Tracy concluded here, "that I realized just how serious things had gotten."

Tracy had a relative who worked for a lawyer out of

Athens. Tom Camp was a seasoned criminal defense attorney. Maybe it was time to make a call and lawyer up, just in case.

"My family rallied around me and we retained Tom right then," Tracy said. "I knew what was coming at me: a runaway freight train."

24.

CSS TERRY COOPER MADE a significant find on Doug's truck when he analyzed it inside Tommy James's wrecker lot. Cooper photographed the entire truck before touching anything. Then, as the CSS began searching for evidence, one of the first things he noticed was a piece of tape used to attach the note that Doug supposedly had left on the driver's side window. But it wasn't just any piece of tape.

Before analyzing the tape, however, Cooper read the note. In almost grammar-school-like handwriting, messy and scribbled, perhaps made by a child just learning to write (or even made to appear that way), the note said:

> *Please take care of my truck for me(.) I have to leve (sic) town for awile (sic)(.) I know I can trust you. I will call you when I can(.) Don't say anything to anybody. Thanks(,) Doug. Don't try to call me. I will call you. Hide my truck if you can.*

Cooper was more interested in the tape, which he photographed. It was not your run-of-the-mill Scotch tape we all use to wrap gifts—but a very specific type of tape Cooper immediately recognized.

He slowly peeled it off the glass. When he realized what kind of tape it was, Cooper stopped. An idea struck him.

So he walked around the garage where the truck had been parked.

"Has anyone else processed this truck?" Cooper asked. He was confused. The tape had momentarily thrown him off.

"No," he heard over and over.

It might have seemed like a bizarre question. But there was no good reason for a CSS to reprocess a scene a colleague had already completed, Cooper explained later.

What had made him think the truck had already been processed?

It was "fingerprint lifting tape." Whoever had attached that note to Doug's truck had the same tape a CSS might use to lift fingerprints from windows, doors, knobs and any other surface or object. Who would have access to such tape? If Doug had attached the note, why would he use fingerprint tape?

Cooper seized the tape. He then had a good look at it and dipped a sample into Crystal Violent, a chemical solution that reveals fingerprint impressions on the sticky side of tape or any adhesive material.

He found nothing more than a flat outline of possibly a finger.

Cooper took the tape and poured magnetic powder on the smooth side of it. Maybe he could get an impression there?

Both areas provided "smooth impressions."

Gloves again.

Why would Doug Benton wear latex gloves and use fingerprint tape to secure a note to his truck?

None of this made sense.

Cooper took Doug's note and applied a purplish colored chemical called n-hydrine, mainly used on porous objects, to check for prints on the note itself. Paper absorbs moisture and amino acids. This chemical extracts the impression, lifting it from the surface.

After applying the solution, Cooper found nothing.

25.

ATTORNEY TOM CAMP CALLED Tracy at her mother's house. In her letter to the media later on, Tracy had the date wrong, but the phone call had to have taken place somewhere around June 20 or 21, Tuesday or Wednesday of that same week Doug's body was found.

"Madison County has a warrant for your arrest," Tracy claimed Tom Camp told her. "You need to meet me at the Sheriff's Office to turn yourself in."That was quick. Within hours of Doug's body being found encased in concrete and an investigation going on as fluid as the Mississippi River— evidence being collected, tests being conducted and a murder weapon not yet determined or found—Tracy Fortson was arrested for Doug Benton's murder. It screamed of cops putting on blinders and focusing the investigation on one suspect, rather than allowing the evidence to direct them to a person. Why make haste of an arrest? If Tracy were the top suspect, where was she going, and why wouldn't you want to question her more—without the scar of a warrant hanging over the interview?

According to Tracy, after she hung up with Tom Camp and realized she was going to have to go down to the sheriff's department, she took a deep breath and thought about the days ahead. Her family was looking at her "longingly," she remembered, as she hung up the phone and collapsed into a nearby kitchen chair.

"What is it, Mom? What's wrong?" Tracy's daughter, Elise, then 15, was particularly concerned and taken aback by the look on her mother's face: Tracy looked as if she carried the weight of the world on her back, compounded by the worry she saw in Elise's face.

"My daughter," Tracy explained, "looked like her world had just crumbled around her feet."

The relationship she had with Doug, Tracy later told me, was unlike any other relationship she'd ever had.

"I am not necessarily a believer in 'love at first sight,' " she recalled. "But I am truly a believer in the power of attraction. Attraction can be so overwhelmingly powerful that two people can be in a crowded room and still be drawn together like a magnet to steel. Yet, what begins as an overwhelming attraction to each other can swiftly turn to the same kind of overwhelming love. That is what Doug and I shared."

Being a cop and dating Doug, Tracy maintained, came with a cost.

"I have been told, more than once, that being with Doug did not make me look good as a law enforcement officer. Maybe it didn't. But when you really love someone, you look beyond their faults and try to help them. I admit that I didn't know all the details of what Doug had been involved in before I met him, or what he continued to be involved in afterward, but I was convinced that he was making the effort to change and I loved him enough to give him a chance."

Now Tracy was being accused of murdering this same man. Still, being a cop, understanding the realities of small-town, southern living, not to mention the denigrating mentality of a woman in a sexist, man's world, Tracy went on to note, she was never naive or ignorant as to what was going on during this time. Tracy said she knew that while sitting in her kitchen, the phone cradled back on the receiver after just having spoken to her attorney and now staring at her daughter, one thing became perfectly clear to her.

"I would never see my family again outside of prison walls."

26.

JEFFREY SMITH ATTENDED UNIVERSITY in Auckland, New Zealand, from 1979 to 1984, where he earned his doctorate in medicine. For six years after that, Dr. Smith practiced in several of New Zealand's emergency and family medical facilities before returning to the United States to begin his career in the Atlanta area.

Arriving in Georgia with a career ahead of him, Dr. Smith spent the next three years, 1992 to 1995, studying pathology. During that interim, he worked two years for the Fulton County Medical Examiner's Office and wound up working for the GBI in Decatur, where he began working on all sorts of criminal cases under the State Medical Examiner.

Before Smith began, Special Agent J.C. Maddox photographed the crudely painted galvanized watering trough, and how the CSSs had cut the bottom of the trough out so they could remove Doug's body. Maddox documented several items within the concrete that were going to, at some point, play a vital role in the investigation. One was a "maroon in color plastic shower curtain," Maddox noted in his report, along with "a clear shower curtain with blue, red and yellow designs"—sea shells and starfish—"and a beige in color floral print (bed) sheet." No one could tell what color the bedsheet had been because of the massive amount of body fluids drained from Doug's body, soaking the sheet through, changing its color.

"There's also a cord there, isn't there?" one agent said as they hoisted CASE NO. 2000-1021325 onto the gurney. Indeed, there was. It was tied around Doug's waist. But there were also two thin ropes tied around Doug's feet, with a piece of red and white plastic covering both. As Smith washed his hands and put on long rubber gloves, he thought about the idea of seeing a man murdered and set in concrete inside a galvanized horse/cattle-watering trough. It was surely a unique—perhaps unprecedented—way to try and hide and ultimately dispose of a body to cover up a murder. Here, in the case of Doug Benton, clearly, that plan had not worked.

On Tuesday, June 20, somewhere just after the noon hour, Smith got to work on Doug's body, which had been removed from the concrete and watering trough by CSS, placed on a gurney, and then wheeled into Smith's autopsy suite at the GBI Division of Forensic Sciences in Decatur. From this point on, Douglas Benton would be referred to as CASE NO. 2000-1021325.

As Dr. Smith would later refer to it, the "puzzle-solving process"—or, rather, the "*medical* puzzle-solving process"—was now officially under way.

"Body is morbidly decomposed," Smith noted in 2002, having called Doug's body "moderately decomposed" in his 2000 autopsy report, further stating that "skin slippage" had occurred, especially Doug's hands, which Smith described as having been "de-gloved."

A terribly horrific image, if there ever was one.

There was "bloating of the body cavities, greening, and intense odor of putrefaction," Smith put in his report, which was what Rob Poston and his wife had smelled coming upon the watering trough out in back of the cattle ranch. Partially mummified (one might reckon because of the concrete), Smith reported Doug's "underlying soft tissues" to be in "very good" shape.

Doug measured in at average height: 71 inches, or 5 feet 9. His body, in the state it arrived, weighed a mere 113 pounds. Doug was twice that, easily. Being encased in the concrete, however, had vaporized most of the liquid from his body (sort of like using rice to dry something out), leaving just bones and decomposed tissue. All of the organs in Doug's body had decomposed to the point of being nothing more than dried mush, allowing his body that great reduction in weight.

Of added significance, Dr. Smith noted in his 2000 report (concurring later during his testimony in court), Doug's body was wrapped in a shower curtain, a sheet and a second shower curtain—those same items Maddox and other CSSs had photographed and reported.

Checking Doug's underwear, one side—his right buttock—was riddled with slits from what was presumed to be the blade of a knife. Doug had been murdered while lying on his side.

The location of the injuries told investigators they were probably correct in speculating Doug had been on his couch sleeping on his side, wearing only his underpants, when his killer snuck up from behind and surprised him. After all, there were no defensive wounds found on Doug's body, information that posed several scenarios. For one, Doug trusted his killer and/or knew the person. Or perhaps the person blindsided Doug and he had no time to respond or react. If it were a sneak attack, one had to ask: was Doug's killer weaker and smaller and concerned that Doug could somehow overpower him or her?

A question not brought up here, though, might have been: were those "knife" wounds on Doug's buttocks and the midsection area of his torso made when the concrete was chipped away with a screwdriver back at the cattle ranch? Or when the trough itself was hoisted off the ground with pointed pitch-fork-like levers placed on Rob Poston's tractor?

They certainly could have.

As Dr. Smith began his general external examination, inspecting Doug's entire body, the pathologist uncovered the manner of death almost immediately: "Specifically, I found a total of 10 stab wounds on the body and a single gunshot wound to the head."

Smith was certain of it.

The gunshot wound to the top of Doug's head showed a blackening of edges around the entrance hole, somewhat of a starfish-shaped pattern. Yet "no stippling," Smith wrote in his 2000 report, "is seen on the surrounding scalp skin," which was too far along into the decomposition process to obtain a good read on, anyway. Still, there was no question or disagreement about Doug being shot at very close range—possibly even with the barrel of the murder weapon butted directly up against the top of his skull.

After studying the entrance wound, Smith dug into Doug's skull with tweezers and searched for a possible bullet or fragment.

"When I saw him, the brain had pretty much liquefied, so the bullet was within what remained," Dr. Smith later testified.

Landing on something, with a pair of forceps, Smith carefully removed the bullet, dropping it with a clank into a stainless-steel dish. Later, he placed it inside a sealed and labeled container. Smith called the fragment "a greatly deformed small caliber" bullet in his report, saying nothing more about it.

Heading toward Doug's midsection, Smith found "a couple of small puncture wounds" on the right side of Doug's belly. A stab wound to his right buttock. Similar wounds to his right flank and on each side of his right buttock. Doug must have been sleeping on his left side.

But why shoot *and* stab him?

The one finding regarding those wounds Smith would later be certain of had to be when they occurred, thus casting aside any theories of a screwdriver or the tractor forks being responsible. According to Dr. Smith, there could be no doubt that each wound had been sustained at or near the time of Doug's death. Post-mortem injuries are vastly different—for one, there would be no blood evidence left behind inside the wound itself—from those sustained after death. When death occurs, blood stops flowing.

Simple science.

This was important because Rob Poston, who had found the body, had indeed used a tractor with pitchforks to lift the watering trough out of the ground. He had also tried to bust up the concrete with the tractor and forks to some extent. In addition, investigators on scene went at the concrete with a screwdriver and mallet. Smith and the GBI had to determine if Poston or the others could have inadvertently caused the injuries with the forks on his tractor or a screwdriver. "Smith was certain of his findings: Not a chance the wounds were created post-mortem." The wounds Doug sustained to his body were administered with a very sharp object, sans a knife, and had been made while blood was still flowing through Doug's body. What's more, the stab wounds were inflicted in areas of the body for one reason: to kill. Several penetrated deep into Doug's stomach, one entering his colon. Another had nicked a bone near Doug's midsection. These were violent injuries, perpetrated with careful precision and significant force—all meant to cause the most amount of damage as possible.

In the end, Smith determined that Doug Benton "died of consequences of a contact range penetrating gunshot of the head and multiple stab wounds," the cause of death the "combined effects of multiple stab wounds and gunshot of the head" and the manner of death "homicide."

WHILE THE AUTOPSY WAS under way, SAs Ben Williams and Jesse Maddox sat down with a young neighbor of Doug's. The 15-year-old girl lived next door.

"Go ahead," Williams encouraged.

It was May 25 or 26, just a week before Doug went missing, she could not recall the exact date. Yet she knew she was at home that weekend. She was outside in the yard. She could hear Doug and Tracy. They were outside and yelling. It was as if the argument had started inside and spilled out into the yard.

"You're a slut!" Doug had said to Tracy, the neighbor remembered. Doug sounded angry, as if Tracy had done something terrible to him.

"Yeah, you're no man," Tracy came back with, apparently going straight for the jugular. "Your dick cannot even please me." She laughed.

"And that was it?" Williams asked.

"Yeah," she said.

27.

ON TUESDAY, JUNE 20, investigator Mike Smith got a tip about a guy who had painted an SUV with what Smith had been told was a "similar camo design" as to what had been painted on the watering trough Doug's body had been recovered from. Smith and SA Ben Williams got hold of the man and had him come down to the OCSD for an interview.

He seemed a bit fidgety, maybe more out of having to disrupt his life by answering questions regarding what everyone in town was talking about: the murder of Doug Benton.

After they settled into an interview suite and sat down, Williams spoke first: "We have information that a camo design we've come across through our investigation is consistent with a design on a 1979 Chevy Blazer you own or owned."

The man looked at the two of them. "Yes, I have a Blazer. It is camouflaged and I painted it." He also added that he had a friend who had once dated Tracy Fortson. He had broken up with her, however, prior to September 1999. That friend actually owned some property adjacent to the RSE Farms acreage, he explained. "Roddy Sturdivant," who owned the farm where Doug's body had been found, "thought I was hunting on his property and told me to stay off."

"You mind if we take a look at your Blazer?"

"Not at all."

They headed out to the guy's house where he kept the Blazer.

Smith photographed the vehicle.

"There were no visible signs of the design (I) had observed on the water trough as was on the 1979 Blazer," Williams concluded in his report of the visit.

28.

LATE THAT SAME AFTERNOON, June 20, those investigators involved believed law enforcement now had enough probable cause for an arrest warrant issued in the name of a former fellow cop. As hard as it was to fathom, Tracy Fortson, a woman who had once professed a desire and will to uphold the law of the land, seemed to be the most likely suspect responsible for Doug Benton's murder. Tracy had motive, means and opportunity, according to law enforcement at this very early stage of the investigation.

Scoggins had spoken to the assistant district attorney, Marsha Cole, and everyone was on the same page regarding enough probable cause not only to obtain that arrest warrant, but a search warrant for Tracy's house. After all, it was clear the cover-up behind Doug's murder had been an elaborately planned, carefully thought-out set of circumstances: wrapping Doug's body in a shower curtain and tying his feet with rope, moving Doug's body from his house into the trough, pouring and mixing the concrete, cleaning up inside Doug's house, realizing there was an investigation going on and going *back* into Doug's house to pour kerosene all over the carpet and light candles to burn any forensic evidence left behind and, finally, getting that watering trough full of concrete with a dead human being inside out to the RSE Farms and dumping it.

Tracy and her team were tipped off from someone on the inside as to what was going on. As Scoggins later reported, "Prior to the issuance of the arrest warrant, a fax was received from the office of" Tracy's attorney, Tom Camp, who indicated he "was the attorney on record for" Tracy and she would arrange to surrender herself.

What did that fax mean, however, in the scope of the investigation?

Tracy had lawyered up, as they say, and was not going to willfully submit to any sort of interview with cops. She knew better. Guilty or innocent, the last thing you *ever* want to do is open your mouth to a cop. No matter how much you want to say, how much you want to stand on top of a table in a packed room and announce your complete innocence, you should never, ever speak to the police, whether they believe you are responsible for a crime or not. Everything you say, as the Miranda warning spells out, *will* be used against you. You might even be lied to. You might even be tricked. You might be bullied. And you might even get the idea that someone else is fingering you for the crime.

EARLY WEDNESDAY MORNING, JUNE 21, that signed search warrant came in. By 11:30 a.m., the troops had rallied at Tracy's Smithonia Road home in Winterville. A quiet, rural street with small, clap-boarded ranches, hidden behind thick Georgia foliage, dense shrubs and trees.

After a few knocks on the front door, the team determined nobody was home.

Ben Williams and Mike Smith led the search. Smith had interviewed Tracy four days prior. He'd also interviewed Jeff Bennett and Jerry Alexander, two of Tracy's most ardent opponents, both of whom had decried how volatile and even violent Tracy and Doug's relationship had been. Bennett and Alexander had told police on more than one occasion that if there were someone out in the world who would want to take revenge on Doug, that person was Tracy Fortson. She was a menace. Had always been a problem and was extremely insecure.

Something wasn't adding up within it all for law enforcement. The more they looked into Tracy's life, the more they thought maybe that violent streak they had heard about manifested into murder.

Mike Smith had been out to Doug's house two times, June 17 and 20. Noticeably, Smith said later, there was no odor inside Doug's beyond that bird smell the first time they went in (on the 17th). In fact, Smith later recalled, "It was warm and hot and we enjoyed all the air that we could get." But when they went out that second time (the 20th) and discovered the bloody couch and candles, "As we entered," Smith added, "(there) was a very strong smell of kerosene."

It almost felt as if somebody had gone inside in between both times the MCSD, GBI and OCSD had gone out there. Had Doug's killer been watching the situation unfold from behind the scenes, seen that law enforcement went into his house, and then before they could come back and search it, try to clean up? But when that plan failed, he or she decided to torch the place in hopes of getting rid of all the evidence at once.

It seemed, without much evidence of it being a fact, that only someone privy to how the investigation into Doug's disappearance was unfolding could plan such an event so timely and perfectly.

Then there was that CSS fingerprint tape used to secure the note to Doug's truck.

Another sure giveaway?

Was it all fitting together and pointing to one suspect— someone either involved with or close to law enforcement?

Still, Tracy would later say, she had given investigators Bill Strickland and Mike Smith plenty of information when they interviewed her that Sunday, June 18—two days, incidentally, *before* they went back into Doug's house, one day *after* they had first spoken to her—about a possible suspect in Doug's disappearance: Painkiller, that drug dealer Doug had, working as a confidential informant, allegedly help put behind bars.

"(When) I was asked to come to the Madison County Sheriff's Department for an interview, I talked with ... Scoggins and ... Bill Strickland," Tracy explained to me. "I had known Bill Strickland for approximately 15 years. I told them everything I could think as to where Doug could have gone, his friends, family, the last weekend we spent together, including the argument we'd had. When asked if Doug had enemies, I told them about (Painkiller, who) ... Doug had worked for years ago. When Doug decided to make a change in his life, he helped prosecute (Painkiller). Doug had also told me that (Painkiller) had threatened to kill him when he got out of prison."

Nowhere in any of the reports had I seen where a law enforcement investigator mentioned that Tracy had given them this information during any of her interviews while Doug was considered missing.

BY 12:20 P.M., CHIEF DEPUTY Bill Strickland arrived at Tracy's residence.

"I've got an indication from the DA there is probable cause here to detain and tow Miss Fortson's black 4x4 truck. Is it here?" Strickland wanted to know after getting out of his vehicle and approaching the team.

It wasn't, someone told him. But they knew Tracy was at her mother's house, where the truck was likely parked. Tracy's mother lived on Arnoldsville-Winterville Road, not too far away.

"Williams, you come with me," Strickland said. "Let's head over there." Strickland had the actual search warrant for Tracy's house in hand. "Smith, Cross, Scoggins, here," he added, handing the warrant over. "I'm leaving this with you."

MCSD investigator Cody Cross had done only basic

work in Doug's disappearance up until this point. At Tracy's house, Cross took out the MCSD's video camera and made sure there was a fresh tape in the deck. His job—beyond helping in the search—was to videotape the process.

Good thing, too, because the MCSD was about to uncover the mother lode of evidence collection.

The first thing Cross and the team noticed was Tracy's mailbox—and the fact that it was painted in a camouflage, leafy green pattern.

Same as the watering trough?

Could be.

Inside the house, investigators found a litany of additional items that seemed, in nothing else, suspect—if not entirely related to the murder of Doug Benton: the arrest warrant indicated an open box of "small gloves, rubber micro flex," "CCI brand .22 LR ammo" (in Tracy's bedroom), "1 22 cal. Stevens model 15 bolt action" rifle (in a second bedroom), "1 22 cal. Stinger ammo" (in the kitchen), "3 spray paint cans, blk, grn, khaki" in the "small building" (garage), "a spent 22 cal. round in the yard beside carport," "2 towels from bathroom w/stains consistent w/blood," "2 22 cal. bullets from back bedroom dresser," "rolls of white tape from 1rst bedroom beside desk," and a host of other items, many of which could be considered incriminating.

Cross found the door into the bathroom and videotaped the room before stepping inside. What he noticed was the odd smell. But then again, in the totality of what they were uncovering, the smell fit in with everything else. There is nothing more potent, prominent and maybe synthetic smelling than that of a brand-new plastic shower curtain inside a small bathroom.

"All the creases were still in it, like it had been freshly unwrapped and more recently unwrapped and it still had that, I guess I would say, plastic odor," Cross mentioned later.

Another interesting find came from GBI SA Terry Cooper, when he came across "some … surgical-type tape and a white, possibly 2-inch wide paper-type tape present in the first bedroom to the right when coming down the hallway."

Cooper requested all of it "seized and secured."

Someone asked about the significance.

"For comparison to the tape which had been discovered on the body," Cooper remarked.

In other words, was this the same tape used to secure the shower curtain to Doug's body and the plastic around his feet?

OCSD Deputy Charles Morgan was also on scene at Tracy's house. As he helped participate in the search, Morgan came upon Tracy's duty belt, that black leather, bulky belt cops fasten around the waist to hold the tools of the trade: weapon, handcuffs, flashlight. Morgan knew Tracy fairly well. He'd once worked with her. Morgan later said that Tracy, unlike other deputies he knew, had an extra leather pouch on her belt where she kept a knife.

Picking up the belt, Morgan opened the pouch.

The knife was gone.

29.

THE FOLLOWING DAY, JUNE 22, first thing in the morning, Cody Cross and Bill Strickland, Sheriff Ray Sanders, Terry Cooper and Ben Williams headed out to the farm where Doug's body had been recovered. There had to be evidence on the farm of maybe a vehicle transporting the watering trough out to the farm. Doug's killer had to have used a truck to transport the trough. Moreover, how had Doug's killer gotten that trough off of the truck bed and onto the ground? If the killer acted alone, which had not yet been ruled out, and committed the crime him- or herself, there could be evidence on the farm of how the trough was removed from the vehicle.

They had a look around.

Cross estimated what he referred to as "the scene" to be about two to three miles from the main road. They stood at that exact area of the farm where Rob Poston and his wife had come upon the trough.

Cross took out the video camera and started recording.

"Upon walking up to the scene," Cross wrote in his report, "I detected a foul odor which was emanating from a pile of what appeared to be potting soil—I noticed bugs, maggots, and flies in the pile of potting soil."

They collected a sample of the soil. A bag of potting soil had been recovered from Tracy's carport garage.

Would the soils match?

The fact that Doug's body and the watering trough were now gone from the location for several days and the smell stayed around told them Doug had been encased in the concrete for an extended period of time.

Next, Cross and the others noticed a nearby tree with markings on its outer skin, or bark, some of those nicks and scrapes about waist-high, others a bit lower.

"The markings [indicated that] something had been tied to it and pressured exerted," Cross said later.

It appeared as though someone had tied a rope or some type of cable to the tree and pulled on it tight enough to leave a marking (indentation) in the bark around the circumference of the tree. As they stood and thought about it, an image emerged: Doug's killer tying one end of a rope or wire to the trough, positioned on the back of a truck, the other end to the tree, and then driving away, using the tree as leverage to pull the trough off the bed of the truck and onto the ground.

Another, small tree, according to law enforcement, "show(ed) skinned marks on it."

What Cross and the others established with both markings was that on this particular limb of the smaller tree, there was "a skint mark and it looks like something either pushed it down and scraped it going in or vice versa, scraped it coming out."

The bumper or fender of a truck, perhaps? Or maybe the tractor used to hoist the trough off the ground and move it around?

A CSS started up a chainsaw. The buzzing noise was loud and obstructive. As he cut into the two trees, carving out those chunks to tag as evidence, it appeared everything they were uncovering led to one conclusion: Tracy Fortson killing Doug Benton, using her truck to transport a watering trough with his body in it onto a portion of farming/hunting land she knew very well and had hunted on herself.

Looking at it all, it was almost too obvious. Like

breadcrumbs leading investigators not only to what had happened to Doug, but who had done it and how it all had been carried out. As if someone had left behind such a trail of evidence it was going to be impossible for law enforcement not to figure it all out. And to think a cop—experienced in how investigations are conducted— had done this?

Still, if you're an investigator looking into Doug's murder, all you can do is follow the evidence.

The situation became worse for Tracy from there. Her 1998 Ford F-150 truck was brought into Madison County for a full forensic examination. Cody Cross began by a visual inspection.

"Cement splatters were visible in the bed of the truck." As if somebody had been mixing concrete in back of Tracy's truck and splashed splotches of it. "Also in the bed of the truck were several bags of potting soil." The rear driver's side taillight was broken. There were several cans of spray paint—those camo colors—found inside the cab.

Slam dunk.

Slam dunk.

Slam dunk.

All of the reports referred to the findings in and out of Tracy's truck as, oddly, "significant items of evidence."

How could one know a piece of evidence was significant without having the entire case at your disposal?

This was all more like a smoking gun in Tracy's hand. The crime on video, for crying out loud. Was there nothing she hadn't left behind? What's more, Cross took out a tape measure and noted the height measurements of the broken taillight and the truck's bumper. In addition, along the bed of the truck, Cross found scratches of paint consistent with metal against metal, watering trough verses the bed of the truck.

"These measurements correspond to measurements of a damaged tree near where the body of the victim was located."

Yet another slam dunk.

So, if there were any indication that all of this evidence seemed too good to be true—or, as Tracy would later suggest, put in place to frame her—Tracy would still have a hell of a lot of explaining to do.

30.

TRACY WAS FORMALLY ARRESTED and taken to Jackson County Jail, only because Madison County did not house females. She was placed in protective custody, which she described as "the hole." Solitary confinement, Tracy knew, was standard practice simply because Tracy had been a cop and there was no telling who she would run into in the general population—women she had arrested, maybe others who would want to settle a score, or those who just wanted a feather in the cap from beating the snot out of a cop.

Either way, it was not a nice place. Tracy said that for 23 out of each 24-hour day she was in her "hole of a cell" with "no electricity, no hot water," with the fluorescent lights constantly on, buzzing and flickering. "I learned to sleep that way."

She said there were many "nights she would wake up from a dream only to realize I was living a nightmare."

Tracy adapted rather quickly. Because she was only allowed to shower three days a week—if, that is, she claimed, the jailer allowed her to—she washed herself in the sink inside her cell. She heated up hot water in a plastic foam cup on the radiator attached to the wall.

In her cell one night during those first days after her arrest, Tracy got to thinking: "It didn't take me long to decide that I needed to drop my sexual harassment claim against

(Ray) Sanders. I was able to contact (my sexual harassment suit attorney) and tell her what I wanted to do. She asked me several times if I was sure. I said yes! I thought that if I dropped the case, then Sheriff Sanders would back off."

Tracy made the decision to call Sanders and tell him about what she'd done. The implication she later gave me was that if she went along with the good ole boys' club and dropped the suit, the avalanche of evidence against her in Doug's murder would all soon be forgotten. She implied that dropping the suit would back the dogs off—that it was all some sort of elaborate set-up to scare her into dropping those charges.

If Tracy is correct, it means there would have been four types of investigators—a state crime lab, the state medical examiner, countless officers and deputies, along with the DA and the assistant DA—involved at some level. Or, at the least, several investigatory cops doing it all and convincing the others. Tracy was alleging that they had put all of this evidence against her in play because of a sexual harassment charge.

Either scenario seemed a bit far-fetched. Maybe even impossible, considering the logistics, set of circumstances that would have to line up, coincidences that would have to occur, and the information about Tracy's life her framers would have to have known.

For one, that she had gone out and bought a new shower curtain. Two, that she had purchased camouflage type paints and painted her mailbox. And three, that she and Doug were fighting.

There is so much more.

"Ray, listen," Tracy said over the phone from jail (according to her recollection of the phone call), "I dropped the case—it wasn't my idea to begin with." According to Tracy, she then explained to Sanders that it had been Doug's idea from the get-go—that "sitting on a gold mine" comment that initiated the entire sexual harassment suit.

"I already knew that," Tracy claimed Sanders told her over the phone. "No hard feelings. Call me anytime."

And that was the end of the call.

31.

SA BEN WILLIAMS WAS busy investigating what turned into a fluid, rapidly developing case of murder building against a former deputy sheriff. No one came out and directly said it, but an unspoken melody playing in the background had to be that the case would have to be well-defined, rock-solid and thoroughly investigated more so perhaps than your average suspect's simply because Tracy Fortson had, in fact, been a cop. In that manner of speaking, one of two key witnesses so far, one of the men who had gotten the ball rolling for investigators in the direction of Tracy Fortson, Jerry Alexander, would have to be, himself, carefully vetted and excluded.

One Friday, June 23, as Tracy sat in jail thinking about and preparing for her bond hearing, SA Ben Williams asked Jerry to come in for a polygraph.

Later, Jerry said, "I never would want to try to put something this serious"—Doug's murder—"on anybody … I didn't want to put this on Tracy, saying she had something to do with (it. Even though) I might have thought she did."

In the totality of the investigation, despite the amount of evidence seemingly piling up against Tracy, those who accused her had to be considered suspects themselves. This was one reason why Jerry Alexander sat down in the polygraphist's chair on that Friday morning and agreed to prove he was not lying.

Thus, GBI polygraphist David Rush came out with it right away and asked Jerry if he'd had anything to do with Doug's murder.

"No," Jerry said emphatically.

Rush, after concluding his examination, was "in the opinion ... that Alexander was truthful in the questions about the death of Doug Benton and that Alexander was not involved."

Jerry Alexander had passed a polygraph test.

IN ATHENS, GEORGIA, GBI SA Jesse Maddox stood in the manager's office of The Home Depot on Epps Bridge Road. A friend of Doug's worked at the popular home improvement center and Maddox had a hunch that perhaps Doug's friend might have some insight to offer. There was an indication that Doug had recently poured some sort of concrete patio or foundation. Maddox was there asking how recent that weekend project had been and if Doug's Home Depot friend had known anything about it or even sold him the concrete.

Patrick Longfellow (a pseudonym) not only worked at the Home Depot, he was also one of Doug's neighbors from the John Sharpe Road neighborhood.

"Six years," Longfellow said after Maddox asked how long he and Doug had been neighbors. "Tracy and Doug came into this store often to buy items."

"Have you seen Tracy come in recently and purchase any concrete?" Maddox wondered.

"No, not her," Longfellow said. "But Doug did. He purchased several bags of mix to lay a concrete slab in front of his house. I do not know where those bags were purchased." Longfellow made it clear he wasn't speaking as a Home Depot employee here, selling Doug the bags of cement. He was speaking as a neighbor who watched Doug work on his house, adding, "I do know he had several of those bags left over after he poured the foundation. To the best of my recollection, approximately six or seven bags (were) left on a pallet."

Maddox asked about Longfellow's relationship with Doug. How they fared as friends. Did they hang out a lot? Coffee? Shoot the shit on the front porch on a cool summer night over iced tea?

"I have not really been associated with Doug for quite some time," Longfellow explained.

Maddox wanted to know if Longfellow had ever seen Doug and Tracy together in The Home Depot.

"The last time I would have seen Doug and Tracy in this store," Longfellow explained, "would have been on the last Tuesday or Wednesday of May. They bought small walkie-talkie handset-type radios." He remembered seeing them because "Doug asked me at that time if his exotic birds had been bothering me any. I told him they had not."

Maddox asked about Tracy next. Had Longfellow interacted with her at all while she was over at Doug's? Seemed some neighbors in that John Sharpe Road neighborhood law enforcement had spoken to thus far had a story to tell about Tracy Fortson.

"She's a fairly sizable female," Longfellow said. "When I say sizable, I mean she is *very* strong. I believe she's a weightlifter. In fact, I've seen Doug and Tracy horse-playing, you know, around Doug's yard. Tracy once picked Doug up over her shoulder."

Indeed, that would make Tracy Fortson an incredibly strong woman. Doug had Tracy by about 75 to 80 pounds.

Longfellow had a look on his face. Something was bothering him.

Maddox wondered what.

Longfellow indicated that he was scared of Tracy. "Look," he said, "she threatened to shoot my dogs. She told me that if the dogs came near her, she would *shoot* them."

Maddox gave Longfellow his card and told him to call if

he remembered anything else.

Maddox left The Home Depot and drove to the Southern States Lawn and Feed Store in Athens on Atlanta Highway. The GBI had just determined that an employee by the name of Scott Knowles had waited on Tracy on June 4, 2000. Another Southern States employee, Sherry Michael, called into the MCSD and said she remembered Tracy coming into the store on that day to purchase several items.

Those items, when Maddox found out what they were, told an incredibly interesting and incriminating story.

32.

SCOTT KNOWLES SAID HE remembered Tracy
Fortson specifically, because he had helped her select the
items she wanted to purchase.

"Yeah," Knowles said as he and Maddox walked around
the store. "And I also helped her load the items onto her
truck."

Maddox took out a photo of Tracy. "That's who we're
talking about?"

"Yup, that's her." Knowles turned, picked up and heaved
a bag of feed onto a pile in front of where they stood.

Maddox showed Knowles a Polaroid of Tracy's truck.

"And that's the same truck we loaded the items into,"
Knowles said, looking at the photo, slapping the dust off his
gloves.

Knowles explained the sale. It was about 1 p.m. that day,
he said. "I know that it was about 1 because I arrive for work
on Sundays at 12:45 to begin my shift at 1. We're open on
Sundays from 1 to 5:30. She was here as soon as we opened.
She was alone. She walked in and first started talking to
Sherry Michael. I was in charge of the warehouse on that
day. Sherry came back to ask me a question."

"Hey, Scott," Sherry had said, "I have someone out here
looking for a watering trough, can you help her?"

Maddox was interested in this bit of what seemed to be

astounding information. Tracy Fortson buying a galvanized horse-watering trough on the weekend her boyfriend went missing.

"I took her out to the warehouse," Knowles continued. "I helped her select a 2-foot wide, 2-foot deep, 6-foot-long water trough." The store clerk couldn't recall if that particular watering trough Tracy was interested in had what he called "a bar" across the middle of it for support. But then remembered, in fact, it was likely Tracy who asked him if "that bar could be removed?"

While discussing the sale with Tracy, Knowles said, he grabbed the bar, noticed it was loose and told Tracy, "Yes, it can be removed, no problem."

As he explained this to Maddox, Knowles then changed his mind. He was now unclear, adding, "I am not certain if (Tracy) was that particular customer (asking if the bar can be removed), however, it just stands out in my mind that it was."

"No problem," Maddox said. "Continue."

"Well, I took the trough out of the warehouse and placed it on the dock." The idea was that they would both load it onto the bed of Tracy's truck.

Tracy then went back into the store. She wasn't yet finished shopping. Sherry Michael was in the store when Tracy walked back in.

"How much concrete mix would I need," Tracy asked Sherry Michael, "to pour a foundation for a dog pen?"

Sherry wasn't sure. She called Knowles up to the front of the store and asked him to call the local Lowe's to see if anyone there could figure out the ratios of concrete mix Tracy Fortson would need to pour a foundation.

Knowles dialed up the Lowe's and got someone on the line. He asked about the number of bags it would take to pour a dog pen foundation.

"I do not recall the exact amounts they advised," Knowles told Maddox. "However, Miss Fortson decided to purchase

10 bags."

Tracy indicated to Knowles that she would back her truck up to the dock.

Knowles waved and said he'd meet her out there with all the items she had bought.

Knowles placed two 8-pound bags of concrete mix into the trough before placing the trough in the back of Tracy's black 4X4 truck.

"Don't put any more bags into the trough, please," Tracy told Knowles when it appeared he was going to load the remaining eight bags into the trough. "It'll be too heavy."

Knowles put the eight additional bags—80 pounds each—on her truck bed alongside of the trough.

Maddox never indicated whether he asked or what prompted the response, but Knowles added here: "I did not notice anything out of the ordinary in the back of the truck. I did not see any blood or flies collecting in the back of the truck."

Odd thing to add, but anyway ...

Tracy was at the store for about 30 minutes, Knowles recalled, explaining how she was a "husky woman" who, wearing Carhart brand blue jeans on that day, appeared to "work out."

There was one other purchase Tracy made on that day, Knowles remembered just before Maddox was about to wrap things up.

"What was that?"

"Trace mineral salt block," Knowles said.

THE TRIP TRACY TOOK to this store and the items she purchased is an interesting fact in this case. For one, Tracy would later indicate that she had, in fact, gone to the feed store that afternoon and made those purchases. She never tried to hide this. The salt block and the watering trough were for her horse, she said. Salt block being a common mineral given to livestock.

"The medical examiner's report said Doug was encased in the metal trough with at least 25 bags of concrete," Tracy told me in 2016. "When I bought Sakrete at Southern State's … I had to ask how much it would take to pour a concrete pad, 6x6, two- to three-inches deep."

There was no mention in the reports of Tracy giving Sherry Michael or Scott Knowles specific measurements of what she wanted to build.

"I was told 10 bags (80 pounds each)," Tracy continued. "Where did the other 15 bags come from? I certainly didn't have it."

Tracy would later question why, if she were planning on murdering Doug that weekend and using these items to hide his body, she would even ask about the bags of cement and buy the watering trough and other items in town? She was a cop. She knew law enforcement would ultimately find out where she purchased these items if she purchased them in town.

Made sense.

Looking at these purchases through that prism, one would question Tracy's decision to not even try to hide the purchases or where she purchased the materials. Maybe the timing, too. If you ask her, Tracy claims those innocent, fairly common purchases on her behalf became part of an elaborate set-up put in place to frame her.

But what if Tracy were simply setting up an alibi for herself and why she needed the concrete and trough by asking them about the measurements? She specifically stated to the clerk what she was building with the concrete.

SCOTTIE KNOWLES BROUGHT MADDOX around the store and showed him duplicates of the same items Tracy had purchased.

Maddox photographed each one.

"Thanks," Maddox said when he was done. "I'll be in touch."

33.

AS JESSE MADDOX UNCOVERED what must have felt like an overabundance of evidence against Tracy Fortson, Capt. Bill Strickland got busy taking care of the public's growing interest in what was shaping up to be one hell of high-profile murder case in this otherwise quiet south central Georgia county.

Speaking to the media, announcing Tracy's arrest, Strickland stepped out on that Friday afternoon, June 24: "No one else has been implicated as an accomplice" in Doug Benton's murder. The sheriff added how they'd recently uncovered where Tracy purchased the concrete mix to encase Doug's body, but did not say where.

Wasn't this an odd statement to make at such an early stage of the investigation and arrest? Law enforcement had not yet recovered a murder weapon, as reported by *Mainstreet News*, a local website covering Madison County, citing Strickland in the same unscheduled press conference. Didn't mean they didn't have the weapon in evidence, but ballistics and evidence examination took time to make or break matches. Still, why give this type of sensitive information to the public within such a short period of time after making an arrest?

A spokesperson for the GBI then came out this same day and said the note found on Doug's truck was a piece of evidence they were carefully looking into. The sheriff interrupted, calling the note "short and cryptic," with the GBI spokesperson adding, "We suspect she (Fortson) wrote it."

One other fact the GBI made public was that Jerry Alexander and the man who owned the farm where Doug's body had been recovered were "still under investigation." Both men were considered suspects, in other words, and no scenario had been ruled out as of yet. The assumption was that the investigation was still open to interpretation.

Yet they had a suspect in custody?

"Some feel she is capable of doing it herself," the GBI spokesperson concluded, "but I don't think she could have."

The *Mainstreet News* interviewed one of Doug's neighbors, Lisa Watson, Larry Bridges' girlfriend. Lisa had two daughters, both of whom knew and liked Doug. Both girls explained they valued Doug as a neighbor always willing to give of himself, a guy who had no problem helping them and others in the neighborhood whenever they needed it.

The one aspect of Doug's life that Lisa's oldest daughter talked about was Tracy and her presence around the otherwise peaceful John Sharpe Road neighborhood. Doug "seemed different, more reserved" whenever Tracy was around, the daughter told the news site. He just wasn't himself. In fact, the daughter added, "She tried to make him stop seeing all of his friends." The daughter then gave an example of Tracy's behavior, saying whenever she walked by Doug's house, waved to Doug and said hello (and Tracy was around), she noticed how Tracy always said something to Doug like, "Don't say 'hey' to her!" It rubbed the daughter the wrong way. Gave her and others the impression that Tracy was domineering and controlling, like she might have been pushing Doug around, bullying the guy.

When investigators spoke with Lisa about the last time she saw Doug and Tracy, like everyone else in the neighborhood, Lisa Watson had a story to tell.

It was Sunday, June 4. Lisa heard Doug start his motorcycle and take off out of his driveway about 9:30 or close to 10. She then heard Doug return home about 5 p.m., a timeframe consistent with what others had reported.

Same as her boyfriend Larry Bridges had described, Lisa noticed Tracy's truck parked in front of Doug's garage—a familiar sight. She first recalled seeing Tracy's vehicle that day around 3:30, which might indicate—if the timelines are accurate—that Tracy was at Doug's *before* he got home. Lisa said she knew for a fact that it was Tracy there that day because she saw Tracy leaving Doug's (alone) between "5 o'clock and ... no ..." She stopped herself while dredging up the memory. Then adjusted the time: "I would say it was between 6 and 7 o'clock that evening."

The timeframe is important when put into the matrix of the shocking allegation Lisa Watson next reported: At around 5 or 6 p.m., Lisa explained, "I heard a gunshot and looked over and I didn't see anything."

The gunshot had come from Doug's yard, Lisa was certain. She looked into Doug's yard after hearing the loud crack, but saw nothing. That is, until about an hour later—when she watched Tracy Fortson walk out of the house and leave.

A gunshot.

Some time passed.

Tracy Fortson leaving Doug's house.

Doug was like clockwork with those birds of his: Every evening, right around 6 p.m., Doug was outside tending to the birds. But after hearing that gunshot and seeing Tracy walk out of Doug's house, Lisa Watson never saw her neighbor again.

34.

TRACY FORTSON'S BOND WAS set at $500,000 cash.

"No way I could *ever* make that," she said later.

The state waited until October 2000 to indict Tracy.

In any case, Tracy was indicted on charges of malice murder, felony murder, two counts of aggravated assault and attempted arson. Prosecuting her case was now in the hands of Northern Judicial Circuit District Attorney Bob Lavender.

In January 2001, Tracy was transferred to Franklin County Jail in Carnesville, and no longer in protective custody. Her trial was scheduled for late summer or early fall. All involved believed it was not going to be pushed back or bumped into the following year, which was a good sign for the prosecution, but not for the defense. The state wanted the case resolved. Lavender and his team believed they had more than enough evidence for a conviction.

"My first year in prison," Tracy told me when I first started talking with her via email during the early summer of 2016, "I thought I had gone to hell. I was dogged out by staff, threatened by inmates, and went to protective custody four times, one of which I stayed 60 days."

As to the overwhelming amount of incriminating evidence against her, Tracy explained to me that it was all part of a carefully, well-thought-out plan to frame her because she had gone and brought a case of sexual harassment against the sheriff. Or, in fact, that Doug was murdered because of his work as a confidential informant. Maybe even a combination of both.

Sounds incredible, I know. Yet you listen to Tracy talk about her case and all of the evidence against her—much of which simply fell into place, like dominoes, one clue leading to the next—and there are moments when you think: *You know, she might have a point.*

"Why would I paint a container that held the body of a murder victim the same as my mailbox?" Tracy rhetorically asked me in one email exchange.

I thought about that.

Who the hell would do this? Better yet, a former cop.

That missing knife from Tracy's duty belt became a problem for Tracy as she thought about it. On the evidence list of items taken from her house, there were no knives. Tracy claimed she had a home full of hunting and cooking knives, even collectors' knives. Yet none were taken and logged as evidence?

Why not?

"One of the OCSD investigators said there was an empty scabbard on my duty belt where he had seen a knife while I was working," Tracy remarked. She's speaking of Charles Morgan. "I never carried a knife on my duty belt! That was not part of my uniform or weapons I carried. Deputies do not wear knife scabbards on their duty belt. I had my service weapon/holster, OC spray, speed loaders, handcuffs, and maybe a flashlight ring, but not a knife scabbard."

This was just one more piece of misinformation that made her look guilty and set in place by those looking to hang her, Tracy purported.

The so-called missing shower curtain was another point of contention for Tracy.

"Shower curtain, rods and rings? Not sure why they listed this (on the evidence list of items). I had a shower curtain, rods and rings in my bathroom, they did not take (any of) it. I had purchased it at Walmart. The old one, (which) did not match the description of the one found with Doug, was put into a trash bag left on the carport and was never seen again. It disappeared about the same time as the trough and concrete. It was clear and had no pattern."

One report from the GBI noted that on June 23, 2000, at 8:59 a.m., Doug's body and "the physical evidence" in the case had been driven to the crime lab for processing.

Pretty standard procedure.

The person transporting it all?

Sheriff Ray Sanders.

That, in and of itself, following along the lines of Tracy's conspiracy to frame theory, might seem to fit congenially with her core argument: the notion that Ray Sanders was behind all of this.

Left there, you might think: *Well, she has a point.*

What's missing from that report, however, are three words: *at the time.* Sanders transported the evidence they had at the time. Because on June 27, SA Jesse Cooper "transported all items of evidence for comparison to the Crime Lab." These items included samples of concrete that had encased Doug's body and "any other items located in the concrete."

Adding a bit of ambiguity to this, however, clearly documented in that same report was the fact that when the watering trough arrived at the Crime Lab, Patty Price, a CSS, poured Clorox bleach on part of the trough and its contents after Doug's remains were extracted from it, thus possibly contaminating any forensic evidence that would have been uncovered inside the concrete or the trough itself: blood, hairs, fibers, nail shavings, skin—anything.

Whomever killed Doug and placed him in that watering trough and encased his body in concrete, Tracy said, "Would have left some sort of DNA behind, but that would have been destroyed with no possible way to recover it once Clorox was poured on it."

This could or could not be true.

We will never know.

In an affidavit produced by the state medical examiner, who did not perform Doug's autopsy, he disagreed, saying he did not think pouring Clorox over evidence would contaminate it.

That's ignorant. Of course it would.

It's easy to write off a person decrying they've been set up and framed—especially in Tracy's case—when you look at all of the incriminating evidence from so many different sources against her. It's almost too much, as I have stated. Like a trail of breadcrumbs led directly to Tracy Fortson's door, which then led to a narrative of the murder, it seems too, well, perfect.

There are pieces of her case that Tracy pointed out to me as we got to talking that still baffle me. As I headed into reading through the transcripts of her first trial and all of the evidence and witnesses brought forward against her, Tracy asked me to keep several points in mind that she believes are vitally important when looking into the potential of her being innocent:

"Number one, the presence of blood (DNA) of a male on the hall closet door (inside Doug's house) that was never identified."

That is a true statement. CSS found blood no one was ever able to identify.

"Number two," Tracy noted, "no blood was ever found in my truck, clothing, or on any of my possessions."

With the amount of blood spilled inside Doug's house during the course of his murder, save for Tracy wearing a full protective Hazmat body suit—which she certainly could have—there would have been some blood left inside her truck.

"Number three, the audio tapes of the sheriff (Ray Sanders uttering sexually harassing comment Tracy secretly taped) disappeared during the search of my house—why?"

The problem I have with this is that there is no objective, independent corroboration the tapes existed or were inside Tracy's house at the time.

"Number four, how could Doug's truck be in two places at the same time on the same day? A neighbor saw it Monday morning, June 5 at 6 a.m. Jerry Alexander claimed he found the truck Monday morning at 6 a.m."

In defense of Jerry, he wasn't all that sure of the timeframe regarding when Doug's truck mysteriously appeared in his driveway.

Furthermore, Tracy explained, two witnesses "changed their testimony as to the position of the truck seat" in Doug's vehicle.

One said it was farther back; the other said it was not.

"Number six," the most polarizing, substantial claim Tracy would make to me about her case: Two main witnesses, she said, "claim to have been coerced and forced to testify, but are afraid to (now) come forward (and state as much). I believe they both would talk if the right person went to them."[4]

"We have an audio recording of (one witness)," Tracy added, "that was submitted as evidence, but it has not been released to the public yet. I don't want to do anything that will put him in danger."

This "secretly" recorded phone call between this witness and Tracy's daughter supposedly tells a far different story from the narrative uncovered by law enforcement. If true, it puts the entire case made by the GBI, the MCSD and OCSD into a tailspin heading toward a fiery crash.

Lastly, Tracy has an issue with, as she called it, "The alleged date of the crime," noting how it has been referred to as "June 3rd," a date I never came across, "or 4th," which is the most likely day of Doug's murder.

"Now look at the incident report and interviews of June

---

4   I reached out to both. Never heard back.

17," Tracy pointed out to me. "His neighbors saw him return on his motorcycle on Sunday, June 4. They also said they saw my truck at his house between 2:30 p.m. and 5:30 p.m. There was a Walmart receipt showing that I was checking out at Walmart during the time that they supposedly saw my truck at Doug's."

That Walmart receipt, which indeed shows that Tracy was at the Athens Walmart, time stamps her checking out at 3:51 p.m. Thus, it proves nothing. It bears no proof of her not being at Doug's when witnesses in the neighborhood claimed to have seen her and her truck near 5 and 6 p.m. At the most, Athens is a half-hour ride from Doug's John Sharpe Road home.

Tracy claimed later that when investigators first "went into Doug's house on the 17th to do a wellness check after neighbors reported him missing, there was no evidence of a crime." She said it was not until "the 19th or 20th, when officers *returned* to Doug's home, that they found evidence that a crime had been committed and that someone had tried to burn the house."

All true.

So there you have it: several of Tracy's most important points to hold close and think about as we move into her trial.

35.

THE HONORABLE LINDSEY TISE, representing the Northern Judicial Circuit, convened his courtroom on July 9, 2001, well before that fall schedule some had claimed Tracy's trial had been scheduled to start. Twelve jurors were seated to hear the *State of Georgia v Tracy Lea Fortson.* Bob Lavender and Marsha Cole were there to represent the state with Tom Camp and Deidra Schad fighting for Tracy's life.

Here now was Tracy's opportunity to argue her case for a careless and close-minded investigation, targeting the wrong person. If Tracy had been set up and targeted, now was the time for her and her attorneys to lay out any evidence they might have developed and prove that theory to a jury. Pointing a finger and saying you were the victim of a frame-up was not the same as providing proof in a court of law.

Tracy had not really changed much, appearance-wise, since her arrest the previous year. Nor would she change—save for hair color and length—throughout the years her case would take to be completely adjudicated. Generally, Tracy had just-past-her-shoulder line-length brown hair and thin eyebrows—all set against an almost flawless, southern-bleached complexion. She maintained the same weight range of about 140 to 160 pounds.

As a sheriff's deputy, she'd favored a more mullet-type haircut, short bangs, flat and straight edges across her forehead, well-defined around the ears, and that long, Billy Ray Cyrus tail made popular in the '80s. Mostly, Tracy had what was a defining, stoic look of determination about her, almost military, drill-instructor-like.

Yet, when she smiled, her pudgy cheeks puffed up and out, displaying a bit of girlish charm. As court proceedings began on this first day of her trial, Tracy came across as determined: ready and willing to face those she believed had set up this entire murder, literally planting evidence in her home and fabricating forensic evidence collected, simply to get back at her for the sexual harassment case she'd lodged against the OCSD and Ray Sanders.

I wondered about this. In presenting this narrative, Tracy is asking us to believe the unbelievable, essentially. Although we live in a day an age where—if one were to believe there are no bad cops who do this sort of thing in the world—he or she would be ill-informed and close-minded.

Tracy insisted it wasn't solely about an unassuming harassment case and a sheriff maybe losing his job and pension; there was far more at play here. The basic substance of the case went to character and id, a man's dignity and severely bruised male ego—and maybe even an undercover case against a drug dealer. Tracy believed Ray Sanders had become so angry with her for lodging the complaint that it had hurt his reputation and standing in the community. Whether he was guilty or innocent, he was about to show her that she could not fuck with a man in a position of power like him. And if she did, there would be a price to pay.

I still wasn't convinced. It seemed beyond a stretch, even if Ray Sanders had an ego as large and fragile as Tracy had explained. To believe all of this was the result of an ostensible harassment case argued before courts every day in this country was pretentious and naïve.

One has to go back to May 11, 2000, almost a month before Doug's murder, to understand where the plot to murder Doug began, according to Tracy. Tracy explained to me that when *The Oglethorpe Echo*, a small local newspaper, ran a large headline on page 12—SHERIFF SANDERS SAYS HE WILL FIGHT SEXUAL DISCRIMINATION COMPLAINT—that was the day her fate was sealed.

The headline and the accompanying article was the spark, Tracy insisted, lighting a fire that ultimately set her up for Doug's brutal murder. The article named Tracy as the plaintiff, quoting Ray Sanders as saying: "There is nothing to it." Further on in the same article, Sanders added how he had a "number of witnesses" lined up who were "willing to testify about the working conditions ... and to Fortson's behavior."

For the first time, on that day, Tracy's complaints had been aired publicly. She had resigned in February 2000 because she claimed she "could no longer handle the working conditions and unfavorable wages." She went on to accuse the department of subjecting her to "sexually explicit comments made by her supervisor and that she (had been) denied a pay raise."

"I was told," the newspaper quoted Tracy's complaint, "that females don't need a raise and their pay has to be cut."

Incredibly, though, when you look at the facts, her comments and even the suit itself don't gel. Tracy had received a raise one month before resigning. She had also been, according to the county's attorney handling the matter, subjected to "discipline for violations and departmental rules."

What was the impetus for Tracy to be disciplined?

She had been "cautioned about her speech and remarks while on duty." There were, the attorney noted, shop talk "remarks in the Sheriff's Department in which Miss Fortson willingly participated."

It seemed that Tracy herself was part of the actual problem she was accusing the sheriff of.

PICKING A JURY IS not the most exciting part of a murder trial—though it could be said to be the most important. As Tracy sat and watched the *voir dire* process unfold before her, she didn't have many issues with the proceedings until a woman named Sandra Banks (a pseudonym) was questioned by the lawyers. For one, Tracy recognized the name. The woman was Painkiller's sister-in-law, that purported drug dealer Doug had allegedly helped law enforcement put away.

"I remember (the) woman … (as) being part of the jury pool," Tracy said later in a letter to the FBI she wrote about her case. "Tom Camp asked (her) if she knew anyone by the name of (Painkiller. She) replied, 'I have a brother-in-law by that name; his real name is …' Tom planned to keep her, but Bob Lavender struck her from the pool immediately; the look on his face was priceless. … I recently found that (Painkiller) was prosecuted in 1987 and again sometime in the 90's for cocaine possession and yes, he did go to prison. I have tried to locate a statement or transcript that would prove Doug's involvement in his conviction, but have not been able to obtain it." Tracy maintained that it was this incident—Doug acting as a confidential informant, helping law enforcement put a major dealer away—that could have led to his death. She claimed that when she did an open records request to Madison County Superior Court years after her case was adjudicated, she "could not get the information," adding, "I believe … they are not going to give that to me. If I had had an investigator when all of this occurred, I believe I would have had a better chance. However, I have never had anything close to an investigator and no one made an effort to obtain any kind of evidence for my defense. I wonder why?"

Painkiller's sister-in-law was never chosen as a juror.

After several legal matters were sorted out on July 10, 2001, a jury was finally chosen.

Thus, with Tracy sitting in a Madison County courtroom next to her lawyers, thinking to herself she did not have a chance in hell at being acquitted, DA Bob Lavender stepped up to deliver his opening statement on behalf of the state.

36.

BOB LAVENDER WAS 51 and the county DA for six years. He had been inside of a courtroom, however, for more than two decades. He'd tried death penalty cases and argued dozens of similar and unrelated cases in front of the Georgia Court of Appeals. Lavender understood the process, that ebb and flow of a courtroom within the scope of a murder trial. He knew he had a rock solid case against a former deputy, but had to tread carefully. One can never be overconfident in a courtroom because anything can (and will) happen. After all, human beings are in charge of the process—and human beings, despite how often they get it right, can also get it wrong.

Lavender was smooth and elegantly polished. In his opening statement, he stuck to the facts of his case developed by law enforcement. He mentioned how Larry Bridges had noticed Doug missing and walked over, consequently coming upon those dead birds. Realizing he had not seen Doug for a few weeks, Larry Bridges knew something was wrong.

Next, the DA talked about how a routine "welfare check" by several law enforcement officers from different agencies turned into a missing person investigation. Jerry Alexander's name came up next, as did Tracy's and Jeff Bennett's. Lavender spoke of how a note had been found on Doug's truck, which experts were going to testify had not been written by Doug, and how a man out on his four-wheel ATV motorbike with his wife one Sunday afternoon came across a watering trough filled with concrete and that the two—Doug missing and this watering trough—were connected in an extremely violent, deadly manner.

The plainspoken DA explained how the state was going to bring into the courtroom part of a tree to show evidence that Tracy's truck had nicked the tree and left marks on the bark when it was used as a lever, effectively, to drop that watering trough on the farm.

The gruesome discovery out on the farm and one of the deputies there recognizing a rather distinct tattoo Doug had on his arm led everyone back to Doug's house for a second look. That was when, Lavender said, they discovered someone had gone *back* into Doug's modular home to try and cover up the murder by burning the place down. Only the plan had not worked.

He then described the scene at Doug's and how Doug was murdered by a gun and sharp object.

"You are going to find out that it was a .22 caliber bullet," Lavender said, using a subtle tone, "and that in all probability it was a special .22 caliber bullet called a .22 *stinger*."

This was important, because Lavender then added sometime later the fact that the jury would hear from an expert how "the rifle that (came) from Mr. Benton's house absolutely did *not* fire the bullet that killed him."

He promised, in addition, how they were going to prove that the rifle they recovered from Tracy's house was, in fact, "consistent" with the same type of weapon that had fired the bullet that killed Doug. They couldn't go so far as to say for certain, however, "because the bullet was so mangled."

As he began to lay out all of the evidence the state was prepared to present, it became apparent law enforcement had developed what could be considered an airtight case. Each piece of evidence pointed to one person.

Tracy Fortson.

Each witness would utter testimony that spoke of one person.

Tracy Fortson.

And each time law enforcement tried to exclude Tracy and focus on perhaps another suspect, Lavender articulated, the case went back to only one person.

Tracy Fortson.

Lavender did not spend a long time, maybe 15 minutes, laying everything of importance out in his opening. The seasoned DA knew that long openings or closings were subject to nodding out and disassociation by juries. You give the jury the summary, let them know what's coming, and get on with the meat and potatoes of your case.

"At the conclusion of this trial, we are going to come back and ask that you find the defendant guilty of the murder charge, malice murder, felony murder … (and) we are going to ask you for a verdict on two counts of aggravated assault, one for the gun, one for the knife or sharp object … and then also for attempted arson, the attempt to destroy the evidence there at the scene by burning Mr. Benton's house."

There were a lot of charges at stake, any one of which could put Tracy in prison, if not for life, for many, many years.

In the end, Lavender took a breath, played with a pen in his hand and resolved: "I think at the conclusion of the case, after you have heard all of the evidence, it will be clear that this defendant"—he looked over at Tracy, just stopping short of pointing at her—"is guilty of all of those charges. Thank you."

TRACY'S ATTORNEY, TOM CAMP, was admitted to the Georgia bar in 1988. Camp worked for the U.S. District Court (Northern and Middle) until 1991, before breaking out on his own. A Mercer University, Walter F. George School of Law graduate, Camp had a Johnny Unitas, all-

American look about him—that sharp and clean-cut image of wholesomeness. Yet make no mistake, when it pertained to fighting for his clients, Camp was a warrior inside a courtroom.

After clearing his throat and staring at the ground a moment before looking up and addressing the jury with appreciation and humility, Camp said, "I want to tell you again that I feel that it is an honor and a privilege to stand before you in my representation of Miss Tracy Fortson, an innocent victim herself, who has been wrongly accused of these charges."

Right away, it was clear Camp was sticking to a carefully written script. Tracy wasn't about to claim self-defense, battered women's syndrome, or that some random nut job broke into Doug's and killed him. She was stating right out of the box through her powerful and competent attorney that these were erroneous charges of murder and assault and arson. This was a crime she had had *nothing* to do with. She had been framed.

Tom Camp stuck to the same defense attorney opening argument tact many use at some point, saying, "Open and closing statements are not evidence."

From there, the defense attorney outlined how the state goes about presenting its case with witnesses and evidence and gets to question all of those witnesses first, making it seem as though he and Tracy were fighting an uphill battle from the get-go. The "defendant," Camp added here, "may or may not put up any witnesses depending how the state's case goes." And because of that, he said, Tracy Fortson was "somewhat at a disadvantage throughout … and the reason is because I *always* have to go second."

Excellent point.

Camp explained they were not going to be disputing many of the facts as brought forth by the state. However, "you will not hear any witness say that they saw Miss Fortson come to Mr. Benton's home, kill him, put him in a metal container, fill it up with concrete and drive him out to a farm ... and we will suggest to you that it certainly did not happen. ... I anticipate that it will all be circumstantial evidence." Then an important, often understated disclosure: "Remember, it is not the *quantity* of the evidence; it is the *quality* of the evidence."

Camp then amplified the fact—a simple fact many defense attorneys ignore—that jurors needed to understand, that not only direct testimony mattered, but cross-examination of those same witnesses mattered just as much.

He mentioned there was going to be "gaping holes" in the evidence.

"Serious questions about what happened."

"There are some facts we are not going to deny."

He listed several.

He talked about how Tracy and Doug had dissolved the relationship before the murder—a fact they would not dispute.

How the investigation into Doug's murder "was botched."

How the state "failed to follow some very obvious leads."

How the investigation "focused on Tracy."

Far shorter than Bob Lavender's opening, Camp ended by encouraging jurors to acquit Tracy of all charges.

37.

CONSTRUCTING A NARRATIVE IS the smart DA's principal way to deconstruct his investigation point by point so the jury can easily digest it. He might say: *Fact A led to Fact B, which led to Fact C*, and so on. So calling Larry Bridges first was Lavender's way to begin getting that job done as efficiently and effectively as possible. Bridges had been the first person to realize something was amiss at Doug's house when he stumbled upon the dead birds, thus sparking a missing person investigation.

Larry sat and told his story with no big surprises. Doug's neighbor and his girlfriend walked the 50 yards across the road to Doug's modular home weeks after last seeing him, noticed the dead birds, and knew right away something was amiss. Doug would have never left his birds unattended or never left them for any length of time without having someone look after them.

Maybe the only argumentative testimony Larry Bridges offered was the timeline he provided. Larry said the last time he saw Doug was on June 4, 2000. Somewhere close to 10 a.m., Doug took off on his loud motorcycle. Then, at 5 p.m. that same day, Larry said he saw Doug return. He added how he'd seen Tracy's truck parked in Doug's driveway around 3 p.m. that same afternoon, where it stayed until about, he guessed, 5 p.m.

"But I never did see her leave," Larry concluded.

This timeline of Tracy being there between 3 and 5 p.m. would not juxtapose with other timelines, one of which had been given by the woman standing next to Larry on that same day.

In cross-examining Larry Bridges, Tom Camp began right away on that timeline and how Larry supposedly saw Tracy's truck parked at Doug's.

"That is right," Larry said after being asked again if he could say for certain it was Tracy's vehicle.

"You do *not* recall seeing anything unusual in the back of her vehicle, correct?"

"No."

Besides a few additional (inconsequential) questions, and maybe a missed opportunity to poke a hole in Larry's memory, that was it. Camp cut him loose.

MCSO Deputy Tom Lutz sat in the witness box next. Lutz was a cop who would bring to the trial its first taste of surprise and controversy, while simply laying out the facts as he uncovered them.

Lutz first spoke about how his role in the investigation began by heading out to Doug's on June 17 to conduct a welfare check—before coming upon all those dead birds.

As Lutz spoke of interviewing Larry Bridges, who had sparked the inquiry Lutz had made, he brought up something Larry had said to him: How the last person Doug was with had been Tracy Fortson. Larry had recalled this fact because he remembered them having an argument, Lutz explained, a fairly common point of theatrics over at Doug's for them during those last days he had seen Doug around.

After being told of the argument from Larry Bridges, Lutz said, and learning Tracy had been a sheriff, Lutz sought to speak with her. Maybe she knew where Doug had run off to? The way he framed it was that he had simply wanted to talk to Tracy to see if she knew Doug's whereabouts, nothing more. A routine inquiry any cop would have made with regards to a missing person and the information he was gathering.

"Did she contact *you?*" DA Lavender asked.

"Yes, sir, she did."

"Did you query her as to where Mr. Benton might be?"

"Yes, sir. I did."

"What, if anything, did she indicate?"

"She said she had broken up with Mr. Benton."

"Did she indicate the last day she had seen him?"

"The fourth day of June."

Lutz went on to note how it was Tracy who had given him Jeff Bennett's name and phone number, pointing the deputy in Jeff's direction. And after he called and spoke to Jeff Bennett, Lutz heard, for a second time, about an argument Tracy and Doug had most recently.

So Lutz called Tracy back.

"What did you ask her about?" Lavender queried.

"I asked her about an argument between her and her boyfriend ..."

As he was speaking, Tom Camp objected under hearsay.

The judge overruled and Lutz was told to continue.

"What was her response, if anything?" Lavender asked again.

Lutz sat up straight, cleared his throat: "Her demeanor was changed all of a sudden. And she wouldn't answer any further questions and therefore, the phone call immediately came to an end."

This sent up a red flag, Lutz seemed to suggest. However, if one is to look at this objectively, within the situation, Tracy Fortson could have been only reacting in kind because of her days as a police officer. Once she felt the "conversation" about Doug and his whereabouts had gone from merely talking to accusatory, Tracy decided to terminate it. She knew her rights, far better than any civilian. If she felt threatened, why not end the call? If they were beginning to use an accusatory tone toward her, why would she want to continue to talk to them?

The way Lutz explained it on the stand sounded as though Tracy had something to hide; that once she felt a finger being pointed at her, she decided not to help. Lutz never mentioned if Tracy sounded concerned for her former boyfriend who, at that time, would have been gone, and not heard from, for almost two weeks.

Lutz told jurors he went over to Jerry Alexander's and uncovered the now questionable note Doug had allegedly left on his window.

Lavender produced the note inside a plastic evidence bag, asking Lutz if it was the same note Jerry Alexander handed him on that day.

Lutz said it was.

From there, the sheriff explained how he called a towing company to impound Doug's truck, which, Lutz noted, was where his role in the investigation ended.

Tom Camp began his cross-examination by asking Lutz about the first time he spoke to Tracy. It was cordial and Tracy was polite, providing information she hadn't even been asked for, Lutz agreed. But during that second call she became "upset," Camp noted, giving the tone of the conversation a different feel (upset and angry being two different ways one can respond to a situation), after being asked about the break-up and an argument she'd had with Doug.

"And it would be *natural* for somebody to be *upset* about breaking up with their boyfriend, correct?" Camp asked Lutz.

"Generally."

Camp broke the subject there and moved on to Jerry Alexander's house.

After being asked, Lutz agreed that yes, Jerry Alexander was extremely mad after he realized the MCSO was going to impound Doug's truck.

Another important point Camp made during his cross

was that Lutz had not actually found the note on Doug's truck. It was Jerry Alexander who claimed to have found the note and brought it into his house.

Lutz told jurors, after Camp pressed him, that the truck, according to Jerry, showed up in his driveway somewhere around June 4, 5 or 6. He just couldn't be certain of an exact date.

Pressed further, Lutz testified, "(Jerry) said the middle of the night on Sunday. I don't remember what date that was."

It would have been the 4th.

Later, on re-cross, Camp asked Lutz if he was an investigator. Just because you're a sheriff's deputy, it did not mean you were part of the investigatory division of the sheriff's office, or that you knew and understood how to investigate crimes.

"No, I'm not," Lutz clarified.

Then they got into how the note had supposedly been attached to Doug's vehicle—with law enforcement fingerprint tape.

"And is it not formal for you to carry fingerprint tape around with you in your vehicle?"

"Yes, it is."

"You *do* carry it?"

"Yes." Lutz seemed a bit perturbed by the question, as though Camp was suggesting something nefarious went on.

"Can you say for sure with 100 percent certainty that is what that is (fingerprint tape)?"

"Yes, 100 percent!"

Camp was done.

38.

AFTER A SHORT BREAK, the State of Georgia called Lisa Watson, Larry Bridges' live-in girlfriend.

Lisa was in court for one purpose: to establish how Tracy was at Doug's house on the evening of June 4. Bob Lavender wasted little time getting into that moment.

Lisa said she saw Tracy's vehicle parked in front of Doug's garage around "3:30 that afternoon." Later on that same day, Lisa testified, she actually saw Tracy herself in the yard.

Then: "I saw her at Doug Benton's house leaving," Lisa recalled.

Lisa Watson could be considered an impartial witness; someone without any skin in the game, per se, if the frame-up angle is where you are heading with your opinion of the case. Lisa had no reason to lie, to embellish or to recall things that weren't so.

Lavender asked Lisa to think about what time, exactly, she'd seen Tracy leaving Doug's house that evening.

"I want to say it was between the hours of 5 and … no," she stopped herself. Then took a moment of reflection, staring up at the ceiling.

A brief pause.

"I would have to say it was between 6 and 7 that evening."

This timeline entirely contradicted Larry Bridges'

testimony.

Without having any knowledge of a Walmart receipt the state would soon produce (unless she was told about it before her testimony), Lisa Watson's timeline fit into a timeline the investigation had constructed with hard, documented evidence of Tracy's movements that day.

Lavender asked if anything "unusual" occurred at Doug's that evening while Tracy was around. Something that might have "caught your attention?"

"Sometime that afternoon," Lisa explained, "I want to say around 5 or 6, I heard a gunshot and I looked over (toward Doug's) and I didn't see anything."

"And about how long after that (gunshot) did Miss Fortson leave?" Lavender asked several questions later.

"I am going to say it was about an hour."

Lisa Watson said she never saw Doug again after that.

This was powerful testimony. It put a gun in Tracy's hand and gave her enough time to clean up inside the home and prepare to get Doug's body ready for the watering trough and his concrete burial.

Tom Camp now had a big problem. A witness had just put a smoking gun and the sound of it firing coming from the victim's house and his client leaving that house an hour later. This was as close to an eyewitness account of Tracy killing Doug as the state could produce, which Camp had promised in his opening to jurors they were not going to hear in this case.

During his cross, all Camp could do was focus on Tracy's truck. Where it was parked. What, if anything, Lisa saw inside the truck bed. He could have gone back to Larry's testimony and asked about the contradiction in times, but he did not.

Lisa said she never saw the truck drive around to the back of Doug's house, adding that she did not see anything "unusual going on over there" that day. She never saw a watering trough or metal container in the back of Tracy's truck and never saw any concrete being mixed. However, she added without being asked, "I couldn't see the back of her pickup truck from my house."

The theory was that Tracy had backed her truck up to Doug's deck, where law enforcement found tire tracks, heaved his body out of the house inside a shower curtain, and placed it into the metal tub. Then, using the hose Doug had left on to water his birds, poured the concrete, filled the trough with water and took off for the farm.

Regarding that gunshot Lisa had supposedly heard, Tom Camp brought up an excellent point in that Lisa Watson never mentioned that gunshot—a *significant* piece of information, one might assume—when Lutz came out and spoke to her and Larry Bridges on that first day. It wasn't until SA Ben Williams showed up on Sept. 12 (three *months* later) that Lisa recalled a gunshot going off in the vicinity of Doug's yard and seeing Tracy leave an hour later.

If one was to take a little detour down Conspiracy Road, heading toward Frame-up Avenue, well, this might feed into that idea.

Lisa countered with an equally important fact, explaining that when Lutz came by to speak with them, there was no murder investigation going on. Nobody really knew of the facts or if Doug had simply taken off somewhere without telling anyone. Lutz was there to conduct a welfare check. Not to poke around and take statements about what may or may not have happened.

"As far as talking about the gunshot," Lisa told jurors, "no, I didn't talk about it until the day of the investigation."

Day of the investigation? What did that mean?

Camp didn't go near it.

"After that date," Camp asked a few questions later, "that afternoon, June 4, when you said you heard a gunshot, you didn't really think anything at all about that, did you?"

"No, sir."

"You didn't call the police or anything, did you?"

"No, sir. Because people around there shoot all the time."

"That is all the questions I have."

Rob Poston took to the stand and explained how he and his wife had come upon the watering trough in the cattle patch out on the farm while tooling around looking for another bike with a flat tire he had set out to fix that Sunday afternoon.

What was interesting about Rob Poston's memory of events was that Bob Lavender used Poston to explain to jurors how familiar Tracy Fortson was with the farmland where Doug's body had been found. The DA asked: "If you see a strange vehicle on the premises, what would you do?"

"I normally go find out who it is and what their desire is," Poston said.

"If you saw Miss *Fortson's* vehicle on the premises, what would you do?"

"Well, if I knew it was *her* vehicle, probably nothing."

Tracy knew this land, had hunted on it in the past and was on good terms, if not friends, with the man who owned the land.

Under cross, Tom Camp established that it was quite possible for those pierced wounds in Doug's body to have been made—hypothetically speaking—by the forks on the front of the John Deere tractor Rob Poston had used that day. Rob said he used the tractor, mainly, to try and hoist the metal trough up and out of the ground. Poston described the forks he had on the tractor that day as being "three feet long and ... in the shape of a pen or a pencil," Camp finishing for him, calling the forks "sharp and pointed at the end."

A motorized pitchfork on the front of a tractor was the image. You stick those forks into the bottom of a trough—which Poston had done—filled with concrete and a human body and it's likely you'd poke a few holes into the corpse, especially around the midsection, or exactly where the puncture wounds had been found on Doug's body.

The point Camp made was that the forks could have made

all of those puncture wounds found in Doug's midsection, not a knife or other sharp object—even though a forensic examination would maintain that the wounds Doug sustained had not been made postmortem. And by most accounts, Doug's body had been in that trough, on that farm, for nearly two weeks.

OCSD Sheriff Mike Smith was up next. Smith basically reiterated what Poston had told jurors: the events as they unfolded out on the farm, how Doug's body was located and then how it was handled from the time law enforcement arrived on the scene.

The only question for Smith that truly mattered became: "Did you identify that person or have a good idea of who that person was?"

"Yes," Smith told Lavender. "I had a good idea who he was."

"Why was that?"

"Because of the tattoo on his arm. I had (seen) it before."

"Where had that been?"

"At the Oglethorpe County Sheriff's ..."

WHEN WE DISCUSSED MIKE Smith's identification of Doug, Tracy questioned Smith's veracity, which made me wonder if Tracy was sitting in the same courtroom when Smith testified.

"As for the ID of Doug by his tattoo," Tracy told me, "I find it (hard) to believe that someone like Mike Smith was able to identify Doug from a tattoo unless he knew him prior or knew he was in that container as well as how he got there. It seems like a family member would have been called to give a positive visual identification."

There are many problems within this statement. For one, this was not a "positive" identification—it was informal, at the scene, yet enough for them to believe they had found Doug Benton. Second, Mike Smith had surely seen Doug around the OCSD. Tracy had been reprimanded at one time for having Doug hang around so often. Finally, law enforcement would never, under these circumstances, ask family members to come out to a crime scene to identify a victim.

The guy saw the tattoo, recognized it, realized Doug Benton was missing two weeks by then, and put two and two together.

Not a big leap there.

CONCLUDING MIKE SMITH'S DIRECT testimony, Lavender had the sheriff look over several documents with Tracy's handwriting. Official stuff, from when she worked at the OCSD.

"Do you recognize that writing?"

"It looks like Tracy Fortson's writing."

"How do you recognize that?"

"By when I looked over her reports. It looks similar to her writing."

Not quite the scientific statement you'd like to have claiming a note written by a murder victim had been forged by the person who had taken his life.

39.

BEFORE THE FIRST DAY of testimony ended, Tom Camp took a crack at Mike Smith. Camp needed to choose his jabs carefully and specifically—and know when the right moment to make contact revealed itself.

"Afternoon, Mike," Camp said first thing. "Where are you now?"

"I am between jobs."

After establishing that Smith was working for the OCSD on June 19, 2000, Camp walked slowly into the fact that Mike Smith was, back then, the chief investigator.

"That is right," Smith agreed.

They talked about crime scenes and Smith's experience, Camp focusing on the policy of when the GBI was called in to look at scenes for the sheriff's department. At one point, Camp mentioned how Smith had GBI SA Ben Williams with him when he went out to the farm after the call came in that day.

They discussed the tractor and its pointed implements.

Where the "container" was located.

How Rob Poston "poked some holes in the container" with the forks of his tractor and how, when he did it the first time, "a bunch of fluid of liquid ran out of it," Camp said.

"Yes, sir."

"And smelled pretty bad, didn't it?"

"Yes, sir, *very* bad."

"And that smell was pretty consistent with the smell of a decaying body?"

"Yes, sir."

Camp brought in SA Terry Cooper, the GBI's crime scene specialist Smith had worked with in the past.

"And you and Mr. (Ben) Williams, you all just didn't think about calling Mr. Cooper out there to the crime scene, did you?"

"I didn't."

Camp spoke of how they all stood around and "tore up" the container without a crime scene specialist on site and Smith responded by saying, "they did," meaning the GBI and Rob Poston.

Smartly, Camp had Smith establish how Doug's body was "face up" inside the container, which put his buttocks and midsection, where the wounds were ultimately found, on the bottom of the container, the same place Poston had poked at it with those forks.

Even more interesting was a fact that had not been known until Smith talked about it: How they actually pulled Doug's entire body out of the container out at the farm.

"Did Mr. Williams have a camera with him on that day?"

"I don't think so. No, sir."

"You don't *ever* recall Terry Cooper, the crime scene specialist, coming down there on that day prior to the container being hauled off?"

"I don't remember."

Tom Camp paused. Gave Smith a quizzical look. A gaze, really, as if to say: *Come on!*

Then, without anything further, Camp said he had no more questions.

The judge recessed court for the day.

40.

THE CRIME SCENE WHERE Doug's body had been recovered was an important point of contention within the scope of my conversations with Tracy Fortson. She had a lot to say about it. And to be honest, much of what she says about this particular portion of her case makes perfect sense. What's more, Tracy has a tremendous amount of respect for Terry Cooper, having worked with the guy on a number of occasions.

Tracy mentioned to me how, for example, "Oglethorpe County is full of old dirt roads that go for miles. A person can travel from one county to another and never touch asphalt. There are places where bridges do not exist, where creeks run across the road, always have. There are old rock quarries where companies have mined granite (before abandoning) the areas, leaving what looks like a bottomless pit full of water. Bodies have been recovered from such places as well as stolen cars."

There was one call, Tracy remembered, when a body was reported being found in a ditch.

"This call got everyone's attention."

They drove out to it: Sheriff Ray Sanders, investigators Mike Smith and Rollins Skelton and the Chief Deputy, Billy Melton, along with Tracy. Arriving at the scene, they noticed the body of a black male lying face up in the ditch.

It appeared to everyone that the guy had been tossed out of a vehicle.

So they secured the scene. As they did that, GBI crime scene specialist Terry Cooper was contacted.

"I remembered Agent Cooper from the Police Academy," Tracy explained. "He had taught a class on crime scene investigation while I was there."

Here she was, however, at this scene, now prepared to put that training into action.

After waiting for what amounted to four hours for Agent Cooper to arrive, they "got down to business, literally," in Tracy's words. "We went into the ditch, up close and personal with this body that had been in this ditch for what looked to be at least 48 hours."

Decomposition had set in. The guy's skin had leathered over from the elements and the insects had gone to work on him.

"Most everyone was putting Vicks VapoRub under their nose, but I had been taught that doing that would cause your brain to associate the Vicks with the smell of human decomposition, so anytime you smelled Vicks, you would automatically smell human decomposition and I didn't intend to have that odor association."

Working with Agent Cooper was the highlight of Tracy's day, she said. Although it had been under tragic circumstances, "Working side by side with someone who was considered an expert in his field was exciting to me."

Her point was that policy and procedure, in that circumstance, had been dictated by the crime scene they had come upon. As a sheriff, one would evaluate. If there were any question or even a slight chance a homicide had occurred, one would call in law enforcement specialists before touching anything.

"Although I will never forget the experience of working side by side with Agent Cooper on a murder case that day, never, in my wildest nightmares, would I have thought two years later Agent Cooper would be investigating … a murder where I was the accused."

I asked Tracy specifically about SA Ben Williams and Mike Smith being out at the scene that day on the farm. What she thought they might have done wrong. How the process they followed might have had a detrimental effect on her case later on.

Tracy had a strong opinion about this. Speaking specifically about a search warrant associated with her case filed by SA Ben Williams, Tracy said: "SA Ben Williams just *happened* to be at the Oglethorpe County Sheriff's … at 3:45 p.m. when the call came in from (Rob) Poston? Then responded to the scene?"

I don't have a problem with an SA hanging around a local sheriff's department talking to the cops he works with. Plus, Williams had been working on a case nearby and had stopped in. This is not unusual.

"Williams and Smith attempted to remove the contents by the use of a tractor," Tracy continued. "Why a tractor? Then a hammer and screwdriver were used to remove the bottom of the container, revealing a human body identified as Doug Benton. Who identified him? Who knew him that well? If his body were in an advanced state of decomposition, someone would have to know him *very* well to make that ID. Was his body in advanced state of decomp as the medical examiner stated or did Williams and Smith already know who was in the container?"

For me, Tracy's argument here becomes weak and accusatory. I firmly believe that Doug's tattoo was enough to identify him. As far as why a crime scene specialist had never been called out to that scene at that time (the bigger of the problems here), no one could answer that question for me.

41.

THE FOLLOWING MORNING, JULY 11, 2001, Lavender called MCSD investigator Jimmy Patton, who had gone to Doug's after a missing person report had been officially filed. Patton's testimony was vital because Lavender needed to show that when the MCSD went inside Doug's trailer on that first day, there was no smell of kerosene or gasoline. Yet, when they returned two days later, the first unusual condition they ran across was a potent, vapor-like smell of an accelerant. Think of standing by the side of your car while filling it with petrol. There's no mistaking that aroma. The implication Lavender tried to get across became that someone had been paying close attention to the investigation, and might have been watching stealthily from afar, or had some insight into how law enforcement investigations worked. That person, so said the DA's implicit theory, gauged how the investigation was progressing and decided to torch Doug's trailer to cover up any lingering forensic/trace evidence.

Patton said he went over to Doug's with Amory Scroggins and Bill Strickland on June 17, hours after the missing person report had been filed. Subsequently pulling open the back door, they walked through the entire residence. At that time, nothing seemed unusual or out of whack. The house was quiet. Nobody was inside. There was no particular smell.

And that was it from Patton. The scene, it could be said, had been set for the DA's next witness.

Tom Camp asked one question of Patton twice: the date. Was he *certain* it was the 17th?

Patton said yes both times.

Cody Cross walked into the courtroom and took his seat in the witness chair. MCSO Investigator Cross went over to Doug's after his body had been recovered. It was here, upon entering Doug's modular home, the smell of an obvious accelerant overtook Cross and the others as they entered.

The other purpose of Cross's testimony was for Lavender to begin entering all of the evidence they'd collected from Doug's on that day. But before he got into any of it, Lavender asked Cross about a search they'd conducted at Tracy's house.

Cross went through each piece of evidence there and Lavender entered each into the record. As Cross and Lavender discussed each item, it felt as if a devastating blow to Tracy's defense was being unleashed.

They discussed that Walmart receipt. Rubber gloves. Guns. "A box of CCI brand stinger .22 caliber long rifle ammunition" (the same type of ammunition used, as far as ballistics was concerned, in Doug's murder).

Lavender asked Cross to explain what was now referred to as State's Exhibit Number 19.

"Yes, sir ... a cartridge or a box of .22 long rifle hollow point ammunition."

Lavender then asked about a list of items Tracy purchased, which were detailed on a Walmart receipt, including a shower curtain.

They went through each, one by one. Most of time there was no explanation needed; the fact alone of mentioning the evidence in the context of what jurors already knew from prior testimony was a shattering enough blow. For example, Cross said he found "three cans of spray paint."

"What are the colors?"

"Black, green, a dark green and an off-beige color."

Camouflage.

After several additional questions, Lavender entered a videotape into the record and asked Cross about it. There was some back and forth with the lawyers and judge regarding what was on the tape, but after sorting it out, Cody Cross stood and narrated as the tape played for jurors.

He next talked about how they had videotaped the back porch area of Doug's house and there "were some old tire impressions or what we *thought* were tire impressions in the grass there, but unfortunately, we never did get any pictures of it."

Inside Doug's modular home, Cross explained, pointing to the screen, "That is the carpet and it was very wet and smelled of kerosene. ... That is the cushion of the sofa. That, I believe," he said, "is candle wax. That is actually a cushion. They tore the cover off the sofa cushion. ... Candles. ... Above it, a burned spot on the cushion."

Through the video and his testimonial narration of it, Cody Cross talked jurors through Tracy's house and carport garage, the farm where the watering trough had been found, more detail inside Doug's home and an area in back of that farm not too far from where the watering trough and Doug's body had been recovered.

Then it was on to Tracy's truck: "Cement splatters and the scratches on the edge of the bed," Cross said as the video showed all of it in real time. "That was sort of powdery cement right here, still in powder form."

All of the pieces formed a fairly clear picture—that is, if one was sitting, analyzing this murder, trying to find a way to pin it on Tracy Fortson. The concrete mix. Where she bought it. How much she had purchased. The shower curtain, later found inside her bathroom.

On and on, evidence against the former deputy piled up.

They talked about trees on the farm and injuries, if you will, to those trees and how likely it was that a wire or some other type of material had been tied around the tree so the watering trough could be pulled off the back of Tracy's truck. Within that, Cross mentioned nicks and cuts and damage done to the tree and also Tracy's truck. And when they matched Tracy's truck—the height measurements—up to the tree, it all gelled.

"IN THE VIDEO, INVESTIGATORS are comparing a scrape on a tree where the trough was found to the bumper of my truck," Tracy explained to me in 2016. "The scrape on the tree was *not* there when the farm manager took still photos of the trough prior to moving it (this comment I could not verify). The scrape they were comparing to my truck was made by (Rob Poston's) tractor used to remove the trough."

AFTER ANOTHER ROUND OF questions relating to some of the evidence Cross had videotaped, Lavender had him explain how they found a notepad with some writing on it inside Tracy's house. But before they could get into talking about what was written on the pad, there was an objection, which was ultimately sustained.

With that, Lavender passed his witness.

Tom Camp stayed on the evidence, not really getting anywhere other than to confuse the situation, which was perhaps his intention from the start. Tracy's lawyer was stuck on the sofa inside Doug's where all the blood and candle wax and kerosene had been found. He wanted to know if all of the blood had been collected and sent over to the lab.

Cross said as far as he knew, it had been.

Then Camp moved onto the search of Tracy's house. He hammered on the idea of Doug's killer using kerosene. He asked Cross about the kerosene smell at Doug's and then moved on to Tracy's residence, saying, "(Y)ou *didn't* find any kerosene at all at Miss Fortson's house, correct?"

"Yes, sir. That is correct."

The one smart tactic seasoned defense attorneys employ quite often, especially when they sense a setback, is to question the evidence itself and how it was collected, including chain of custody. It's the only way to supplant the notion of an internal problem into such seemingly unimpeachable evidence, which appears to be, if only by circumstance, burying your client. And in this situation—even for someone on the fence about Tracy's guilt—you'd have to agree there was so much evidence pointing at her, it was hard to ignore. Much of it, on top of that, Tracy had no explanation for, other it all being planted.

Camp asked about the inside cab of Tracy's truck and pointed out what law enforcement had uncovered there, adding how, in the bottom of the floorboard, "There were lots of rocks and dirt and stuff in there as well, right?"

"Yes, sir."

"And *none* of that was collected or tested at all, either, right?"

"Not to my knowledge."

That statement was incredible, actually—evidence of perhaps dirt from the farm inside Tracy's vehicle left untested. You have to ask why. Was it deemed unimportant? Had those CSSs scouring Tracy's truck unknowingly brought it into the vehicle on their own shoes? There were so many questions. So many possible scenarios.

None of which were ever answered.

Still, it was an ideal way for Camp to point out that perhaps some shoddy police work had gone on here. That maybe tunnel vision took over as they focused on Tracy. In doing that, Camp suggested, could investigators have looked only to broaden their investigation into Tracy as a suspect? Why test what was found in the back bed of Tracy's truck and not what you found inside the cab?

TRACY TOLD ME: "**THEY** never found any articles or items (of mine) stained with blood. However, they claimed that there was cement residue in the *back* of my truck. Of course there was residue! I had 10 80-pound bags loaded into the back of my truck on Sunday, June 4, by ... forklift. When I was trying to unload them by myself, without a forklift, one of the bags ripped as I was tugging it across the bed of my truck. I rinsed the bed out, but I didn't scrub it or use anything to actually clean it. No reason to. I had no clue that I would be accused of mixing concrete in the bed of my truck. Had concrete been mixed in the bed of my truck, there would have been a *lot* more than just splatters or residue."

BACK QUESTIONING HIS WITNESS, Tom Camp added how crime scene specialists searching the inside of Tracy's truck had come across an "item on the armrest ... some sort of light dot or something and that wasn't collected and no test was attempted on that."

"That is correct, sir," Cross stated.

This was an incredible statement on fact alone. CSSs had swept the inside of Tracy's truck for forensic evidence and did not collect a "white dot" on an armrest?

Why not?

ONE OF TRACY'S ARGUMENTS to me has been the lack of forensic evidence inside the cab of her truck. If she had shot and stabbed Doug to death, why wasn't there any blood found inside the cab of her truck, which she had supposedly used to transport his body out to the farm?

One has to consider this.

"There was no blood inside my truck, on my truck, or in the bed of my truck," Tracy told me. "One of the reports claims there were deep scratches in the bed of my truck as if something heavy had been dragged from it," Tracy added. "Yet there was *no* paint transfer from the metal bed of my black truck to the metal trough. I did not have a bed liner in my truck, therefore any metal-on-metal contact/friction would have left paint from one to the other."

Tracy is spot on with her comments.

TOM CAMP THEN ASKED Cody Cross a smart question, one surely any top-notch major crimes investigative squad member would have answered yes to. Camp wanted to know if any agency had gone out and purchased the same watering trough Tracy had allegedly used to bury Doug in to see if it matched up to the scratches left behind in the bed of her truck. Kind of like a set of teeth put up against bite marks.

"No, sir, not to my knowledge," Cross answered.

Tom Camp's job was to cast doubt on the evidence and how that evidence had been collected, how much of it was collected, what might have been overlooked, and what law enforcement failed to do. He was doing a superb job of that with his cross-examination of Cody Cross, who had to answer no to a lot of straightforward, Investigation 101 questions.

Near the end of his cross–examination, Camp asked Cross, first warning him that he was about "state the obvious here," if they had searched "anyone else's home other than Miss Fortson's and Doug Benton's."

"To my knowledge, yes, sir."

"There was never a search warrant obtained for Jeff Bennett's home, was there?"

It was the first time an alternative suspect—without calling him such—had been brought up.

"Not that I know of."

"There was never a search warrant obtained for Jerry Alexander's home, was there?"

"Not that I am aware of, no sir."

"Are you aware of the fact that both of those people own pickup trucks?" Camp asked.

"I don't know what they drive, sir."

"You don't even *know* what they drive?" Camp thundered, asking a few more questions about the video, before indicating he was finished his cross of Cross.

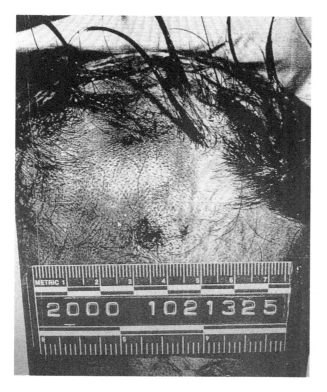

A single bullet wound to the top of his skull was found to have killed Doug Benton after his decomposed body was found and extracted from a cement tomb.

Doug Benton was 38 years old when he went missing in early June 2000.

An amateur bodybuilder, some claimed Doug Benton was heavily into steroids and, at one time, other illegal drugs— which might have been the motive behind his murder.

Tracy Fortson was the first and only female deputy sheriff in Oglethorpe County, Georgia, at the time the law took a turn in her life and she found herself facing a murder charge.

With her strong personality and aggressive way of dealing with others, Tracy Fortson made an excellent sheriff's deputy. She had not one blemish to her career at the time of her arrest.

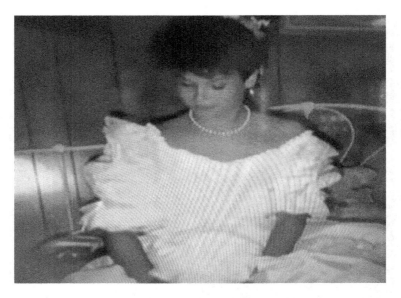

Married and divorced twice, when Tracy first met Doug Benton she wasn't thrilled about the prospect of dating him and soon shunned his advances.

Tracy lived with her daughter just a few miles from Doug Benton's modular trailer home. She claimed that the concrete and horse watering trough she purchased near the time Doug Benton went missing had been stolen from a carport attached to her home.

Tracy Fortson owned her own horse, which she kept on a spread of land just down the road from her house—hence the reason why she bought the watering trough and mineral block near the time Doug Benton went missing.

Doug Benton had been heavily involved with drugs and, according to several people who knew him well, had worked as a confidential informant for law enforcement to bust a local drug dealer—which was, those same sources claim, why he was later murdered.

The horse watering trough, with Doug Benton's body encased in cement, as it sat in the middle of the same cattle field where Tracy Fortson hunted.

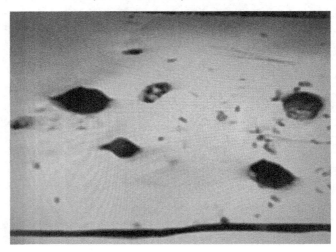

As a point of contention throughout the case: Did these holes on the bottom of the cattle trough, made by the pitch forks of a tractor, also make the wounds on the lower-mid portion of Doug Benton's torso?

Crime scene experts later busted up the concrete inside the trough with pick-axes and hammers. A portion of the concrete was then doused with Clorox bleach.

Was this scuff mark on the bark of a tree near the watering trough made by Tracy Fortson's truck or the tractor used to hoist the watering trough from the ground?

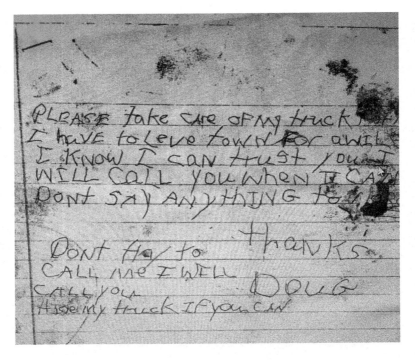

Was this note allegedly found on the window of Doug Benton's truck actually written by Doug, or had his killer forged his handwriting?

Years after her arrest, being found guilty twice, Tracy Fortson continues to fight for her innocence.

She's been in prison nearly two decades, but Tracy will never, she says, stop trying to convince the world she did not kill Doug Benton.

At 52 years of age, in 2017, Tracy Fortson sent me this photo. As we corresponded over the course of nearly a year, Tracy and I butted heads and fought like enemies. The one thing that never changed was Tracy's narrative. I never caught her lying to me.

42.

MCSD SHERIFF BILL STRICKLAND took a seat in the witness box. After being asked, he explained to Bob Lavender his role in an investigation that seemed to have utilized every available investigator the county could spare. Above all, Strickland reiterated what Mike Smith had previously laid out: those dead birds, going into Doug's house under that "welfare check" status, not seeing much of anything out of the ordinary, opening a missing person case.

Leaving Doug's, Strickland explained, he set out to talk to Tracy (that first time), but only under the pretext of her having "possible knowledge of Mr. Benton's whereabouts." The way he described this first contact with Tracy made it sound as though it was routine, which was certainly true.

Lavender asked Strickland to give an overall assessment of the conversation with regards to Doug and Tracy's relationship.

Strickland said Tracy was open about their relationship being "rocky" and "on and off" again, mentioning the fact that they were separated.

Then Tracy gave Strickland a date: June 4, the last time she saw Doug, according to Strickland. That date—which would change throughout the course of the case—was the starting point. It matched up to the date Larry Bridges and his girlfriend had given to the sheriff's department.

They moved on to Jeff Bennett and Jerry Alexander, both of whom Strickland interviewed, but failed to discuss what information Strickland was able to glean from those interviews.

Lavender asked about going back into Doug's home for a second time.

Strickland said they smelled an intense odor of kerosene.

The DA wanted to know if Strickland had been involved with impounding Tracy's truck.

"Yes," Strickland said. He'd gone out to Tracy's parents' home to secure Tracy's truck under a warrant. When he arrived, Strickland testified, "It had debris in the back: splatters. It had potting soil. Bags of potting soil in the back and it looked like quite a few scuff marks in the bed."

All incredibly condemning testimony.

After discussing the couch Doug was likely lying on when he was murdered and how GBI SA Terry Cooper was called out to Doug's house to process that scene, Lavender passed his witness.

Camp didn't have much. He asked about Tracy and that interview Strickland conducted, getting Strickland to agree Tracy had actually come down to the sheriff's department under her own volition and "appeared to be cooperative in talking to you about what she knew."

"That is right," Strickland agreed.

"And she, in fact, talked to you about her relationship with Doug Benton, is that correct?" Camp asked.

"Yes, sir."

"And she actually, at times, got a little bit tearful about that—I mean, that is what it states here (in your report): 'Tracy spoke of her relationship with him (Doug), which at times were tearful'?"

"That is true."

Camp was done.

SCOTTIE KNOWLES CAME IN next and spoke of how

he helped Tracy choose a watering trough and the concrete mix and helped load it all into her truck.

When Tom Camp took a crack at Knowles, he focused on Tracy's demeanor that day, first asking if she appeared "nervous in any way."

"No, sir," Knowles said.

"She did not appear to be really upset about anything, did she?"

"No, sir."

"She certainly wasn't crying or anything of that nature, was she?"

"No, sir."

"And she told you she was going to be building a pad, a concrete pad, for her dog pen, is that correct?"

"Yes, sir."

They talked about how Tracy had asked for calculations and how to gauge how much concrete she'd need for the dog pen. Hearing this, Knowles and his boss called a big-building supply competitor and asked for help.

Camp asked Knowles about several photos and how the bags of concrete mix Tracy bought were dusty with concrete residue all over the outside of them, same as the ones in the photos.

To which Knowles agreed.

Sherry Michael followed and gave the same basic narrative as Knowles. Only difference that came up, which might be deemed relevant, depending on which side you leaned, was that Sherry and Tracy knew each other.

How, Camp asked Sherry.

"We've ridden horses together on several occasions."

Camp keyed right in on that acquaintance, asking, "And she shopped in the store before?"

"Countless times," Sherry Michael said, adding soon after how Tracy did not seem at all unnerved or upset that day.

One might wonder why Tracy Fortson, preparing to bury

her boyfriend in concrete and entomb him inside a watering trough, would go to a store and purchase those items from a woman she knew personally?

They then discussed how common it was for the store to sell watering troughs. People who owned horses and other farm animals often came in and bought the troughs. It was a common sale item.

Smartly, Camp asked if Tracy had purchased any potting soil, rope or cable that day.

"No, she did not."

Yale alumnus Paul Schroeder, a geologist, sat in the witness box next and gave the State of Georgia its scientific link to the concrete. Schroeder explained to jurors how GBI SA Ben Williams brought him several samples of concrete to analyze. After schooling the courtroom with regards to how geologists examine concrete and stone to determine their origins, Lavender asked the most important question of his witness: "Did you compare ... scrapings and what was taken out of the bed of the truck?"

"Yes. The observation that I made was that the scale and size and texture of the fragments from the truck (Tracy's) and the concrete block (where Doug's body was recovered) were similar."

After a long, tedious and, quite honestly, boring discussion about something called X-ray powder defraction (XRD),[5] which Schroeder admitted "involves a lot of theory," Lavender and Schroeder gave a second geology class to jurors, banging on and on about ridges and hardness and textures in stone and rock.

In the end, Schroeder said it was the same stone in both Tracy's truck and the sample he'd been given by SA

---

5   According to serc.carleton.edu, XRD is "is a rapid analytical technique primarily used for phase identification of a crystalline material and can provide information on unit cell dimensions. ... The analyzed material is finely ground, homogenized, and average bulk composition is determined."

Williams from the concrete block in the watering trough—the sole reason the DA had put the respected scientist on the stand to begin with.

During the cross-examination portion of his testimony, Tom Camp and Schroeder agreed to disagree, mostly, with Camp pointing out somewhat obviously that all of this so-called "science" was actually based part and partial on opinion.

Schroeder agreed.

Then there was a brief re-direct and an even briefer re-cross. All this back and forth did was tell the jury that the information Schroeder provided was probably more important than it was, simply because of the amount of time they gave to it. The more the attorneys argued their respected points, the more the jury sat up and paid attention. What it came down to was rather simple: would a guy with Schroeder's reputation and standing at Yale University give an opinion the DA needed? Or was he simply banking on his experience to dictate the facts as he saw them?

The jury would have to decide.

Jeffrey Smith sat down next and took a deep breath. Forensic pathologist, Dr. Smith, a licensed physician, hailed from the State Medical Examiner's Office at GBI headquarters in Decatur. Smith had performed the autopsy on Doug Benton.

THIS NAME WAS A problem for Tracy Fortson as we talked through her case. Tracy truly feels Smith got it wrong—if not purposely, incompetently. At least that was the impression Tracy gave me as we went back and forth about Smith's findings.

"The medical examiner's report stated that the cause of death was a combination of a gunshot wound to the head and 10 potentially fatal stab wounds," Tracy told me. "Those stab wounds were found to be made by the hayforks used to move the trough as well as the screwdriver and mallet used to open the trough (there was never any solid proof offered to prove or disprove this outright). You would think that a medical examiner who is considered an expert would be able to distinguish between postmortem wounds and wounds made at the time death occurred. Look at the testimony of Dr. Jeffrey Smith."

And so, here you have it—that testimony Tracy asked me to review.

RIGHT OUT OF THE gate, Dr. Smith explained how unusual the case was as compared to those he normally looked into, mainly because of how the body had arrived at the M.E.'s office encased in concrete, inside a watering trough. Then, after being asked by Bob Lavender, Smith called his job a "puzzle-solving process." Most importantly, Smith restated, part of his job was to work "in conjunction with the information I get from investigators."

They discussed Doug's height and weight, as Lavender introduced a series of autopsy and crime-scene photographs they'd be referring to during the course of Smith's testimony.

Lavender asked about Doug's wounds.

"Specifically, I found a total of 10 stab wounds on the body and a single gunshot wound to the head," Smith said.

The DA then wanted Smith to look at a photo of the gunshot wound. He asked if there was anything "significant" about the "area *around* the wound."

Smith gave an opinion of the wound being "inflicted at a very close range" because he had found "blackening of its edges."

The next photo Lavender brought up on the screen was a picture of Doug's underwear.

Smith talked about the "back of the underwear" and "defects" in the material he'd reviewed. The defects had actually "corresponded" with two stab wounds he found on Doug's body.

This was interesting, because if Doug was lying face up

in the trough and he had stab wounds to his buttocks and Rob Poston had picked up the trough from the bottom and penetrated it with those pointed pitchfork-like tongs on his tractor, well, this was evidence that those two stab wounds, at least, could have been made by the forks.

Lavender moved onto the stab wounds around Doug's belly, which had likely not been made by the forks of the tractor, hence Doug's stomach facing up while inside the trough.

"Could you determine what made those stab wounds?" Lavender asked the pathologist at one point.

"A sharp object, such as a knife."

Lavender countered with when the wounds might have occurred.

"Well, because of the postmortemental number of the injuries, they are different from what they would be in a freshly deceased individual," Smith said. He added how "a number of the injuries had somewhat was apparently some older blood corresponding to the wound track. It is my opinion that these injuries occurred after about the time the deceased died."

That was very vague, however, not to mention oddly worded: *Somewhat was apparently some older blood.* Still, he admitted several of the wounds had been likely made afterward.

"Is it possible that the wounds occurred as a result of removing him from the trough?"

Smith was specific here, contradicting himself: "No."

Lavender asked about the bullet wound and Smith's opinion of it.

Smith was certain the gunshot killed Doug. When compared to the stab wounds, Smith said he disagreed Doug might have died instantly from the gunshot wound. Instant unconsciousness, yes. But not immediate death. Only if the bullet went through the section of the brain controlling the heart and his breathing would death occur instantaneously,

Smith explained. And there was no way they could tell because Doug's brain had been dried out like a prune, most of it gone.

Lavender's next question was, perhaps, a bit of a stretch to ask a pathologist, though the polished DA was on a roll. Why not give it a go?

"When you saw this bullet, did you have any comment about what kind of bullet it was, et cetera?"

Smith called his knowledge of identifying bullets "rudimentary." The ballistics descriptions he normally used in his reports came in the form of "small, medium or large caliber," he said. So he was not the best expert to ask such a question. That being all said, Smith sat up straight, leaned into the microphone and gave his best analysis: "I felt confident this was a small caliber bullet," he told jurors, referring to the moment he pulled it out of Doug's head, briefly examining it before tossing into a plastic evidence bag.

Part of Smith's opinion regarding the caliber was based on the damage the bullet had caused to Doug's skull. In a longwinded, run-on response, stumbling through his explanation, Smith said he considered the bullet to be more than your "normal size small .22 bullet and you don't actually see this sort of damage to the head from a small .22 caliber bullets and I might have offered an opinion at the time that it *could* have been, but basically the understanding there is, I package it up, I label it, and send it to the experts up in firearms to make a definitive identification."

In his report dated June 20, 2000, Smith called that same bullet he took from Doug's body "a greatly deformed small caliber bullet." There was no ambiguity of it being a small caliber projectile.

I guess, if one is keeping score, you'd have to look at Smith's testimony here and call it what it is: backtracking. Smith was changing his opinion, which, now in court, did not include the words "greatly deformed."

Why?

When asked by Lavender what had ultimately killed Doug Benton, Smith believed it was a "combination" of multiple stabs wounds and that gunshot wound to the head.

The DA passed the witness.

43.

THAT ALL-AMERICAN LOOK of Tom Camp gave him a rather comforting edge while inside a courtroom. Camp came across trustworthy and intelligent, and those who knew him well agreed the guy fell into both categories.

No doubt about it, Tom Camp had some work to do with his cross-examination of Dr. Jeffrey Smith. The combination of a knife and gun attack worked well for the prosecution's case, mainly because Doug was a massive man, in bulk and strength, and the DA's killer, though quite tough herself, is female. The idea of knife and a gunshot wounds spoke of a tacit theory that one or the other had incapacitated Doug first, so the other could deliver the fatal blow. It was clear within the testimony thus far that while neither was an immediate killer, gunshot and stab wounds alone would have eventually caused Doug's demise.

Camp directed his cross-examination at those stab wounds, getting Smith to agree that all of them were "from about the midline of the torso down."

Tracy's defense attorney stayed there for about five minutes, indicating quite early into his cross he was done, no more questions.

Which felt odd.

Why not question Smith about his opinion of the bullet?

"IN HIS TESTIMONY, DR. Smith says he has no idea how long Doug had been dead," Tracy explained to me. "(Then he says) he did not know that Doug had been removed from the trough (and) placed back in it. He did not know that the container had been speared with the hayforks of a tractor and slammed repeatedly on the ground. So some of his conclusions came from photos."

Tracy is correct in her assessment. Smith, during a later court proceeding, testified on all those accounts and, he said, he relied mainly on photos to draw his conclusions. DA Bob Lavender had, in fact, pointed this out during his direct examination: pathologists sometimes depend on photos and reports, and speak with investigators, along with many other pieces of evidence they uncover themselves during autopsy, to evaluate a case.

Problem I find with Tracy's argument here is that it doesn't matter if Smith's testimony was flawed (which one could argue for or against), or if those wounds were made by the tractor forks or not. Fact is, it doesn't clear Tracy from the murder.

Still, the preponderance of evidence is purely overwhelming. I guess if one wants to claim innocence, which Tracy has, one would have to, in this situation, assert that it was a frame job. Because it's truly the only way in which all of the evidence against Tracy could be disregarded. Otherwise, you're left with one suspect. At the same time, when you dig deep, and truly take into account all of that same evidence, you have to question how perfect it all is and how magically it lines up to prove that Tracy Fortson killed Doug Benton. This became the lingering question that bothered me the more I looked at the entire picture.

44.

BERNADETTE DAVY WALKED INTO the courtroom after Dr. Smith concluded his testimony. If Tracy Fortson had a true archnemesis in this trial, a villain to hang her core argument of incompetence and nefarious allegations on, Davy was that person.

A State Crime Lab forensic examiner working out of Atlanta, Bernadette Davy had over 10 years' worth of experience behind the microscope. She had been qualified as an expert in a court of law 450 times (many of those murder trials).

After having Davy, a California State University graduate, list her qualifications under direct testimony, Bob Lavender asked Camp if he had any objection to qualifying Davy as an expert in this trial.

Tom Camp said he did not.

There you have it: qualification number 451.

Davy had run the tests to determine if any of the weapons found inside Tracy's or Doug's house were a match to the bullet fragment pulled out of Doug's skull. Because the bullet had been so badly deformed—photos show it was significantly distorted—while traveling through Doug's skull and lodging itself inside his head, definitive proof—more commonly known as ballistics—was going to be controversial, at the least.

Generally, a ballistics expert in Davy's shoes studies what are candy cane-like, raised striations inside the barrel of a weapon and compares those markings to any striations or markings left on a bullet or bullet fragment provided to him or her for comparison. A fingerprint-worthy match can be what some ballistics experts rely on when these types of tests are conclusive: the bullet was either fired from the weapon or it wasn't.

Davy's job included test-firing weapons, collecting those test-fired bullets and looking at cartridge cases (casings: the empty shell left behind) under a microscope to determine if there are any similarities. She might also examine any unfired bullet ammunition found at Tracy's or Doug's to determine if it was the same ammunition used in the crime. This type of forensic work is all about consistency in the samples as compared to the barrels of weapons—in addition to consistency in the projectile evidence and any bullets or unfired ammunition recovered. Test firing gives the examiner a base on which to judge those comparisons. Bullets and casings from the same weapon should match up to the barrels they were fired from. This is sometimes called "ballistics fingerprinting," a science the FBI and most law enforcement agencies throughout the world have relied on for decades to help convict defendants. However, in one study by a group of scientific experts who looked at 2,500 cases the FBI used ballistics in, there was a problem. The National Research Council panel, after a year-long study of those cases, found the FBI's science was fairly "sound," but that "examiners had sometimes overstated its reliability in court testimony ... 'The bottom line,' said Barry Scheck, (then) president-elect of the National Association of Criminal Defense Lawyers, 'is that FBI experts have been going into courts for years and definitively saying that particular bullets found at a crime scene came from a certain box of ammunition or were manufactured on a certain date, and the researchers are now saying that is wrong. These cases have to be re-examined.' "[6]

So, although ballistics was purported to be an ironclad forensic science, which many considered either black or white, add a human factor into it (a gray area, per se), and you have a science fated to sometimes fall apart.

BOB LAVENDER HANDED DAVY State's Exhibit 42, a Remington .22 rifle. There was a package attached to it with a test-fired cartridge (casing) and bullets Davy had test fired herself with that particular weapon for comparison purposes. Davy said GBI SA Terry Cooper had brought the weapon to her lab.

State's Exhibit 40 was then put in front of Davy. "A box," Davy explained, describing the exhibit, "that contains a .22 caliber lead bullet."

Lavender asked Davy if she had made a comparison between 40 (the bullet) and 42 (the Remington).

"Yes, sir."

"What was the result of that comparison?"

"That the bullet, State's Exhibit 40, was *not* fired from this rifle, State's Exhibit 42."

Thus, within that statement, Davy was saying under oath with an emphatic *hell yes* that she was able to use the bullet—however deformed—taken from Doug's skull in her testing.

State's Exhibit 21 was put into Davy's hands next—a Stevens .22 rifle with no serial number. Davy explained that the first time she saw this particular weapon happened to be when Amory Scoggins turned it over to the crime lab on April 25, 2001.

Ten months after the murder.

Exhibit 43 was next: "Numerous .22 cartridge cases and .22 caliber bullets"—all test-fired evidence Davy had

---

6 New York Times, February 11, 2004: http://www.nytimes.com/2004/02/11/us/report-questions-the-reliability-of-an-fbi-ballistics-test.html?_r=0

produced herself in the lab from the Stevens .22 rifle.

Asked about this evidence, Davy's testimony came across a bit confusing: "(B)ased on the microscope comparison, I was unable to eliminate this weapon as having fired the bullet, but I could not identify this weapon as having fired the bullet."

Davy seemed to be saying both were possible: the weapon *could* have fired the bullet that had been extracted from Doug's head, or it *couldn't*.

"What does that mean to the ladies and gentlemen of the jury?" Lavender asked of his expert witness, hoping to clear up any of that confusion. "What did you find when you made your examinations?"

This was the most vital answer Davy would be asked to give within her brief direct testimony. She cleared her throat, beginning: "When this rifle was made, the manufacturer put six raised ridges into its barrel incline with a right-hand twist." She added how within those ridges was "a certain width between the raised area and the groove area," before explaining how each ridge is different, thus giving the bullet its so-called metal fingerprint. "When I test fired the weapon"—Exhibit 21, the Stevens .22 rifle found inside Tracy's home—"and collected the test fires, the land impressions or the raised ridges, there was the same number. There were six of them and a right-hand twist and they were the same width as the ridges and impressions that are on the bullet that was received from the autopsy."

A match, in other words.

Davy continued, clarifying how the markings of the barrel had been transferred to the bullet.

The damage for Tracy had been done: That weapon they found inside her home had, according to this expert, fired the bullet that killed Doug Benton.

"WHAT I GLEAN FROM her testimony is bull crap," Tracy told me as we began a long conversation about Davy, her career, and her testimony. "She could tell the bullet *wasn't* fired from the Remington .22, but it had the *same* class characteristics being fired from Stevens .22?"

To Tracy, this was inconclusive. You cannot have it both ways.

"Since the bullet was too distorted to make a definitive match," Tracy continued, "she could not (draw) the conclusion that it was fired from the Stevens .22, yet she *could* determine the exact brand, caliber and velocity of the bullet by comparing it to the ones she had on hand in the lab? Really?"

Tracy Fortson had a point.

AS DAVY CONTINUED ON direct, she explained her findings more clearly, adding, "The next step was to see if the markings from the barrel that are transferred to the surface of the bullet, if they matched between the test-fired bullets and this evidence bullet."

Indeed, tests of which would truly tell the tale.

"Due to the mutilation that the bullet sustained," she continued, "… those individual characteristics, or those markings from the barrel, were pretty much obliterated and I was unable to find them, or they were not there on the bullet due to the mutilation." She went on to call the markings "obscured by mutilation," not mincing words. Concluding this thought, Davy added, "So the best that I can say is that the bullet from the autopsy … has the *same* classic characteristics or rifling structure as this rifle, State's Exhibit 21."

Not that metal fingerprint the prosecution was hoping for, but enough to lean in that direction—at least according to Bernadette Davy.

"IN ONE OF MY open records requests to the GBI (later on)," Tracy told me, "I specifically asked for the weight of the recovered bullet in grams. I received a response from Special Agent Lisa Harris who said that a search for the records was done and according to this search, the bullet was not weighed." Tracy wanted that weight of the bullet, she claimed, "due to the fact that Dr. Smith stated in his (autopsy) report ... that the bullet was pancaked and too distorted for ballistic comparisons."

Smith did not use that precise language. In an eight-page report, Smith only mentions the bullet once, calling it, again, "greatly deformed." I never saw another report indicating Smith thought the bullet was "pancaked" and "too distorted for ballistic comparisons." Furthermore, why would a pathologist ever make such a bold claim? In all my years of studying hundreds of autopsy reports, I do not ever recall this type of analysis being made by a pathologist in his or her autopsy report.

"If the bullet was not weighed, then there was no way to tell if the bullet was complete or whether it had lost some of the lead content, which would have altered the weight from its original state," Tracy continued. "In other words, how did she do a comparison and come to her conclusion if she didn't even know if she had a complete bullet? And how did she determine from a pancaked, distorted bullet that it was a CCI brand .22 Stinger?"

Several issues here. A ballistics expert does not need a complete specimen to do a comparison analysis. Also, we're back to the pancaked bullet. It was not 100 percent pancaked, thus allowing Davy to put it under a microscope and have a look. Lastly, Davy certainly knew she had a distorted bullet to work with—she mentioned as much during her testimony.

BOB LAVENDER'S NEXT QUESTION to Davy came off a bit strange, yet he was able to get his point across:

"Would it be fair to say that it would be consistent with being fired from this rifle but *not* this rifle?"

"That is correct," Davy said over Camp's objection to a leading question.

Lavender simplified his query: "Can you make *any* comparison between the bullet in 40 and the two rifles?"

"Yes, sir," Davy clarified. Then she explained, in great detail, how she went about doing that. It came down to simple science, Davy seemed to say. The ridges on the test-fired bullets from one weapon were "much smaller" in comparison to the ridges on the test-fired bullets from the other weapon. Thus, she could easily eliminate that one weapon when she compared both weapons to the bullet extracted from Doug's head, regardless (though she never said this) of the shape the bullet fragment was in.

Bottom line here was that although she could exclude the one weapon entirely, she could not exclude the other weapon, saying how "the classic characteristics are completely different." As for the other weapon—Tracy's—those "classic characteristics," Davy was comfortable saying, "are identical, meaning that they have the same number of lands and grooves, the same direction of twist and the widths of those lands and grooves are identical." Adding further, "The only reason I cannot say that it was fired from this weapon is because the individual characteristics that are unique to each barrel are obliterated from State's Exhibit 40, the bullet from the autopsy."

To prove that the bullet extracted from Doug was a CCI brand .22 Stinger, same as they had found inside Tracy's house, Davy said she compared the autopsy bullet to "several different manufacturers' brands." A rather simple, straightforward comparison test.

Lavender asked a few more questions and completed his direct.

The jury, as well as Bob Lavender's team, must have expected a long and complicated cross-examination by Tom Camp, with the potential here for a good, old-fashioned Southern courtroom tongue-lashing. At the least, a quarrelsome back and forth fest of how, what, where, why, when, by whom, between the defense attorney and his witness. Yet, Camp asked only two questions of Bernadette Davy, each of which focused on how Davy was unable to determine "for sure" that the bullet was fired from the weapon in question; how she was certain it was "consistent with having been fired" and how the bullet itself was "consistent with a CCI brand Stinger, but you cannot say with 100 percent certainty that *that* is what it is?"

Davy answered, "That's correct," to both.

Camp was done.

Immediately following Davy's second response, the judge piped in and said: "Bye, see you next time." And the ballistics expert got up and walked out of the courtroom.

I WONDERED WHAT TRACY thought while sitting there, watching Bernadette Davy walk out of the courtroom, having to answer only two questions from her attorney.

"Well, I feel like Tom just didn't have the knowledge about ballistics that he needed to ask the right questions. It would have been helpful if he had researched more. He just didn't have the experience. I've contacted a forensic expert (in 2017) who says he can examine and weigh the recovered bullet to determine if it is actually a CCI Stinger. ... Hopefully, I can pursue this."

This would not be the last time the name Bernadette Davy came up in Tracy Fortson's life.

45.

NO ONE IN THAT 2001 Georgia courtroom had a crystal
ball, obviously. But had a medium been sitting next to
Tracy, watching the proceedings in the *State of Georgia v
Tracy Fortson*, and by a stroke of reality that person saw
the future, here's what he or she would have witnessed: A
damaging blow—a death knell, actually—to any prosecution
Bernadette Davy had *ever* been involved in.

To back up a bit, Tracy Fortson, in her criticisms of
Bernadette Davy, was not at all off the mark. Tracy had
sensed something in Davy and, as it turned out, the former
cop's instincts were spot on.

Fast-forward to April 2009. Bernadette Davy was set
to walk into a courtroom and testify in a murder trial. The
prosecution in that case, however, made the decision—just
before proceedings began—to have Davy's results in the case
re-tested. When the prosecutor asked the GBI about the case
and Davy's work, officials within the GBI, claimed a memo I
later uncovered, came forward and explained that Davy had
"admitted" to "falsifying a test report in an unrelated case
the month before."

Simply devastating. For a defense attorney, this was jaw-
on-the-floor information.

But there was much, much more.

In those same documents, which included internal GBI

memos, a letter and several emails, the GBI stated that Davy had "intentionally fabricated data on a firearms worksheet that was part of the official crime lab case file."

For any crime lab to hear a revelation of this nature was beyond monumental—the last thing a forensic crime lab wanted to face: the idea that one of its forensic examiners had falsified a report. It calls into question, by itself, all of the work the lab has ever done, not to mention any of the work that particular examiner had ever done in any case.

The specific case relating to Davy dated back to Sept. 8, 2006. It involved a .22 caliber six-shot revolver. During her testing of the revolver, a crime lab scientist conducting an audit discovered that Bernadette Davy "had 10 trigger pulls on a weapons worksheet when the actual number should have been 12 trigger pulls," those same documents claimed. Because of that seemingly small discrepancy, the crime lab scientist conducting an internal audit of paperwork sent the case for peer review. Just a few hours after Davy's case had been sent for review, the scientist conducting the investigation received an email from Davy stating that "the trigger pull function of the procedure had been completed."

That immediate email response from Davy raised a red flag for the investigating scientist.

Why?

"Because she was not expecting to hear back from Davy that quickly," explained one of the documents.

So the scientist checked in-house chain of custody records and found that the "firearm in question was still locked up in evidence."

Those two additional trigger pulls had *never* been completed, which meant Davy had lied about it in her email.

The deputy director of the crime lab, along with several higher-ups, called Davy on the carpet and questioned her about the discrepancy and her subsequent email.

"Did you retrieve the revolver out of (the) evidence locker and complete the two trigger pulls that you had placed on your weapons worksheet?" Davy was asked by one official.

"I did not retrieve the weapon out of evidence and I used the average number of trigger pulls that I had already conducted to complete the analysis."

Clearly, Davy had fabricated the report and then lied about it.

In the internal report of the matter, "Davy admitted that by her not retrieving the weapon out of evidence and conducting the trigger pulls, she fabricated data on the weapons worksheet."

Davy argued that "time factors" were the reason—not enough help juxtaposed against too many cases on her plate. A letter accompanying the internal documents I discovered clearly explains that the lab was stressed and in desperate need of additional scientists to keep up with demand from the various district attorneys' offices they worked for.

"(N)ot completing the trigger pulls," Davy said during that interview about her conduct, "did not impact the quality of the case."

Although this is probably accurate to say, it becomes an insignificant, irrelevant factor in the totality of the situation.

As they talked about the matter back and forth, Davy said the scientist who suggested the peer review had always been a bit of a thorn in Davy's professional side. The woman "constantly nit-picks (Davy's) work on peer reviews and she (Davy) was fed up with it and that is the reason she fabricated the data," the internal documents I uncovered went on to say. "(She) stated that she has never fabricated data in her cases in the past, or done anything similar to fabrication."

One of Davy's bosses stepped up in her defense, however weakly, and explained how he had once reported that Davy was in dire need of "a break from working rush cases and if she didn't get one she was going to end up doing something stupid."

This was not an overstatement by any stretch of the imagination. Since July of the previous year (2008) to April

2009, Bernadette Davy had worked more than 300 cases. That's a little over 33 cases a month—that is, with a seven-day workweek.

Nonetheless, the final results of the internal investigation found that Davy, whom they referred to in several emails while discussing her cases by her nickname—"Bernie"—had "violated" crime lab policy and procedure.

A fair assessment.

An isolated case is one thing, obviously. But a pattern, of course, is an entirely different matter.

Thus, this one discovery set off a whirlwind of re-analysis of Davy's cases by scientists in the lab. And as they began to go through her cases, more red flags were raised. One scientist, a man who had sparked the new audit, wrote in an email how he had "noticed some things in a couple of (Davy's) cases that I have (re)worked that cause me some concern and I need to know if there is a pattern developing." He listed several of his findings.

Among them was a "weapon worksheet of 6R rifling" that had been noted by Davy "when in fact the weapon was 4R." In another, "listing of weapon worksheet of 'safeties OK' (when) in fact the Lorcin 9mm manual (thumb) safety was entirely missing as well as the safety retainer spring." A third said Davy had listed on a weapon worksheet a magazine "capacity of 13 but 14 was easily fit." She had also made note of a "cartridge case worksheet (whose) primer color (was) 'gold' when in fact it was 'silver' (nickel)."

This particular scientist indicated at the end of his email that these seemingly minor discrepancies, which could be detrimental to a prosecution if discovered by the defense, were "at the very least ... concerning."

A second email I found from another scientist working out of the Central Regional Lab in Dry Branch included a discovery of five additional discrepancies within re-evaluated cases where mistakes had been made. In one instance, Davy described an item in a case as "simply a lead core," when it "was lead core and several lead fragments." In another, she made errors of color again, indicating on a bullet worksheet a "non-metallic" substance that was actually "silver/gray metal fragment."

In another particularly interesting case of re-analysis (especially if you are Tracy Fortson), there was a discrepancy; the scientist re-evaluating Davy's work found in a ".45 metal jacket bullet (where) Bernie had some agreement (in) ... both .45 metal jacketed bullets that ID'ed with each other." The scientist went on to note how this one piece of misinformation "changed the Conclusion of the related case."

There was another "change in conclusion" attributed to Davy that a third scientist had uncovered while going through Davy's old cases. This one involved a word Tracy Fortson was all too familiar with in regards to bullets: "mutilation." In this case, "Bernie did a (test) on this bullet as a ... 'mutilation.'" But when the scientist went back and looked at it, "In my opinion, there are no definite shoulders visible to measure (the bullet)." Consequently, Davy was saying in this instance, according to re-analysis done by a former colleague, that she was *able* to measure a bullet fragment and evaluate it, but when he went back to look at it, there was no way that he could. In addition, this particular bullet had "been run over and had abrasions across the entire bullet (and) what was visible of the rifling is very shallow." In this case, "should a gun be submitted for comparison," the scientist wrote in the email, "there are not enough discernable characteristics ... and very minimal individual characteristics." He even had another colleague look at the same case and that scientist agreed. The conclusion they came to, if they were ever to be asked about the case, would have to include: "fails to reveal sufficient characteristics to determine what type of weapon it was fired from."

Which spoke directly to Tracy's case.

The re-evaluations went on and on, well into June 2009 and beyond. Those scientists taking a second and third look at Davy's cases found discrepancy after discrepancy. Some extraneous, others more complicated. Either way, the fact that a scientist had made so many errors and admitted to fabricating a worksheet in a case—and then lied about it—was enough to question everything she had ever done, which would have to include the work she did on Tracy's 2001 case.

"THE GBI DOES NOT give out info readily," Tracy explained to me in 2016 (she had no idea then that I had dug up these reports about Davy and the re-examination on her cases, or how many discrepancies I had discovered). "There were times when I had to re-word a request just to get what I was asking for. If I asked for any and all information pertaining to the firearms expert, ballistics, etc., in my case, I would get A) a copy of Bernadette Davy's 'Report and Conclusion,' which consisted of one sentence: 'The bullet in question is consistent with a .22 CCI brand Stinger'; or B) a copy of the 'Official Chain of Custody Evidence Report,' which listed all of the evidence the GBI had and that's it."

Meaningless paperwork meant to satisfy Tracy's request, as opposed to fulfilling it. Why would they not give Tracy Fortson the same documents I had uncovered? She was asking specifically about Bernadette Davy.

Tracy said she "finally asked" the GBI "for 'the weight of the recovered bullet in grains' and that's when I got the letter stating 'the bullet had never been weighed'—a data sheet with no information on it concerning 'Item No. 0026 Lead bullet from Douglas B. Benton.' "

Another "discrepancy," at the least, by Bernadette Davy.

THAT 2009 CASE had opened up a can of embarrassing mishaps, became subject to reassessment by the courts, but also made it clear that any of the cases Davy had testified in would now have to be looked at and re-examined. How would anyone know if Davy had only falsified one report? After the 2009 announcement, her entire credibility was now in question.

"I think we're going to see a lot of inmates saying, 'This person testified against me,' and demanding new trials, which is reasonable when a lot of cases come down to the ballistics expert," Christine Koehler, president of the Georgia Association of Criminal Defense Lawyers, told *Online Athens* in 2009 after Davy's fabricated report sheet was made public.

For Tracy Fortson, however, the reality was that she could not see into the future, and Bernadette Davy had just told a jury (in 2001, eight years before the bottom fell out of her career) that, according to the tests she'd run, the gun that fired the bullet killing Doug Benton was found inside Tracy Fortson's home, along with a box of the same type of ammunition. Tracy and her team, or even SA Lavender for that matter, of course, had no idea that Davy's entire career would be put into question eight years hence.

"She testified to her findings under oath knowing her results were incorrect in several cases," Tracy said of Davy, explaining her frustration in a 2017 email to me, after I sent her the documents I had uncovered and she reviewed them. "I was never able to get any worksheets or notes pertaining to my case. I sent several open record requests and got nowhere. Now I can see why they didn't want me to have them, if they actually existed. In my case, Davy testified that the bullet recovered from Doug had certain lands and grooves, which I have always thought would have been impossible because the bullet was 'pancaked' and distorted. How could she make that determination if the bullet was pancaked and distorted? After all these years ... and this info was there the entire time. I'm at a loss for words. This is what I needed all along. I'm not sure what to do at this point, but I ... credit you for finding this information."

46.

AS TRACY'S TRIAL CONTINUED, the DA's fire debris expert from the Western Regional Crime Lab in Columbus, Brian Hargett, sat in the witness box. After qualifying himself by listing his credentials and extensive training, Hargett explained how he'd examined a section of couch cushion and rug cut from Doug's residence. Saturated into both household items, Hargett testified, was a mixture of "heavy petroleum distillates," including "diesel fuel, kerosene, fuel oils and some other types of products."

From there, Hargett schooled the jury in fuel oils (which I won't bore you with here), after which Lavender indicated he was done with his direct examination.

Tom Camp questioned Hargett firmly on the fact that law enforcement never submitted any type of "raw liquids" from either Tracy or Doug's house, implying that, well, yes, there might have been an ignitable fuel found on the carpet and cushion, but there was no way to tell where it had come from or who actually put it there.

Hargett agreed.

And that was it for the fire debris expert.

The DA's case was now cruising into its scientific groove of experts coming in and explaining the abundance of forensic evidence it had collected. What's interesting is that a majority of this evidence did not point at anyone in particular, especially Tracy Fortson, but the implication—because she was the suspect on trial—was always that it had.

Next up was Mary Elizabeth Horton, a GBI microanalysis expert who looked at the paint found in Tracy's truck, on her mailbox and in her garage and the paint used to disguise the trough, along with any paint scrapings CSSs collected.

Bottom line was, Horton said, the same colors of paint had been used on the watering trough and Tracy's mailbox, which were later found in Tracy's possession. But there was no way to tell that a certain scraping of paint had come from a particular can of paint. Calling her work "color comparison," the only absolute Horton could testify to was that the paints were the same color—which meant absolutely nothing in the scope of proving guilt.

Then, at the very end of her brief period on the stand, Lavender asked Horton about the masking tape found at Doug's house.

It was the same type of masking tape, Horton said, "recovered at the time of the autopsy."

"Was there any comparison between those?"

Horton said she had analyzed the backing portion of both sample adhesives and found they were similar.

What did this mean, however? That the same *type* of masking tape found at Doug's house was then found inside the watering trough? It did not mean Tracy had used that piece of tape. After all, Horton never mentioned any fingerprints found on the tape. It was another piece of evidence presented for the mere fact of guilt by association. Yet, in the reality of inculpatory evidence, it had zero value.

Camp did an excellent job pointing out in his short cross-examination that all Horton could do was draw similarities and state her *opinion*; there was "no way" she could "identify that the paint came from a particular can."

A point of which Horton agreed.

Another factor Camp brought up was the DA's contention that some of the paint might have been transferred to Tracy's truck during the process of dragging the trough off the vehicle, so he asked about it: "You did not find *any* paint on that metal container that would be in any way consistent with these paint scrapings that you were submitted there from the defendant's vehicle, correct?"

"I did not."

"No further questions."

Arthur Anthony, the DA's document examiner, had been with the crime lab since 1981. His role in this case was to compare the writing of Doug Benton to an envelope and handwritten note, and also "further comparisons of writings of Tracy Fortson back to" the same envelope. Anthony was going to make a judgment based on his experience whether Tracy's handwriting compared at all to the note allegedly found on Doug's window and also if Doug's proven handwriting compared to that same note.

Lavender handed Anthony the actual pieces of evidence. Then asked the crime analyst to explain how he had drawn his comparisons. Anthony stepped down from the witness stand to address several charts, explaining: "My opinion is that the writing on the left-hand side of the chart, which is the letter or note (purportedly left on the driver's-side window of Doug's truck), is *not* comparable to the known writing as contained in the marked State's Exhibit 47 (Doug's handwriting)."

After that, Anthony gave a long explanation of how he had drawn this assumption, concluding, "Tracy Fortson probably prepared the writing on State's Exhibit Number 1 (the note found on Doug's truck window)."

Probably?

Interesting.

Could a jury vote that Tracy was "probably" guilty?

Anthony then explained how he'd used a "side-by-side comparison." He talked about arcs and strokes, and how individuals left a distinctive pattern within the way in which they wrote letters. Circular motion was not the same from person to person. He noted in particular the letter "G" and how Tracy's "Gs" were the same as the "Gs" on the truck window letter.

Under cross, Tom Camp went after the idea that the handwriting expert did not know either Doug or Tracy and his analysis was based on an opinion of seeing those handwriting samples for a first time after the prosecution gave them to him. Moreover, Camp made clear, all Anthony had to work with were samples from Tracy and Doug.

After Anthony answered yes, Camp smartly followed up with: "And you were *not* given *any* known handwriting samples to analyze as purported to be the known handwriting samples of Jeff Bennett either, were you?"

"I was not."

"No further questions, Your Honor."

WHEN I ASKED TRACY in 2016 how she felt about what seemed to be a cavalcade of evidence during her trial pointing toward her guilt, she said: "This has been an uphill battle for me since it began. I've faced adversity and contradiction for the past 16 years. That's nothing new. You want me to prove to you that I'm innocent, that's not so easy, especially when people are steadily trying to discredit everything I say. But hey, that's nothing new, either. I've had experienced professionals trying to prove it and they failed miserably. If proving my innocence was easy, I wouldn't be where I am."

AS TRACY SAT AND watched what felt like a piling on of evidence during her trial—a lot of which, I have to agree, seemed to be cut and pasted and designed to see that she was found guilty—she sometimes digressed. Losing her train of thought inside the courtroom, Tracy often went back to her childhood and early adult life. There were lessons—maybe answers, too—for how her life had later turned out, many of which were rooted in her formative years.

47.

TRACY FORTSON WAS 12 years old. She stood outside her Winterville, Georgia, childhood home one afternoon, listening to her mama and daddy argue inside the house. The muffled yelling back and forth, an occasional slam of a door, smack of a table. Not recalling ever hearing a fight between them get this heated, Tracy climbed up on top of a windowsill and peered inside to see if she could better gauge what was happening. Or maybe more to determine if her intervention was needed.

As she focused her vision, cupping both hands around her eyes to block the sun, Tracy saw her parents wrestling on the ground. They were struggling to gain control over an object.

A gun, in fact, Tracy soon realized.

"Daddy was trying to get it away from her."

Tracy jumped down from the windowsill and ran around the corner and into the house. As she made her way to the door of their bedroom, Tracy watched as "Daddy pushed Mama onto the bed, grabbed the gun from her and then hit her with his fist in the mouth."

Terrified, Tracy felt as though she had to do something. Protect her mother. Stop the insanity. So she crept up behind her father, who didn't yet know she was standing just a few feet away.

"Mama was crying."

Tracy looked left and right, searching for something to use as a weapon to stop him.

She spied a flashlight with a hard plastic handle.

She picked it up.

Then she swung the thing like a bat in the direction of her father's head.

He turned just in time to see what she was doing and "snatched the flashlight" from Tracy's hand.

She managed to stop him, however, from attacking her mother. Rattling the old man out of whatever rage-filled tantrum he had been locked in.

As he "came to his senses," Tracy remembered, her mother ran out of the room.

Tracy followed.

"Mama and I did leave that night," Tracy explained to me in 2016. "She took me to my (grandparents') house, but she didn't stay. Mama seemed afraid of Daddy, but she was even more afraid of what he would do if she didn't go back. She always said, 'Things will be worse for me if I don't go home, honey. Please understand.' I always thought that it couldn't get any worse than getting a busted lip, but she was convinced he would kill her."

As the relationship between her parents unraveled from there, with Tracy's mother staying, Tracy found solace in taking off and spending time away from home, losing herself—like most kids amid dysfunction—in activities outside the house.

"I rode the dirt roads with (friends) on our motorcycles and sometimes we ended up in another county. I found more people who had horses and we would all ride for hours. I went to the skating rink every Friday and Saturday night and I had friends from school who invited me over to their houses. I was too embarrassed to invite anyone to mine because I never knew when a fight would break out between my parents."

After Tracy went back home from her grandparents' in the weeks following that fight, the arguments she witnessed had escalated. As Tracy got older, she realized how "things really were" between her parents. "And it wasn't good." She felt for maybe the first time that their marriage was beyond repair.

Then a grace period, when the tension and resentment and anger somewhat relaxed. This gave Tracy the opportunity, she said, to finally invite a friend over for the night.

"You hear that?" Tracy's friend said. They stood outside. The noise came from inside the house. An all-too-familiar sound of two people arguing.

"An eruption," Tracy recalled.

"Let's go to my treehouse," Tracy said, explaining later how that treehouse was one of the places she went to "get away from the yelling."

They sat up in the treehouse for hours talking as the situation inside the house calmed. Eventually, Tracey explained, perhaps thinking that a fresh start in a new house would make the marriage better, her parents built their dream home.

"But the fighting never slowed down ... (and) things only got worse."

Tracy said she made her way through school "as if I didn't have any parents. No one ever came to any of the events that I was involved in. No one came to parent/teacher conferences. They never knew I was in Student Council or the Beta Club. If I needed something signed, Mama would do that. ... No one was able to help me with my homework. The only time either of them came to my school was to drop me off or pick me up."

While the fights between her parents got worse during Tracy's teenage years, she began thinking of ways to leave home permanently. Her love of animals and the outdoors had Tracy daydreaming of going to college and becoming a veterinarian, but the dream dissolved when her parents said they couldn't afford to send her to college.

"So I contacted the Marine Corps recruiter. I knew that the Marine Corps would gladly have me and I could get a college degree. I came awfully close to signing up. Although I wasn't afraid to become a soldier, it just wasn't what I had in mind. Plus, who was going to protect Mama?"

By the time she graduated high school, Tracy said, "I guess Mama had finally had enough. I was thinking that it sure did take a long time to realize it, but then again, she claimed that she was waiting for me to graduate."

When it came time for her mother to file for divorce, "Daddy wasn't having it. I guess he didn't think she would go through with it, but the divorce papers made it clear. Until it was final, Mama stayed in the house—and me too, of course. At first, my father refused to leave, but the law got involved and he finally relented."

But that did not last.

"My daddy just changed tactics," Tracy said.

One particular afternoon that stood out to Tracy later was when her father brought the local preacher over to the house to speak with her mother. This was odd to Tracy and her mother because, she said, "We had never attended a church that I could recall, not together, anyway. I guess he thought she needed some spiritual intervention."

When that didn't work, Tracy's father came back, "with fire and hell in his eyes. He didn't knock politely on the door this time; he pounded and demanded an audience with my mother."

Tracy's cousin just happened to be staying with them at the time. She answered the door.

"She's got a headache and is lying down to rest."

Her father wasn't having it. He pushed his way into the house, past the cousin, and went straight for the bedroom.

"If the preacher couldn't make her see reason by God, well, he was going to himself," Tracy said.

Tracy realized what was happening and jumped in front

of the door into the bedroom. Her father tried to push past her. Tracy grabbed his arm and, with all her might, pulled him away.

"The next thing I knew, Daddy had blood running down his arm where he had scraped it on the doorframe."

Rather than admit he had scraped it on the doorframe, he turned his rage toward his daughter, screaming, "You scratched me."

"I knew that I couldn't have (done it) because I was a nail biter and didn't have enough fingernails to scratch an itch."

Her father looked at his arm, then up at Tracy.

"Look what you've done!"

"I didn't do that. *You* did."

"Daddy was in such a rage at that moment that he swiped his arm across my white shirt, smearing blood all down the front, then he turned around and ran for the kitchen."

Tracy followed. He could hear her cousin dialing the phone, calling the OCSD, so he ran over and grabbed the phone from her hand and started pulling at the wires, trying to jerk them out of the wall.

Tracy approached, grabbed the phone out of his hand and tried to hit him with it.

Daddy ran out the back door.

Watching, Tracy knew from experience he was going for the outside wires, to pull them out of the house.

So she ran out the side door and met him there.

"I had taken as much of this as I could take and if my Mama wasn't going to fight back, well, I was. I became tired of the arguing, the drinking, the fussing and fighting and my Mama getting her mouth busted or her eye blackened. I wasn't scared of him! So when he reached for the wires on the side of the house, I swung (at him)."

He tried blocking the punch.

"I pushed him away."

Her father fell back and screamed, "You bitch."

Tracy stood, stunned. She'd stopped him.

Her father wasn't finished, however. He ran for his truck. Hopped in. Started it up and drove straight toward Tracy.

"Well, it's a good thing we had railroad ties in the yard, because that's what he hit. He sat there for a second, I guess trying to decide what to do next. I just stood there looking at him. I think I was in shock that my own father had just come at me with his truck."

Ultimately, after a brief standoff, he left.

"I went back into the house and locked all the doors. I knew he would be back—maybe not this night, but he *would* be back."

48.

GBI AGENT DAWN PIERCE testified next. As Tracy sat, she dialed out of that childhood memory and refocused on her case. Pierce worked for the GBI Crime Lab. Her specialty was bodily fluids: blood, semen, saliva. She'd been with the lab since 1997.

In total, Pierce had conducted DNA comparison tests with the blood found on a closet door handle inside Doug's residence to Tracy's DNA.

"What were you able to determine, if anything, from that analysis?" Lavender asked.

"I was able to determine that the DNA from that swabbing, which was collected on the hall closet door, excluded Tracy Fortson as a donor. And I was unable to determine if that did match Mr. Douglas Benton due to the known blood sample that was taken at the time of autopsy. That particular sample was very decomposed and I was unable to get a known DNA type from that particular item and was unable to match that back to that particular DNA."

"I have no further questions," Lavender said.

Tom Camp asked Pierce if she had conducted any tests on the blood saturated into the couch cushion underneath Doug's body.

"No," she said. "The only item that I did perform DNA testing on was the sample from the hall closet door."

Why would GBI not test the couch cushion blood against Tracy's DNA? It seemed almost a given that they would want to know if by stabbing someone so many times—as purported by the prosecution—Doug's accused killer nicked herself during the process and maybe left DNA, placing her directly at the scene of the murder.

Camp reiterated the fact that the blood on the hall closet door did not match Tracy's DNA.

Pierce agreed.

Then Camp asked: "And you did not *ever* receive any donated blood from an individual by the name of Jeff Bennett to your knowledge, did you?"

Smart question. Ringing that reasonable doubt bell once again.

"Not to my knowledge."

"And to your knowledge, you did not *ever* receive any donated blood from an individual by the name of Jerry Alexander?"

An even smarter follow-up.

"To my knowledge, no, I did not."

THE IDEA OF THERE being blood found on the hall closet door was as equally baffling as it was significant to Tracy. It seemed to her to be an important clue—like, for example, maybe the killer had left it there unknowingly?

"I never knew there was blood on a closet door at Doug's house until they came to the county jail with a search warrant to obtain mine," Tracy explained. "So why didn't the prosecution test the identity of the DNA when they found out it wasn't mine?"

Was that blood DNA put into CODIS, the national database? Was it tested against any other person besides

Tracy and Doug?

Tracy said the answer to both is no.

WITH DAWN PIERCE RELEASED, yet another forensic scientist walked in, held up her right hand and swore to tell the truth and nothing but the truth. This particular scientist had 20 years' GBI experience. Terri Santamaria had performed tests on a piece of cord—soaked in decomposition fluid and marked as a biohazard—recovered from Doug's body and another piece of cord found on a different section of Doug's body. Those two pieces of cord were tested against a roll of "cordage" found inside what both Lavender and Santamaria described as "a hall closet."

In the end, Santamaria testified, she was able to determine that one piece of cord on Doug's body was a match to the hall closet cordage, but the other was not.

Then the scientist was asked about pieces of cord found attached to a tarp found with Doug's body inside the watering trough.

The cord on the tarp was, in fact, a match to a spool of cordage found (again they said) "in the hall closet."

Whose hall closet was never mentioned—was it Tracy's or Doug's? The insinuation, left there, was that the cordage in question had been recovered from Tracy's house, yet no one had said as much.

Tom Camp went straight at that information beginning his cross, wondering if the roll of cordage was taken "from the victim's home?"

"That is correct," Santamaria said.

Was it lazy prosecution work not to have made this clear during Santamaria's direct exam? Or was it a slight-of-hand trick? By not mentioning which hall closet, was the jury supposed to think it was Tracy's?

With that cleared up, Camp went back to what was became a recurring theme of his cross-examination throughout the trial: "Were you ever submitted any cordage that had been identified to you as being from the home of either a Jeff Bennett or Jerry Alexander?"

"No."

Through his cross-examination of certain witnesses, Tom Camp was showing that the investigation had been blindly focused—either intentionally or not—on one specific suspect, Tracy Fortson, and investigators never once thought to rule out anyone else.

"Or they did not want to," Tracy commented later.

After a brief exchange between Lavender and another inconsequential forensic witness—Tom Camp passing on the opportunity to cross-examine—the gallery turned to see that Jerry Alexander was making his way toward the witness box.

Tom Camp, surely ready to pounce on whatever Doug's old friend was going to say, watched as Jerry sat down.

49.

TRACY MADE IT THROUGH her high school years without any major bumps or bruises—or, rather, any that could be construed as emotionally beating her down. Yet the damage to the family unit had been done, according to Tracy's recollection. Her father's unpredictable, dysfunctional behavior had wreaked havoc on the marriage and home. So when it came time for terminating the union, Tracy did not expect things to end without some blowback.

"Mama and Daddy's divorce was not just a fight, it was an ongoing battle," Tracy recalled in 2016.

Her father at first refused to sell the house or give her mother half when—and if—they did sell. He also refused, Tracy said, "To do anything that would have made things easier" for her and her mother. They were being punished, Tracy saw it, for not wanting him anymore.

"Mama thought she had a good lawyer, but he never fought for her, so when they did finally divorce, she just gave up the fight and settled for a measly $10,000 just to get it over with."

House finally sold, divorce on track, one might think the chaos was over.

"Except, it wasn't. The day the divorce was final, Mama had until 6 p.m. to get everything she had out of the house. My aunt and uncle came to help. We had their truck and my mother's car loaded down. Mama had rented some land within two miles of Daddy, which was the dumbest thing I had ever heard of. And then she bought a small mobile home for us to live in. At 5:45 p.m. that day, Daddy came driving up in the yard to, as he put it, 'stake his claim.' "

He said he wanted them out of the house at 6, no excuses. They had 15 minutes and that was it. Whatever was left behind was not theirs any longer.

Tracy claimed her father made no secret of packing a .45 caliber pistol in a holster on his hip and another in a shoulder holster.

"He was there to intimidate and scare the living hell out of everybody."

He approached them as they packed up the car.

"You have just a few minutes to get your shit and get the hell out of here," he said, making sure to place a hand on his holster to show he was armed.

Then, without saying much else, he unholstered one of the weapons and shot several rounds into the trees to make a point that he was not messing around on this day.

After that, he walked up to the four of them, all of whom were standing, staring in shock at what had just happened. Then pointed the gun at himself.

"Go ahead, pull the fucking trigger," he said, staring into their eyes, standing in front of each, saying it over and over, daring any of them to have the guts to do it.

When he got to Tracy, she immediately reached for the weapon. Her plan was to take the gun away from her father. But with the sort of unbridled relationship they'd had the past five or so years, he must have thought she just might pull the trigger, so he backed away.

"I knew my father," Tracy recalled. "I knew he was putting on a show, but the others didn't know it and his show was having the desired effect."

Tracy's uncle, there to help with the move, walked over to the truck, sat down and froze, not sure what was happening.

Tracy told her father: "I'm not scared of you."

"The others were convinced that he would shoot each and every one of us if we didn't get the hell out of there. I felt like I was in a nightmare. I was embarrassed for him. He was making a complete fool of himself and I was just wishing that I wasn't a part of it. Why couldn't I have a normal family: loving, kind, caring?"

Eventually, they were able to leave without any additional trouble. Tracy said her father was "left to do whatever it was he wanted to do" in that house.

Only the chaos wasn't finished.

"Mama wasn't used to being alone and she was having a very hard time. She just wanted someone to love her and care for her without the drinking and arguing. She began seeing a very nice man who was also divorced. Knowing that my father was still wreaking havoc, they tried to keep their relationship as discreet as possible. But my father was always lurking around. He knew everything."

Tracy was certain her father was plotting and planning something. By that time in her life, Tracy was working at Georgia Square Mall in Athens and the job kept her away from home on most evenings. She'd leave about 6 and come home late, after her mother was asleep. She said her father's drinking had escalated. At one time, he could ride the roads drunk and never get caught, but those days were over.

"I found out he had spent quite a few nights in jail."

Tracy left for work one afternoon. Her mother and her new boyfriend had a nice evening planned. Tracy's father had a habit of calling in the middle of the night when he was drunk, saying things like, "I'm gonna kill that bitch," accusing Tracy's mother of all sorts of infidelity and other nefarious activities, even bringing up things from their past. Tracy would tell him she didn't want to hear about it. The marriage was over. Let it go.

"You're talking about my mama," Tracy would snap back on the phone when he went off into a tirade, calling her mother names.

"It didn't do any good. He kept threatening."

On this particular evening, while she was at work, Tracy took a call from her mother. Her mother didn't sound good. She was scared, Tracy could tell.

"What is it, Mama?"

"Your father came over to the house drunk, threatening to kill us."

Tracy rushed home.

"When I got there, Mama had a black eye, a busted lip and her shirt was torn halfway off. The sheriff's office came by and took a report, but did not make an arrest." Tracy later told me her father was on good terms with the sheriff and because of that friendship, they left him alone. "Mama was a mess. The busted lip came from Daddy, the black eye from the .44 Magnum Super Blackhawk pistol I kept on the headboard of my bed."

In a burst of courage after her ex hit her in the mouth, Tracy's mother had run into the house and grabbed Tracy's .44 Magnum. Tracy kept the gun, she said, because they were two women living alone on a dark dirt road with a madman for a father. Tracy's mother ran back outside with the weapon and fired a round into the air.

The shot scared her ex off.

"The blow she took to the face from Daddy had knocked her glasses off her face and she couldn't see," Tracy remembered. "But she had already pulled the hammer back on the gun for a second warning shot. Well, when she bent over to pick up her glasses as he was leaving, she accidentally pulled the trigger. The gun went off and the recoil caused it to hit her in the eye."

The new boyfriend had seen enough. He disappeared after that. Too much dysfunction and chaos, Tracy surmised.

"Daddy had gotten just what he wanted," Tracy explained. "Mama was heartbroken. Daddy's claim had always been, 'If I can't have you, nobody will.' I don't know why he wanted her so bad. All they did was fuss and fight."

By now Tracy was "hating my Daddy." "He had made my life a living hell and I blamed him for everything wrong in it. I didn't feel loved and I didn't feel wanted. I always felt like I was in the way. Nothing was like it was supposed to be. I shouldn't have to answer the phone in the middle of the night and listen to a drunk man telling me that he was going to kill Mama."

Tracy's impression of a proper childhood was, she described, what she had seen on television, "The Waltons" and "Little House on the Prairie." The fantasy was important to her: The perfect family dynamic. Everyone loves, is loved and gets along.

"That's what a family is supposed to be like. The daddy is supposed to love and protect his family, not run around drunk with a gun threatening to kill everybody. And where were the police when you needed them? They certainly never answered Mama's call for help."

That lack of love and affection at home during her formative years, Tracy added, "was the perfect reason for me to look for love elsewhere."

Just like the classic song says, Tracy concluded, after that last stand at the house, she "started 'looking for love in all the wrong places.' "

50.

JERRY ALEXANDER SAT IN the witness stand and stared at jurors. After being asked by DA Bob Lavender, Jerry described how he and Doug had been friends for about 10 years. They'd met right around the same time Doug was "saved" by the Lord. Though Doug had his issues like everyone else, he was a good guy, a close friend, someone Jerry said he felt he knew quite well.

After that, Lavender didn't waste time getting into the crux of why Jerry Alexander had been called. Lavender brought up the June morning when Jerry realized Doug's truck had been dropped off the previous night.

Jerry said he had not heard "anything" from Doug about dropping the truck off. The truck was not parked in the driveway one night when he went to bed, but the next morning, lo and behold, there she was positioned "backwards" on the side of Jerry's driveway. Kind of strange and not the behavior he had been accustomed to as Doug's friend.

Walking outside, realizing whose truck it was, Jerry explained, he searched the yard, yelling Doug's name.

"I said (to myself) he got to be around here somewhere because he never brings his truck and just leaves it."

"Was he?" Lavender followed up.

"No, I couldn't find him anywhere."

Jerry said at one point he moved the truck, thinking how "weird it was that Doug had left the keys in the ignition."

Then it was onto the note/letter Doug had allegedly taped to, Jerry testified, "the driver's side ... taped on the side of the window."

"Who does the letter purport to be from?"

"It looks like Doug's handwriting," Jerry said. "It looks identical. He always wrote scribbly like I do most of the time. We both always kidded around, said we had Japanese handwriting."

"Did you take the note off the window?"

"Yes, sir."

Jerry said he gave the note to the police after they arrived and started asking questions some two weeks or so after the truck had been parked in the yard. During that entire time, he had not seen or heard from Doug.

As Tom Camp began his cross, he brought up several occasions where Jerry Alexander had charges lodged against him. Serious stuff. Felonies: aggravated assault and possessing firearms and obliterating the serial numbers off of them.

Jerry said it was a long time ago: "Fourteen years."

After a bit of back and forth, Jerry explaining each charge and his version of what happened, Tom Camp changed the subject and said: "You don't particularly care for Miss Fortson, do you?"

"I have nothing against her. She's always been good to me. Doug has, too. And I told them I wanted the best for their lives."

Camp implied that Jerry didn't particularly like it all that much when Tracy, acting in the capacity of sheriff, had once visited his house to "break up an incident of domestic violence between you and your wife. Isn't that correct?"

"It was *not* violence," Jerry said with a deep breath, a shrug of his shoulders. "I mean, people have problems in their marriage. *Nothing* physical."

"A fight between you and your wife, was it?" Camp seized on.

"*No* physical violence."

They talked about the discrepancy in Jerry's memory regarding when he saw Doug's truck at his house and when he first told someone about it being there.

Jerry mentioned at one point how he "had a feeling" that "something happened to Doug," based on his knowledge of Doug being "real depressed a lot of the times." He considered that Doug had parked the truck and run off into the woods to commit suicide, but dropped the idea after conducting a cursory search of the area, failing to find his friend. It wasn't until the cops showed up two weeks later and Jerry learned that many of Doug's birds had died from being left alone that he began to truly believe something bad had happened to his friend.

Still, Jerry reiterated, he wasn't thinking sinister activity. It wasn't until the OCSD notified Jerry about finding Doug's body, Camp made a point. "And then," Tracy's sharp lawyer added, "one of the first things that you started to do was point a finger at Miss Fortson." Camp paused. Took a long few seconds to allow the statement to hang in the air of the courtroom. Then: "Isn't that correct?"

Jerry said he began to go down that road when the only other person who had shown up to help him search for Doug when he put out word was Jeff Bennett.

"And you said," Camp concluded, "that you and Jeff Bennett had *just* gotten together shortly *before* Mr. Benton's body had been found. Is *that* correct?"

"Yes, sir."

"No further questions."

Both lawyers made a few queries on re-direct and re-cross and Jerry was told he could remove himself from the courtroom. The judge then ended what had become a very long day of testimony.

Tracy stood. Sighed. Bowed her head a minute. Rubbed

her forehead. The testimony had been intense.

"It was not easy to sit through all of that," Tracy said later.

ACCORDING TO TRACY, YEARS later when we talked about the trial and Doug's friends, it was Jerry Alexander who had the biggest impact on her.

"Listening to him talk about his life and the things he had done, I couldn't believe this was the same person," Tracy said of a conversation she'd had with Doug once. "Doug told me that his life had been like a runaway freight train. He was heavy into alcohol and drugs. He knew he needed to make a change, but he needed help to do it. So he went to a friend and asked."

That friend, Jerry, prayed with Doug. Picked him up for church. Was with Doug when he accepted Jesus Christ as his savior. It was a turning point in Doug's life. His entire outlook and demeanor changed.

"It was the best decision he had ever made," Tracy maintained. "He quit drinking and got away from the drug scene and the people associated with it. That friend, Jerry Alexander, as it turned out, was someone I had known for years."

51.

WITH THE DIVORCE OF her parents behind Tracy, in addition to all she had witnessed as a child growing up in such a volatile and violent household, one could say she developed a skewed view of relationships and love and marriage. A trait now deeply rooted in her consciousness. Either consciously or subconsciously, however, as she herself began to date, Tracy fell into a pattern. She termed it as "looking for love in all the wrong places." But was it something much more profound than that rather simple explanation?

Let's go back to 1980. Tracy was 15, a few months shy of her 16th birthday. She was invited to her bestie's sweet 16 birthday party. The bestie's brother was there.

"You wanna dance?" Tod Savino (a pseudonym) asked. Tracy had already dated her bestie's other brother (who was her age), but that hadn't turned out so well.

Tod was older. Nineteen.

"He was gorgeous," Tracy told me. "No question about it."

Tod was tall, muscular, dark hair, hazel eyes.

"He was wearing a tan velour shirt that was so soft to the touch, a pair of Levis and boots. He smelled of Jovan Musk for Men and FreshenUp bubblegum. What a combination— one I will *never* forget. I felt like Cinderella at the ball."

They walked out onto a balcony at one point during the

party and Tod kissed Tracy. She saw stars and fireworks.

"I was Juliet. I never wanted that night to end. I replayed it over and over in my mind. I talked about (Tod) all week long. I'm sure (my best friend) got sick of hearing me go on and on about her brother."

In the days after that party, Tod and Tracy became inseparable. Just crazy about each other, she said.

"We were as in love as two people could be, but I was only 15 when we met, so even though we got really close a few times, we never had sex—until, that is, I turned 16."

After consummating the relationship, which they had planned and talked about for a long time, Tod and Tracy felt closer.

"It was quite an experience. (Tod) had only been with one other person, but he was my first."

They were now planning to get married as soon as Tracy graduated high school. It was all they ever talked about.

For her 16th birthday, Tod showed up with a deer rifle, a 30/30 Winchester model 94 with a leather sling. A man after her heart, she said.

"Even though the wives or girlfriends were not allowed to go deer hunting with the men at (Tod's) hunting club, he opted to take me to another place so we could hunt together."

Tracy began dreaming of nobody else.

"But things have a way of changing," she said. "And maybe it was me that changed? Maybe it was too much togetherness? But change did come. Rather than being happy when we were together, we started making each other miserable."

According to Tracy's version, Tod became possessive and jealous. He didn't want Tracy speaking to other guys, even at school. When they were out cruising through the parking lot where other friends hung out, Tod was constantly watching to see if Tracy waved or looked at another guy.

"We got into terrible arguments about it."

There was one day when Tracy was at Tod's house. His

mother asked Tracy and Tod's sister, Tracy's bestie, if they wanted to go to the grocery store.

"Sure."

They hopped in the car and left.

"Where have you gone off to dressed like that?" Tod snapped when they returned.

"What?" Tracy said. She was all at once perplexed and taken aback. This was a new level of control on Tod's part.

Tracy had worn shorts and make-up.

Tod was "livid," she explained. "I just couldn't understand why he was so mad. I was with his mother and sister. We went to the grocery store, but he wasn't having it. I had never seen him act like that."

This was the beginning of the end. Tracy felt smothered, like some sort of object Tod felt he had the authority to tell what to do, when to do it.

She was 16 years old, for crying out loud.

"Finally, I had enough. I could not do it anymore. I loved (Tod) with all of my heart, but I couldn't stand the accusations and the isolation or the feelings I was having. It was only getting worse and I didn't know how to fix it. So I told him it was over."

Even though Tracy was so young, she thought Tod was "the one. And I truly regretted that it didn't work out, but I didn't want to be miserable. I guess the ongoing mess at my house was a contributing factor. I wanted someone to love me and care about me, not treat me like a possession. I think I was looking for that 'father-figure.' But not *my* father figure. I wanted what I was lacking at home. So rather than dating guys my own age, I tended to be attracted to older, more mature men."

AFTER SHE TURNED 18, Tracy started working behind the information desk at Georgia Square Mall. Her job included answering the telephone, assisting patrons and giving directions to customers. It was where, she later believed, the law enforcement bug first bit her.

"My favorite part was dispatching the security officers and using the 10 codes on the radio just like the police department. I also interacted with the local county police when we were in need of their assistance. And so my infatuation with police officers began (while working that job in the mall)."

She also met Joseph Tandy (a pseudonym), an older man who "caught my eye."

Joseph was at least a dozen years older than Tracy. But the age difference didn't bother her.

"I was infatuated. And hell, I was grown. (Joe) was one of the police officers who was hired by the manager of the movie theatre as security. My infatuation with him grew."

Tracy would "linger" around the theater after hours, she remembered, on weekends, knowing when Joe was getting out of work, so she could walk with him.

"You are too young," Joe said one night.

"Come on, I'm 18," she pleaded.

"Too young, Tracy."

But Tracy persisted. Often as she could, she'd show up at the movie theater and try to talk Joe into hanging out. A relationship, at least in Tracy's eyes, was developing.

"Then he went and married someone else and I got the message," Tracy recalled. "I also got my heart broke. I just didn't understand. It never sunk in that he *didn't* want me."

As life went on, Tracy began to realize something: "I attracted plenty of men, but it took a while to understand that although I was pretty and the men were attracted, they were only after one thing. What I wanted was of no concern to them. While I was looking for someone to fill that void in my heart, they were looking for a good time and that was it."

Then she met Billy Jackson (a pseudonym). "And," Tracy said, "my life was changed forever."

52.

OCSD INVESTIGATOR CHARLES MORGAN was part of the search team that went into Tracy's house in June 2000. As Morgan stepped into the witness stand after Jerry Alexander walked out of the courtroom, never once looking at Tracy, Morgan came across as your typical Southern sheriff. There was an almost comforting, Andy Taylor-like nuance in his demeanor, as if here was the friendly town cop, walking the beat, waving to everyone, keeping watch on his community.

Morgan knew Tracy and she had once worked for him as a deputy. That alone, one might think, did not make Morgan the best witness for the prosecution, though there was hardly a cop involved in the case who, in one capacity or another, did not know (or hear of) Tracy Fortson.

Charles Morgan was called to testify for one purpose: To discuss the duty belt found inside Tracy's house. And just a few questions in, Lavender got down to it, asking Morgan to explain to jurors how familiar he was with Tracy's duty belt.

"Yes, as far as I remember, knowing Tracy and her duty belt, she carried a little pouch which contained a knife."

That was the line Lavender needed in order to make the assumption to jurors that Tracy had likely stabbed Doug, not the forks of the tractor.

"Was that *on* the belt?" Lavender pressed.

"No, it was not."

One more question and Lavender was finished. Morgan told jurors he knew Tracy carried a knife in her duty belt and yet when they recovered that same duty belt inside her home under a search warrant, the knife was nowhere to be found.

Tom Camp stood.

Morgan took a deep breath.

Camp bypassed any question about the duty belt and went directly at several interviews Morgan had been present for, including Jerry Alexander and Jeff Bennett. Camp's point as he got into questioning Morgan about those interviews was simple: Not long after Doug Benton's body was found on that farm encased inside a tub of cement, Morgan got together with deputy Mike Smith and GBI SA Ben Williams to discuss what their next move should be. And "y'all talked amongst yourselves" and "decided it would be a good idea to interview a couple of folks right away?"

"Yes," Morgan said, then agreed that Jerry Alexander and Jeff Bennett were among those the three of them talked about and decided to interview first.

"And you became aware that during the interview that Jerry Alexander was pointing a finger almost *immediately* to Tracy Fortson?"

"Not that I am aware of."

"You *don't* recall that?" Camp had a strange, quizzical look about him. That information was in the report: Jerry Alexander talking about the volatile relationship Tracy and Doug shared, mainly because of Tracy's behavior.

"No, sir," Morgan reiterated.

Onto Jeff Bennett.

Morgan said he couldn't recall if Jeff Bennett was pointing a finger at Tracy right away.

"There were also a few facts that Jeff Bennett knew that were really a bit unusual for somebody to know at that point in time in an investigation—isn't that correct?"

"What do you mean, sir?"

"Well, investigator Smith asked Jeff Bennett, you know, if he knew who might have done this and he (Jeff Bennett) immediately piped up that it must be somebody that was familiar with concrete. Do you remember him saying that?"

Morgan said he "remembered something like that."

Camp dropped his shoulders. *How could Jeff Bennett know such a thing?* Camp managed to point out in his next question. Then, without hesitation, he added how everyone in the room listening to Jeff Bennett talk about concrete was "shocked" because the body had just been recovered in concrete. How could he have known that information?

Dodging the main context of the question, Morgan said, "That was a little while after the body was found, yes, sir."

"Just a few hours."

"Yes, sir."

Camp sat. Took a moment.

The defense attorney was done with Morgan.

At face value, Morgan's testimony was stunning. According to what he had said, Jeff Bennett knew merely hours after Doug's body had been recovered that there was concrete involved in the crime. How could someone uninvolved in the investigation know about the concrete?

"AS FOR CHARLES MORGAN," Tracy told me in 2017, "he was … (trying) to say that a knife was missing from a scabbard on my duty belt. I didn't have a scabbard on my duty belt and I didn't carry a knife, except for the little $5 pocketknife ($2\frac{1}{2}$ inches long) that the sheriff bought me, which, incidentally, broke while in my pocket, and almost cut the tip of my finger off when I reached in for it. I had plenty of knives in my house … but they did not take *any* of my knives, which is also strange because they thought Doug had been stabbed."

The other odd part of Morgan's testimony was the Jeff Bennett concrete information Tom Camp was able to get into the record.

"We wondered how Jeff would have known that info before it was released," Tracy added. "Jeff claimed that his friend (a local deputy) told him. I've always wondered why investigators were sharing confidential information with Jeff. That's not normal protocol. At that point in the investigation, no one should have been eliminated as a possible suspect, Jeff included. In a proper investigation, investigators would *never* share confidential info with a citizen, especially in a murder (case). Nothing they did in their so-called investigation reflected proper procedure."

After thinking about it some more, Tracy needed to make an important point, she said.

"Consider this: Jeff was a hunter; he had guns and knives. He had a boat painted in camo pattern. He was pissed off at Doug at that time. He had just as much motive as anyone else. Look, I am not saying that Jeff killed Doug, but he certainly should have been a suspect. And without knowing who actually killed Doug (at that time), they were giving pertinent information to a citizen, the 'best friend' of the victim?"

None of it made sense from Tracy's perspective.

WITH ALL THIS TALK about Jeff Bennett going on inside the courtroom, it was no wonder that as Tracy watched Charles Morgan exit the witness stand and walk toward the door, she turned to see the man in question himself walking through the gallery on his way toward the witness stand.

Jeff Bennett.

53.

TRACY SAT AT HER desk one Sunday afternoon when she "saw the most gorgeous man" she had "ever seen in a police uniform stroll across the atrium in front of me." His name: Billy Jackson. Tall, dark, handsome. A lawman. A nasty combination of man equal to kryptonite when placed before Tracy Fortson by this point in her life. She couldn't resist an older, good-looking man in blue.

"I couldn't take my eyes off him. He ... wore that uniform like a glove."

Tracy didn't utter a word to Billy on that day. She was far too smitten and nervous to open her mouth. But a few nights later, Billy just happened to stop by her desk, put his elbows on the counter, smile, and beckon Tracy over for a little chat.

"I didn't think I would be able to speak, at least not anything intelligible."

"I'm working surveillance on the roof," Billy explained, "looking for people who tend to break into cars while the owners are inside the mall shopping. You mind if I use your phone to call in?"

Tracy said sure. She was in another world. Disappointed it was an official visit, she was still thrilled to be talking to the new man of her dreams.

When Billy finished his call into the police department, he struck up a conversation with Tracy.

"Name's Billy, nice to meet you."

"Uh, Tracy … My name is Tracy."

It was strange. Tracy had heard from a group of kids who hung around the mall that Billy Jackson had an "attitude" and was known for being "an asshole."

"They couldn't have been talking about this same good-looking guy who was talking and smiling at me."

"Nice to meet you, Tracy. I enjoyed talking, but I have to get back to work."

Billy turned to walk away, but then turned back around and approached Tracy a second time.

"You wouldn't be interested in an old man like me would you?" he said.

Tracy thought: *Old man? You've got to be kidding me.*

Billy explained to Tracy how to get up to the roof, where he was working, adding, "Come up some time, visit me, would you?"

"Uh, sure," Tracy said.

A day later, Tracy found her way up to the roof after getting lost and having a security guard friend show her the way. She stuck her head out of the trap door and took a look around. She saw Billy's jacket and radio, but he didn't seem to be around. So she left.

"I was thinking I had missed the only opportunity I would ever have to talk to this man, but that was not the case."

Billy came back to the information desk some time later. After that day, his visits became more frequent and Tracy gave him her number and he started calling.

"He began to ask me to meet him places after I got off work and take rides in his patrol car. One thing led to another. A month flew by and I was head over heels in love. I had never met anyone like this man. He was kind, considerate, loving, and passionate."

The only problem Tracy found out after a month of spending time together with Billy Jackson, all while sending little love notes to each other, the phone calls, and the "I love yous," was that the new man of her dreams had a secret.

He was married.

5 4.

HIS FULL NAME IS William Jeff Bennett. Most everyone, however, called him Jeff. And after Bob Lavender asked the man the court had heard so much about since the start of trial how he knew Doug, "He was my best friend," Jeff answered somberly.

It was clear Jeff Bennett missed his old friend.

They'd met in 1985, Jeff explained. He had known Tracy ever since Doug started dating her. About "eight months."

Jeff then explained how he visited Doug "just about every day" since they'd become friends. "We built a gym (in) his house."

Lavender quickly got into Doug's handwriting, showing Jeff State's Exhibit Number 47, a proven example of Doug's writing. After asking if he was familiar with Doug's handwriting, the DA asked Jeff to take a close look at the exhibit and "tell us if it's his writing?"

"Yes, sir," Jeff confirmed.

They talked about Jeff and Doug's workout schedule and how it became disrupted on May 23, 2000, the week before Doug went missing—the last day Jeff Bennett recalled seeing his friend alive.

Lavender asked why they had stopped working out together.

"Because, basically, I didn't want to come over there

anymore if *she* was going to be over there." Jeff gave a slight glance over to Tracy, who sat motionless and expressionless, staring at Doug's old friend.

"Had there been some problems or something?"

"Well, they had been having problems for a long time. I didn't want to get involved."

Strangely, after a few additional, inconsequential questions, Lavender passed his witness.

Tom Camp went straight at the place where he thought he could do the most damage: "And you all worked out a lot together, right?"

"Yes, sir."

"And also did steroids together, correct?"

"We have in the past."

"You got pretty upset with Doug about Miss Fortson, correct?"

"Yes. I was pretty upset, discouraged, because seeing what was going on in the relationship."

Camp mentioned Jeff telling Sheriff Tom Lutz when they first chatted how he had told Doug not to call him to work out until he severed his relationship with Tracy.

"That is right," Jeff testified.

Camp wanted to know why it was Jeff never "showed any concern whatsoever about him being missing until" about two weeks after Doug was last seen.

Jeff Bennett told jurors he mentioned to Doug in May that when he had broken ties to Tracy "once and for all" to call him. They could then resume their schedule. Once she was out of the picture, Jeff said, he would be glad to "come over and start working out" again. "Until then," he added, "I will not come around anymore because you are playing a dangerous game and you are not going to include me. The last time I saw Doug, I told him that."

Jeff took a breath. Sip of water. Continued.

He added how he spoke to Doug on the phone that spring and explained his feelings. Doug was upset by the call. He said, " 'Will you please come back and start working out with me again? I need my workout.' Sure, Doug," Jeff told him, "I would love to." Doug replied, "'It's OK. She said she would leave us alone. She wouldn't bother us.' The last time I worked out with Doug was May 23 and I am pretty sure it had come to a head again. And I said, I am not coming over there again." This was the reason, Jeff continued, why he had not spoken to Doug during those two weeks he was missing. He was upset with his friend. They'd had a falling out. At some point near the two-week mark, however, after not hearing from Doug, Jeff told jurors he actually picked up his phone and called him. It was near mid-June. Jeff just wanted to "see how (Doug) was doing." But he "couldn't get him." Days later, Jeff found out Doug had been missing. Then he found out Doug's birds had died. "I said, 'Oh, God.' I knew *immediately* right then, you know, (that) she done it and I said it" to Lutz. "I said, 'Oh, my God, his girlfriend finally done something to him.' "

"That's right," Camp countered. "You immediately started pointing a finger at Tracy Fortson."

"I couldn't help it. After everything that I had seen all of that year, I couldn't help it."

Camp then dropped a rather interesting fact into the conversation, trying to drum up some sort of motive, perhaps: "Is it also just a coincidence that your wife wound up being the (administrator) of his estate?"

"His mother asked us (if we) would we do it and (my wife) accepted the job. I said I couldn't do it. So my wife took the job over."

"That's right, your wife did it, not you ... because that wouldn't look real good, would it?" Camp said.

"Excuse me?" Jeff countered, clearly upset and angered by the weak accusation.

"That wouldn't look real good, would it?" Camp repeated.

"What are you insinuating?"

"No further questions."

5 5 .

WHEN TRACY FOUND OUT the man of her dreams was married, she freaked out. She was hurt, of course. Angry as a rabid raccoon, too. She couldn't understand why Billy Jackson had lied to her. She thought they'd share a deep connection.

"Why? Why would you do this to me?" Tracy asked Billy next time she saw him.

"I don't love her," Billy said. "We're getting a divorce. We don't even sleep together anymore. I love *you*. I want to be with you. I'm leaving her. It's been over for a long time."

Instead of running for the hills, however, Tracy said she "believed him." She bought the story.

"I was just like an infatuated, love-struck, 18-year-old. He loved *me*, not her. We were going to be together."

One day, Tracy decided to show up at a Little League baseball game to watch Billy, the new love of her life, coach the kids. He had always talked about how much he loved coaching. Here was the neighborhood cop coaching the neighborhood kids. It certainly added some credibility to Billy's integrity in Tracy's eyes.

As she walked toward the field, Tracy could not believe what she was staring at. By this time, the revelation that Billy was married had blown over and he had convinced Tracy she was the only one for him. At home, Billy told Tracy, he was going through the motions and going to divorce his wife. It was just going to take time.

"Not only was he married," Tracy explained, reflecting on that Little League game. "She was *pregnant*."

This led to another confrontation with Billy.

"I cried, we argued, but he was relentless, telling me: 'She thinks it was an act of God. I wasn't even supposed to be able to have kids. I was injured. We haven't slept together since. I'm leaving after the baby is born.'"

Tracy couldn't let go. She said she "held onto those promises like a lifeline."

No matter how many lies, how many times she caught Billy doing something he said he wouldn't, Tracy hung around for more.

Billy started to take Tracy into the clubs. Tracy wasn't old enough, but Billy was a police officer, so there was never any problem getting her in.

"And we danced. I loved dancing with him. He was fun and exciting. The relationship was exciting. … As time went on, we continued to meet after I got off work. He came to my house while he was working and I would cook dinner for him. My face glowed every time I saw his patrol car coming down the driveway. He was taking a chance by coming to my house while on duty … but it didn't seem to matter to him."

The relationship became Tracy's life. Every chance Billy had, he poured on the charm. They met at the Waffle House one night, a favorite place to go after the bars closed. Tracy had injured her ankle in the days before and wasn't feeling well.

"I'm not much in the mood to talk tonight, Billy," she said.

Billy carried on an entire conversation by writing notes back and forth on a Waffle House napkin, "Looking into my eyes, never saying a word. No one else has ever done that. It was the little things like that, little nothings that meant so much. I kept that napkin in a shoebox for years, along with all the other notes he left for me."

At Easter that same year, Tracy took off to Savannah with a friend to visit her friends' parents. Billy was waiting for them in Athens and presented Tracy with a little yellow stuffed bunny, along with a Happy Easter card upon her return.

"He made me feel special, like no one had ever done before. He called me at work just to say, 'I love you,' and when I got off work, he was usually waiting for me in the parking lot. I would immediately look for his patrol car as I walked out. Sometimes he would hide his car and make me think he wasn't there, and I would be disappointed, then he'd drive out from behind a corner of the building and turn his blue lights on to surprise me."

It was a whirlwind romance, Billy sweeping Tracy off her feet almost daily with some sort of special surprise.

Months went by. The butterfly kisses and unicorns and rainbows passed. The relationship turned into what Tracy saw as "normal," or, as normal as it was going to be with Billy still married. Then, out of nowhere, Tracy said, she saw a jealous side of Billy come out. He started to question where she was, who she was with, why she wasn't home at certain times. She'd walk out of work with a fellow security officer friend. Billy would roll up in his patrol car and say, "Who is that guy? What are you doing with him?"

"Just a friend, Billy. Relax."

Tracy gave a friend a ride home from work one night. Billy followed. Pulled her over afterward.

"Unacceptable," he said after she explained they were just friends and he needed a ride home.

"He didn't care who it was," she recalled. "He did not want me to give another man a ride anywhere."

This caused a big argument between them, which carried on for a few days. Tracy had not seen this side of Billy and it bothered her. "Plus, how could he be jealous when he *still* had a wife at home? Of course, he had an answer for that. 'I don't love her anymore. I love you. You're my girl and I don't want you with any other guys and that includes giving someone a ride. You can't trust anybody. What if that guy had tried to take advantage of you and I wasn't here?' "

The problem for Tracy, which she could not have known, was that she accepted the behavior within the context of someone who was co-dependent: *Wow ... he truly loves me to care that much.* She felt comfortable being treated this way. It spoke to her low self-esteem at the time.

As the relationship progressed, another odd behavior presented itself to Tracy. Billy pulled his gun on someone inside a club one night when the dude pissed him off. It took several security guards to pull Billy off the guy. Someone called the local cops and Billy was reprimanded at work. Put on probation.

"I knew that he had a temper and he wasn't one to mess with, but I had never known him to pull his weapon in a public place."

Billy continued to cross the line. He was now getting into trouble on a regular basis, in and out of work. Whatever was going on with him, Tracy said, she was "oblivious to it." Billy started to spend evening at her house while he was supposed to be on duty.

There was one day near this time that stood out to Tracy. She hadn't heard from Billy at all the entire day, which was unusual. He would call all day, every day and make random stops by her house to say hello.

"I was worried. It wasn't like him to not call or stop by."

Midnight came. The phone rang.

Billy.

He was drunk. Sitting behind the bar at the 5th Quarter, a club in Athens that Tracy and Billy frequented.

"I'm sorry, baby, but I've been at the hospital all day," Billy explained after Tracy asked where he had been. "(My wife) had the baby. A girl."

Billy was crying. He said he needed a ride home from the bar. Could Tracy come and get him?

"So you call *me*?" Tracy exploded.

"Baby, can you come and get me? I can't drive home."

Tracy thought about it. "OK, Billy. I'll be there."

When she arrived, Billy decided to drive his brother-in-law's car home instead of leaving it at the bar. His brother-in-law had already left, hours before.

"Follow me," Billy told Tracy.

"No way, Billy. You're wasted."

"Follow me!" he insisted.

There was no talking him out of it.

So she followed.

Billy made it home without being stopped or crashing the vehicle.

"I didn't hear from him for a week after that. When he finally called, he told me that (his wife) had complications and he had to stay with her, taking her back to the hospital on one occasion. The baby was fine."

Tracy did not know how to respond to this. What could she say?

"I gave the baby your middle name," Billy told her.

"You *what*?"

Billy explained how his wife had no idea that he'd given his child the middle name of his mistress.

As the months peeled off the calendar, Tracy would ask when Billy was leaving his wife. He'd promised her that after the baby was born, he was checking out of the marriage to be with her.

"After (my wife) is back on her feet," Billy said. "I need to be there until she is totally recouped."

Always an excuse, Tracy thought.

The entire thing blew up when a few friends of Billy's family caught Tracy and Billy one day inside his car. They'd just happened to be walking down the street and came up to the window to say hi to Billy, who was kissing Tracy.

They told Billy's wife.

Tracy put Billy on the spot. She explained how every time he said he was leaving his wife, he came up with an excuse. No more. What was it going to be?

Billy said he needed more time. "I'll figure it all out."

"I was so angry and frustrated I couldn't think straight and certainly couldn't make sense out of what had just happened."

When they got to Billy's house later on that day after getting caught in Billy's squad car, all of Billy's clothes had been tossed into the front yard. So Billy gathered his things and decided to go home with Tracy.

"I need a place to stay, baby."

A few days later, Billy's mother called Tracy at work. "You're a homewrecker and a bitch."

"She blames me for the adulterous relationship that I am having with her son," Tracy recalled.

Then came the hang-ups. Billy's wife began calling Tracy at work, calling 15 times a day at one time.

Then the mother and the wife began showing up at Tracy's work. Calling her names.

"These people were blaming me for everything and trying very hard to make my life miserable. And all Billy could say to me was: 'Don't worry about it, baby.' "

Tracy and Billy took a weekend away. They had a blast, Tracy recalled. Just the two of them. Out and about as a couple. A weekend in the country to forget about everything that had happened.

The fun quickly ended when they returned home on Sunday afternoon. Billy headed home to get a change of clothes. A while later, as Tracy waited at her house for him to return, he called.

"She used the weekend to pack up everything she owned, including my baby," Billy said. "She went home to her parents in Alabama. The only thing she left behind was the bed frame."

Billy was devastated.

During the year Billy's wife and child were gone, he turned into someone Tracy said she did not know.

"Gone were the little notes, the flowers, the kind and passionate man I knew. Here was someone who didn't seem to care about me at all. I was thinking that we would be able to get a place together, but he had other plans."

"We cannot live together," Billy said. "I am in the middle of a divorce."

"What?" Tracy was confused. "All this time we've been practically out in the open, now this?"

"Sorry, that's the way it is."

Billy moved out of Tracy's house and started living with a police buddy in an apartment complex on the west side of Athens, just down the street from the 5th Quarter.

From that point forward, Billy started spending more time with his roommate. He became more aloof and secretive. Sometimes he wanted Tracy around, other times he didn't. While she was over to the apartment, the phone would ring and he would answer it, but then disappear into another room to talk. Business, he would say. An informant calling to give him confidential information.

"I was starting to get depressed. Just when our relationship should have been getting better, it wasn't. I loved him. I thought he loved me. We had talked about our future together and now it seemed like that future was further away than ever."

"You need to find someone else," Billy said one night not long after. "I cannot be with you."

"I don't want anyone else. I want you. I want to spend the rest of my life with you."

"That's not going to happen. I'm no good for you."

Tracy couldn't imagine life without Billy.

"After all I had been through with this man, all the love I had in my heart for him, and all the promises he had made that I had been clinging to. This was just too much."

Billy left. Tracy knew he was gone for good. She'd never see him again.

"I laid there and thought about my life. I was hurt. I was tired. I couldn't see past that moment. The man I loved more than life itself had just walked out the door, just like that. Gone. My dad was always drunk, constantly calling at all hours of the night and day, threatening to kill my mama. If it wasn't him calling, it was my grandmother calling at 1 or 2 in the morning, always sick, always wanting to go to the hospital. If no one went over there, she would slit her wrist and call an ambulance. Then the hospital would call. We had to go get her. This had been going on for years. I was 19."

After Billy took off, Tracy thought: *What do I have left?*

"You coming to church this morning?" her mother asked her that Sunday morning after Billy took off.

"No, Mama."

Instead, with her mother gone, Tracy found 29 Valium pills and swallowed all of them.

56.

BEFORE THE NEXT WITNESS, there was a bit of legal business to take care of between the judge and lawyers, without the jury present. Tom Camp argued the legitimacy of the state's next witness, Ralph Stone, a crime scene specialist. Camp referred to Stone as a "tea leaf reader," explaining that he was against Stone's proposed testimony: "I anticipate Mr. Stone to testify as to how this crime happened; and it is my belief that *that* is purely conjecture and speculation and that he has no foundation for doing it."

After a bit of contentious back and forth debate, Lavender said, "Any expert's opinion, I guess you could say, is conjecture."

For anyone who has spent even a minimal amount of time inside a courtroom, however, this was a great oversimplification. Trial experts generally come from a foundational position of fact and speak to those facts as they gathered them. Was there a person's *opinion* involved in that process? Certainly. But the overall scope of expert testimony is driven by the expert's qualifications and his or her interpretation of the evidence. A defense attorney, obviously, had every right to question the expert about his opinion.

Still, if Stone were going to walk in and explain what he *believed* had happened inside Doug's trailer on the day of the murder, there was no other way to put that besides it being an expert's *opinion* of what *might* have happened. If you ask me, that sort of speculation does not belong inside a courtroom during a trial with so much at stake. But this is why we have discussions about witnesses and testimony during trials without the jury present, so the judge can decide relevance.

Regardless, any defense attorney worth his weight is going to have a big problem with this.

The judge ultimately agreed that Stone could keep his testimony to what the crime scene itself and any accompanying evidence indicated. Anything beyond that was going to be a gray area they would have to deal with on a question-by-question basis. Tom Camp had every right to object when he felt the need to.

Onward.

AFTER THE JURY WAS re-seated and Stone was sworn, the crime scene expert explained that he was actually a crime scene reconstructionist. He took a crime scene and reconstructed it in a way that might speak to what happened. All evidence left behind by a killer had the potential to explain his or her crime. It was Stone's job, he explained, to interpret that evidence and detail those findings based on his extensive experience and, of course, his opinions.

Stone had learned part of his trade in Quantico, at the FBI's Behavioral Science Unit. He had been in law enforcement for 31 years. Both of these career qualifications, one might imagine, gave his opinion that much more credibility.

Lavender had Stone talk about how he looked at everything involved in the case pertaining to the crime scene: autopsy, evidence and police reports, DNA results, photographs, videos, interviews with witnesses, blood spatter and forensic analysis. It was through the meticulous study of that information that allowed him to come up with what he termed to be his professional "conclusion."

"And what was that?" Lavender lobbed.

Stone said the first thing he looked at was the potential for there to have been "more than one offender," because "two weapons had been used." He added how, after reviewing more than 400 homicides throughout his career, it had been his experience in a majority of those cases where two weapons *had* been used, however, that "there is only one offender." He explained the main reason for this being that if the offender found the first weapon did not work, he or she chose a second weapon.

"So," Stone clarified, "in my opinion, in this particular case, there was only *one* offender, although two weapons were used."

Was he saying that most killers brought a backup weapon with them to a homicide?

If so, that is a ludicrous statement.

Lavender asked about the gunshot wound Doug sustained to his head.

Based on all the evidence, Stone told jurors, Doug was "likely" asleep at the time he was shot. He was also possibly "caught totally by surprise, or was caught by someone whom he felt comfortable with, whom he may have even let in the house."

For many, this was stretching that opinion vs. fact rubber band to its snapping point. Stone had given jurors a scenario that put Tracy Fortson at the center and none of it was based in actual eyewitness accounts or any other evidence besides what an expert *thought* had happened.

Camp let it go and did not object.

Lavender asked about an "order of events" Stone had come up with after studying all of the evidence.

Stone said he believed, based on the injuries he found on Doug's body, "The gunshot wound occurred first (and) there was a struggle." He added how, after the gunshot, Doug was "incapacitated and then the 10 stab wounds were inflicted ... right immediately after death, or while the individual was dying."

The DA wanted to know what Stone thought about the "location" of the body when it was later found. Did the way in which the body had been dumped and the location itself say anything about this crime and a potential perpetrator?

Stone was firm here. How the body was found, where and by whom, had spoken to him. He began his argument by explaining the section of Doug's house soaked with an accelerant. This told Stone the perp had tried to cover the crime up by torching the house. He called this part of the crime, along with Doug being found in the watering trough, "staging." He said it was all done in this case "to mislead" police: to make it appear as if there were two or more offenders involved in the murder, when there was actually only one.

Truly asking his expert to expand the speculation boundaries even farther, Lavender wanted to know if the "staging" in this case indicated to Stone any type of "relationship" between the offender and victim.

Really?

Shockingly, Camp sat idle. He did not object.

"When staging occurs," Stone said, "it has been my experience it is done by the offender because there is such a close connection either between the offender and the victim, or the offender and the place where it happens, and that if the police are able to discover what really happened here, well, that individual would be the first suspect that they would go to."

This was an incredible statement. It was as if GBI Stone had just handed the DA his entire case in a neatly wrapped package with a pretty little pink bow on top. Both scenarios Stone described—of which were absolutely speculative opinion, at best—fit perfectly (and rather congenially) into Tracy being the killer. In fact, Stone all but came out and said he believed Tracy to be the perpetrator. He gave the jury every possible reason to visualize Tracy as Doug's killer.

"That is all I have," Lavender said with a cozy, confident smile off to the side of his face.

Camp had a concerned, frustrated look about him. He needed to tear apart Stone's "opinions." Rip each one to shreds and point out that none of it was fact; it was only what the guy "thought," and very little of the evidence presented thus far backed him up.

"STONE NEVER WENT TO the crime scene," Tracy told me in 2017. "He never went to Doug's house or where his body was found. Instead, he formed his *amazing* scenario of one-person-committed-the-crime-but-staged-it-to-look-like-two all from photographs."

Reports and interviews, too, Tracy left out.

"Again," Tracy continued, "I believe Stone was the state's storyteller. They used him to narrate their story of what they wanted the jury to believe. I don't believe a person, expert or not, could ever depict what happened at a crime scene without actually going to the location. That is absurd. How could he say the crime was committed by one person, but staged to make it look like two? What evidence supported that? How could one person commit the crime and have enough time to stage a scene? If it looked like two people committed the crime, as was his opinion, then why didn't investigators consider that two people may have committed the crime?"

Good question.

"I don't know how someone could have killed Doug," Tracy added, "and got him out of the house without being seen—that has always been my question. ... Yet someone was able to go inside Doug's house, shoot him, then remove his body, all 230-plus pounds of him, stage a scene, put him in concrete and leave. Nobody sees a thing. Really?"

Another good question.

IT WAS UP TO Tom Camp now to speak for Tracy and

try to dismantle that "one killer" image, along with a visual narrative of the murder that the jury certainly now had after Stone's direct testimony.

57.

TRACY SURVIVED HER SUICIDE attempt. She managed to get over Billy Jackson—a relationship, she realized later, that was never going anywhere from the moment they met. She knew it, felt it, expected it, but went with it anyway, hoping the outcome would somehow be different. There is not a human being alive who hasn't made the same mistake, however different the situation.

Growing up, Tracy was particularly interested in a person close to her who worked for the Oglethorpe County Sheriff's Department. As a child, she looked up to the man. And as she began to think about joining law enforcement herself while into her early 20s, Tracy hoped that familial connection would help her out.

"For as long as I can remember, he had a reputation when he was younger as a no-nonsense bull of a man who would just as soon smack someone upside the head with his Maglite or nightstick, whichever he had in his hand at the time, as look at him. He didn't take any shit from anybody and he had his own way of dealing with folks that didn't comply."

To a small extent, Tracy could relate, especially for a cop out in the world interacting with criminals every day. There was a certain smugness, a certain attitude one had to have in order to be a good, respected cop.

But the crass and arrogance of this person, Tracy soon learned, overshadowed what might have been a street toughness needed for the job. It was the sort of brashness that "might have been acceptable back in the day," she added, "but law enforcement had changed and (that person I knew) seemed to have trouble conforming to more modern-day techniques."

She began working as a deputy, which, alone, seemed to irritate this person. According to Tracy, he had worked his way higher up within the department. Now, he spent most of his time in the office behind a desk. One day, there was a call to the office about a small blue truck weaving as it headed down a local highway.

"I'll check it out myself," Tracy heard over the radio. It was this person. He wanted the call.

"I was thinking that this would be a hoot as I listened to the transmissions over the radio," Tracy recalled, meaning her friend taking this call himself.

As the call continued, Tracy sat and listened.

"(Dispatch)," he said over the radio, arriving and assessing the situation, "I got this little blue truck with a wheelchair tag on it and the man inside has got blood all over himself. I don't know what's wrong with him, but he don't know where he's at and I can't make much sense out of it."

Tracy decided to head out to the call; it sounded serious. Maybe she could help?

"I knew (he) wouldn't like my interference, but that's tough—there was no telling what was going on and I wasn't about to leave him alone with that call."

When she arrived, Tracy saw that man she knew standing beside the truck. So she pulled in behind his patrol car, got out and started toward him.

When he spied her walking in his direction, "What the hell are you doing here?" he snapped.

"I've come to help you."

"I don't need your *got* damn help, Trace. You ain't taking over my call."

"I'm not trying to take over your call, but I came to help, if you need me."

Meanwhile, more cops arrived at the scene—probably out of wanting to see the fireworks explode between Tracy and the man, rather than helping out with the call, Tracy later speculated.

Turned out the guy driving the vehicle "must have had dementia or Alzheimer's," Tracy said. He had also soiled himself and the entire scene stunk of shit.

As Tracy went back to her patrol car, she discovered the driver's side door locked, the engine running, keys inside.

She cupped a hand and peered through the window. Then stepped back, banged on the glass with a fist.

"Darn it all!"

That was all her friend needed to hear. He walked over, saw what she'd done, and went off on her right there in front of everyone.

They argued. He called into question Tracy's competence as a law enforcement officer. The animosity between them sputtering out in words back and forth.

When Tracy later returned to her car after going back to the station to get a second set of keys, the sheriff who had waited behind to make sure nothing happened to the vehicle got out of his car and said, "Hey, Fortson, come here."

They walked over to the passenger's side of Tracy's car.

"Look," he said, pointing.

"When I looked and saw the door unlocked, he opened it. The damn car had been unlocked all along. Someone had locked the driver's side door to make me *think* that the keys were locked in. All that trouble and arguing and cussing for nothing. I had never locked my keys in the car. Somebody was expressing their sense of humor."

Tracy told me this story, she later said, because there always seemed to be someone in the department messing around with her—and it was some of those same sheriffs and deputies who later investigated the murder of Doug Benton.

58.

CAMP BEGAN CROSS-EXAMINING Ralph Stone by asking the crime scene re-constructionist if he believed his "opinion was only really as good as the information upon which (he was) provided." A fair and intelligent question under what were unprecedented circumstances.

"That is correct," Stone responded.

"So, if you don't have all of the information, then it is sometimes difficult to make an appropriate opinion, correct?"

"I can make an opinion," Stone pushed back a little, "but my opinion might change if I am provided additional information."

They discussed the so-called "research" Stone had studied and ultimately based his opinions on in this case, and how much of it, actually, Stone had taken a look at. But before Stone could answer, Tom Camp indicated an interest in something else, a topic of which should have caused jurors to sit up straight: How many times had Stone met with DA Bob Lavender to talk about the case and his testimony?

Stone agreed he had met with Lavender "at least once if not more."

"And you all talked about this theory of the case and all of that, is that correct?"

"He gave me an overview of the facts, I guess, as he understood them."

As he understood them, in this situation, is an incredible statement. It's no secret, of course, that witnesses meet with prosecutors to discuss testimony. Yet, when that testimony pertains to such delicate matters such as opinion and what *might* have happened at a crime scene during the course of a murder, it was important to point out what would become one of Tracy Fortson's main points of contention later—that a murder narrative was constructed by the district attorney and Stone was the chosen storyteller.

Next, Camp returned to the idea of the tractor forks and/ or a screwdriver at the watering trough farmland scene being responsible for the possible stab wounds. He and Stone talked about this for a few moments, Stone agreeing that nobody had ever told him about a screwdriver being at the watering trough scene (a major piece of editing).

After that, Camp took a final look at his yellow legal pad and said he was done.

Lavender produced another GBI crime scene analyst who talked about and eventually qualified all of the photographs taken inside Doug's house. Once again, here was another law enforcement expert talking about what had been established repeatedly as a "very strong odor" of kerosene as investigators and crime scene experts walked into Doug's residence.

This testimony, no doubt one of the DA's final witnesses, carried on and on as Lavender had him introduce photo after photo, depicting nearly every scene inside Doug's house.

From Doug's home, they moved onto Doug's truck, before a series of photographs of it was introduced.

The testimony became so tedious and comprehensive that the judge requested a break for jurors to collect their thoughts and unwind for a few moments.

When crime scene analyst Terry Cooper returned after the break, they moved onto the crime scene, where the watering trough had been found. Cooper talked about all the photos he took, including aerial shots from a helicopter.

After 15 minutes of that, it was on to Tracy's truck and

all of the photos Cooper had taken.

In particular, Lavender had Cooper explain how the photographs of marks on the trees near the spot where the trough was found matched in height to Tracy's bumper, implying that it was likely that Tracy's truck made the markings on the trees.

This was speculation, not science. And Tracy had strong opinions about it when we talked.

"(IN) THE VIDEO FROM the scene where Doug's body was found," she said, "investigators tried to match marks on a tree to the bumper of my truck. In the video, you can see a fresh scrape on a pine tree, a fairly large chunk that was very visible. However, when you look at the still photos taken prior to the removal of the metal container, using a tractor and hayforks, it is obvious that the mark was *not* there. They were trying to connect my truck to a mark that was most definitely caused by the tractor. And you'll notice that they used three (police officers) to simulate the weight of the container (estimated at 1,100 pounds) and the effect the weight had when it came to how far the bumper of my truck dropped. What kind of scientific analysis is that?"

OVER THE COURSE OF that same afternoon, Jessie Mattox, Cody Cross and Amory "Buck" Scoggins concluded the DA's case. Mostly, Mattox and Cross told jurors about the crime scenes (yet again), with a focus on the concrete mix Tracy had purchased, when and where. Scoggins discussed his role in the investigation interviewing Tracy, telling jurors Tracy admitted that she'd had a "rocky relationship" with Doug, and that Doug, in her view, had "become jealous" and wanted to "know her whereabouts at all times."

Probably the most important question Lavender asked that afternoon went to Scoggins when the prosecutor brought up whether the sheriff had "eliminated" Jerry Alexander and Jeff Bennett as suspects in the murder of their friend.

"They were eliminated as suspects," Scoggins testified.

The DA left it there and did not get into how.

Amory Scoggins was the DA's final witness.

To that, a few moments later, the judge asked Tracy to stand. Then: "I have just talked to your attorney about whether or not you would take the witness stand and testify. And he has informed the court that you are not." Further, the judge made a point to say it was his responsibility to make sure that this was a conscious decision on Tracy's part and if she understood it clearly.

"Do you want to testify?" the judge asked pointedly.

Tracy looked toward her attorney. Then down at the table. After a pause. "No, sir," she said.

Quite surprisingly, Tom Camp told the judge that the defense was resting its case—meaning, of course, that Tracy's lawyers were not going to be calling any defense witnesses.

The judge brought the jury back in and explained the situation, adding how the remainder of the trial was set for closing arguments.

During closings, both attorneys tirelessly rehashed their cases, point by point, adding nothing more to the record other than a narrative of the case from his perspective.

By 6:10 that evening, after a week of testimony, the jury was in a room deliberating Tracy Fortson's fate.

Just under three hours later, by 9 that same night, a note was given to the judge that jurors had reached a verdict. In terms of scope and how much information had been detailed during the weeklong trial, this was rather quick.

The judge had the foreperson stand. He then asked if the jury had, in fact, reached a unanimous decision.

"Yes, Your Honor, we have," the foreperson said.

The judge had the foreperson hand the verdict to the bailiff.

Tracy's stomach tightened. She gripped the hand of her lawyer, pinched her face, and prepared herself.

59.

IN DECEMBER 2016, I began sending Tracy questions about various aspects of her case. Namely, a belief of mine that Tracy was reading one particular document wrong and was too focused on the conspiracy aspect of her argument. One of her main contentions throughout has been that many of the people involved in her case lied—that, in effect, either collectively or by themselves, conspired to make sure the evidence lined up to convict her. I need to always question this sort of accusation because, for one, just about every convicted murderer I have interviewed makes it; and two, the chances that so many law enforcement officers got together to falsify and plant evidence to frame a person for murder is, to me, as far-fetched an accusation as there could ever be. I mean, were there mistakes made in Tracy's case? Surely. Were parts of the investigation compromised? Absolutely. Were speculation and opinion put forth during her trial that might have been misconstrued as fact? No question about it. But for me, I have to ask: Did several law enforcement officers walk into that courtroom and lie to make sure Tracy Fortson was convicted?

I am not anywhere near that opinion.

Thus, as I started to ask what I saw as hard, pushback questions, Tracy went after my motives, ethics, how I work and my overall interest in writing about her case.

We got into what was a heated email exchange over the

holiday season 2016. By the start of the New Year, after trying to work through our difficulties and differences of opinion, I received this:

> *Sorry. But I don't believe that you are looking out for my best interests. I no longer wish to participate in your project and request that you do not include any of my personal information, i.e. emails, documents, letters, or any other correspondence relating to my case or my personal life, in your book, if you decide to write one.*

> *Respectfully, Tracy Lea Fortson*

I understood the frustration and anger. It was just a week or so before this email that Tracy had been given some rather bad and final news from an appellate court. She was in the tough position of facing finality regarding her case. On top of that, and maybe most importantly, I sat back in my cozy office and put myself in the position of someone in prison for life knowing she had not committed the crime for which she had been convicted. That would be (anyone would agree), to borrow a cliché, a living hell like no other. The feeling of isolation and no one willing to listen must be immense and overwhelming. Your days are consumed by thoughts of never being able to explain to the world that you are not who the court says you are. I would imagine, speaking for myself, that a final exit enters your mind at some point.

Still, I needed to defend the integrity of what I do, why I do it and how I do it, and fight for Tracy's continued participation. We were, at the time she cut it off, heading somewhere. I could feel it. I sensed a breakthrough. I had been told by a woman in television who studied this case and produced a show about it that I needed to go into it with open eyes and an understanding that Tracy could be telling the truth. You, as a reader, have read most of the evidence presented. You've heard witnesses testify. You cannot, like me, overlook how guilty Tracy Fortson comes across. It's seems so clear to me that only one person had motive, means and opportunity to kill Doug Benton.

I persevered and called Doug's mother.

"She's innocent," Doug's mother, the victim in this case, told me over the phone. "I have no doubt about it."

I spoke to Carol Benton for some time. She insisted over and over that Tracy had been set up and framed.

Hanging up the phone, I sat back and thought about it: *The victim's mother stands behind the main suspect and person likely most responsible for her son's death?*

A bit pissed off at her trying to cut me off and the idea that as soon as I posed some tough questions, she got upset, I wrote to Tracy.

Honestly, this back and forth, passive-aggressiveness, is not good for your cause. And I'm done with it. I thought we were going to chat by phone early next year, hash these things out—the facts of your case— but forget that now!

So you face a bit of pushback, some pressure from me on a few issues (based on speculation and opinion) ... and you decide: You know what, he's getting to close. He's not accepting the applied truth. You're right: I do NOT have your best interests at heart; I have the interest of the TRUTH ... I considered maybe that truth was what you were interested in. Apparently, only when it plays into your arguments and opinions are you interested. I ask tough questions because I need answers. You don't agree, you throw up your hands and give up. That's fine with me.

... PLEASE NOTE: Your case (life story) is PUBLIC. All of the letters I have, the documents, trial transcripts, police reports, witness interviews, medical and autopsy reports, scores and scores of

additional documents, interviews I conduct with all the players, audio and photos and video, a 6-page narrative of events written by YOU, your letters to Carol Benton and hers back to you, etc., ALL of it is public record and fair use for me as a journalist. All of what you wrote to me in your prison emails (which you KNEW could end up as part of my book—the ONLY reason we were corresponding) ... is good to go. You've said a LOT. Thank you for that!

So I will consider that you want no part from this point on. Fine. You can't answer some hard questions the public will expect me to ask, that is okay. I get it. I had a running list of questions based on what I have uncovered that I was just about to send, but forget that.

Tracy wrote back a few days later.

I would have liked to be able to talk to you without you interpreting what I say incorrectly, but no matter what I say or how I say it, you take it wrong. I don't want pity, I'm not asking for your sympathy. I never asked for any of this. You contacted me, I never even heard of you until I got your letter.

The way I understood you when you said you were looking at my case objectively was that you were looking at it from a neutral standpoint, but you're not ... It's obvious that you had your mind made up before you ever contacted me. I didn't throw my hands up and quit because you asked me hard questions. You already have the answers to the questions you asked ... You tell me that you are basing your book on facts, but that isn't true ... You are going to believe what you want to believe about me, about evidence, about testimony and everything else involved in my case, and your book will reflect that. You don't want to be neutral and non-biased, if you did, I would continue, but you slam me every chance you get. ... (Y)ou aren't interested in the truth. You're only interested in a story that will get you recognition, and possibly an award. I'm not angry with you. You are what you are and you're just doing what comes natural to you.

I so wanted to hit back. But as I thought about it, Tracy was in prison, alone, feeling as if some book writer was poking her with a stick to get a reaction to write a juicy, salacious book that made her look like a fool—on top of being completely guilty. Anyone who has ever read any of my books knows that's not me. But she didn't know that, obviously.

I left it there. It was clear to me that Tracy was coming from a place of pure frustration and angst. Taking the environment she was in at the time into account, I knew there was no way, then, I could convince her that it doesn't matter what she thinks of me, what type of book I am writing, what the court found, what I think personally of her, or what the investigation uncovered. What matters, really, in the end, is what the evidence implies. What does that evidence— even when you take out those pieces of the puzzle Tracy calls controversial or contrived—say about who killed Doug Benton? There is so much that points to Tracy as Doug's killer.

Was all of that so-called evidence, however, *too* much? This became the question. Was it *too* obvious that Tracy Fortson was Doug's killer? Were there just too many breadcrumbs leading to Tracy? As a cop, why hadn't she cleaned up her role in the murder better, if she had done it? Why leave so much evidence behind, especially knowing the process of crime scene investigation?

60.

ON A GOOD DAY, most people manage the world in which they live fairly well. In other words, most of us with a solid moral compass make the best decisions we can based on the information we are given, and lead the best life we know how to. Juries, it has been said, do the best they can, given the circumstances and evidence. But at the end of the day, as William Landay so articulately puts it in his book, *Defending Jacob*, "A jury verdict is just a guess—a well-intentioned guess, generally, but you simply cannot tell fact from fiction by taking a vote."

For Tracy Fortson, her life was in the balance. A guilty verdict and it was over. An acquittal and she could pick up the pieces and try to move on. She'd struggled to come to terms with being branded a murderer. And if there were one consistent, undeniable facet of Tracy Fortson's character, it had to be that from June 2000, when she was arrested, until I began speaking with her in 2016, the woman had not once wavered in her resolve and determination to clear her name. Throughout all of those years, Tracy maintained she was set up and framed by a group of cops who had pooled their resources to see that she paid the ultimate price—either because of something Doug had done in his past or that sexual harassment suit she had lodged against Ray Sanders and the sheriff's department.

THE COURTROOM WAS SILENT, waiting on the clerk to read the jury's verdict. It could go either way. The short time span of deliberation didn't mean a damn thing, in the end. Juries were a fickle bunch. They got it right and they got it wrong.

Tom Camp put an arm around his client. "It's going to be OK."

Tracy stared at each juror.

On all five counts—malice murder, felony murder, aggravated assault with a gun, aggravated assault with a knife, attempted arson—Tracy was convicted.

Guilty, guilty, guilty, guilty, guilty.

The worst possible outcome. It was like a burst of reality rushing through her all at once.

The jury believed every argument the prosecution put forth, every witness, every bit of information presented. Within an hour and 50 minutes, 30 of those minutes likely to settle in and grab some coffee, 12 men and women deciphered all of that evidence and convicted Tracy.

On each count.

Tracy's legs turned to rubber and she sat down.

Each juror was named publicly and asked for an oral confirmation of his or her vote.

Each affirmed.

The judge took a 10-minute recess and told everyone to be back promptly so he could render Tracy's sentence.

Before that could take place, however, the judge asked if the lawyers wanted to speak.

Lavender said, "We think the evidence shows, and I think the verdict shows, the jury found this to be premeditated murder with the intent to hide that fact and we, of course, would ask the Court for a stringent sentence."

Tom Camp reminded the judge that Tracy had "no prior felony record."

The judge paused. Looked down at his notes. Cleared

his throat. Then sentenced Tracy to double life plus 50 years. After that, he asked that everyone leave the room in an orderly fashion. As that took place, the judge collected his belongings, banged his gavel, and walked away into his chambers.

The trial and sentencing were over.

At least for right now.

PART III

"Innocence is a kind of insanity."

— Graham Greene, *The Quiet American*

61.

MY EMAIL CONVERSATION WITH Tracy Fortson began during the summer of 2016. Tracy had been down 15 years by then, give or take. Although she'll have a problem with this description, she was a hardened con by now. She'd had time to consider her life and her case. I was essentially just stepping into it then. I had done some preliminary research, but nothing all that investigative. The first several emails we shared did not go well.

A bit of backstory first.

That same year, I had consulted on-camera for an episode of Investigation Discovery's long-running series "Deadly Women," which included a segment about Tracy. "Deadly Women" is a series I have been a part of for almost as long as Tracy has been in prison. I had read through the documents, looked over some of the court record, consulted with producers, and sat down for an interview, armed with the simple and most dramatic public facts from Tracy's case.

As the red light turned green and my producer said go, there I sat, talking about—some might even say trashing—Tracy Fortson. I dug right into her. Gave my usual sarcastic, entertaining (factual) commentary, all based on the court record left behind.

Tracy had been convicted of a violent crime. There is no other crime on the books more egregious, more inexcusable, or more atrocious, than the crime of murder. As I have said many times, there are those in this world who place very little value on human life.

Writing to Tracy via prison email, I knew she was going to bring up my consulting on "Deadly Women." On a website—tracyfortsondefensefund.com—dedicated to her innocence is a disclaimer targeted, I suppose, at TV people like myself:

> *"'Docu-Dramas,' such as the one made by the producers of ID Channel, EXAGGERATE public records of a case to capture viewers. The ID Channel did no investigation whatsoever of the case they are portraying. They have no regard for innocence or guilt of the people involved nor what impact it may have on the ongoing case the families of everyone involved. ... This site is for those interested in the facts and the truth."*

I could tear that description to shreds, of course. But for now I'll leave it be.

I had come right out of the box, in my first email to Tracy, asking what evidence she has to prove her innocence. Not just words on a website or a broad-brush claim of a frame job. I'm interested in evidence. Impartial facts of which speak for themselves. What is it you can show me to back up what it is you are claiming?

"Mr. Phelps ... where to begin," Tracy wrote back. "I suppose your questions. Evidence? The greatest evidence I have to prove my innocence, to me, is the fact that the prosecution had to lie, coerce and intimidate just to convict me."[7]

You see, that response in and of itself is what I am talking

---

7   I am going to present this exchange as a conversation for a more pleasurable reading experience, but please understand that this was an email exchange between the two of us.

about. Tracy's *opinion* is not evidence; it is speculation and accusation. There is no objectivity in any part of it.

"As far as tangible evidence," Tracy continued, "there is the unidentified DNA of a male at the scene of the crime. Then there is (a key witness, who) admitted he (said some things out) of anger, then went along with 'the plan' to convict me. I wish (my daughter) Elise had been able to record the first conversation she had with him, but she had no idea that he would tell her any of that."

Those are serious allegations. Tracy props up her latter argument on a former foundation of an unidentified piece of DNA found at Doug's house (the blood on that closet doorknob) and Key Witness's so-called subsequent recanting of an earlier accusation against her—to only Tracy's daughter—while testifying in court.

For one, every single home in this country has a plethora of unidentified DNA all over it. That is not evidence of someone creeping into Doug's home to murder him.

Then we come to Key Witness's claim?

"Elise originally contacted (Key Witness) because several people, including Doug's mom," Tracy went on, "had told us that (this person) no longer felt the same as (he or she) once did and did not believe that I had killed Doug. So, based on that, Elise contacted (Key Witness) when I came up for parole to see if (this person) would be willing sign a letter of support. When (this person) finally returned Elise's call, (he or she) talked for two hours non-stop, telling Elise everything that had happened during the investigation, bond hearing, and (in court). (Key Witness) told her things I suspected, but couldn't prove, as well as things that I never knew. (I wish you could talk to [this person].) Elise asked (he or she) to sign an affidavit, but (he or she) wouldn't."

Key Witness talked about having a family, according to Tracy, and coming forward would place them in danger.

"The second time Key Witness called, Elise recorded the conversation, but of course (he or she) didn't give near the details as in the first phone call. In the second conversation Key Witness admits being afraid. Key Witness wants to do the right thing, but won't name names. Key Witness is afraid that (certain people) will find out, which would put (he or she and family) in danger. Fear was the issue from the beginning. Fear of ending up like Doug. Key Witness learned the hard way of the corruption within our system."[8]

The problem with all of this is that Key Witness will not stand behind what Elise and Tracy claim he or she has said. Nor sign an affidavit. Nor go on record in any way to support a conversation recorded without his or her permission. This makes what Key Witness has allegedly said entirely suspect and placed into the hearsay category. Beyond that, even if he or she did go on record, what does it prove? That someone else, besides Tracy, is making spurious claims of corruption and framing? Where, still, is the hard evidence backing any of it up? All the evidence in this case, as you have read, points to one person.

Tracy Fortson.

"The majority of the people in the great State of Georgia want to believe in our justice system," Tracy continued, building a case for her argument, "and the people who work within the system. No one wants to believe that the system is corrupt in any way."

That is untrue. Time and again, we all have seen the system failing people. We have all heard the lies many public and professional civic leaders promote. In addition, we have seen people sprung from prison after spending decades behind bars.

"That is," Tracy added, "until something like this happens

---

8   I want to apologize here for the ambiguous "he or she" and "Key Witness" and "certain people" descriptions in place of actual pronouns. But I cannot, without any proof whatsoever, begin to name people in this situation because Tracy Fortson and her camp say so. It's just not fair to all of those involved. Furthermore, I asked for this tape several times, but was never given a copy of it.

to them. We trust the police to abide by the rules and enforce the law by making legitimate, valid arrests. We trust the investigators to gather the vital evidence, not just some, but *all* of the evidence. We trust the experts and lay witnesses to testify truthfully to what they know, based on experience, education, training and methodology, rather than what they are paid to say. We trust the lawyers to defend to the best of their ability. We trust the integrity of the prosecutors and expect them to be honest. Actually, we expect integrity and honesty from all who participate in the case from beginning to end. We trust the judge to oversee the trial with a neutral and non-biased attitude to ensure fairness, to make sure that both sides follow the rules, that due process of law, as guaranteed by our constitutional rights, is not violated. We expect the jury to be fully informed of their duties, rights and abilities, and consider all of the evidence and make a decision based on the evidence presented."

I read that statement several times. It is an astounding—and astonishing—reprimand within the context of this case, made by a woman who has been found guilty of murder. It flies in the face of what sounds like something a murderer who has been caught and convicted might say. Is Tracy saying in this statement that everyone involved in her case—each officer, deputy, GBI agent, lawyer, juror, witness, dozens of people—is railroading her or looked the other way when he or she realized what was going on?

Tracy was found guilty, as we have seen through her trial, based on some rather hard, factual, seemingly undisputed, unimpeachable evidence. If she has been set up, as she has claimed, the coincidences of circumstances and what had to take place in order for this to take place are insurmountable.

"However," Tracy continued, "our system is flawed and the accused is guilty until proven innocent. The rules of court and the rules of evidence are cast into the wind and a trial becomes a game. There are rules for the defense, but the prosecution has none. The truth is no longer the objective;

conviction is. And it's 'anything goes.' Fairness and due process are flushed down the toilet."

That is simply not true. Tracy knows this. Our system in this country works. It works because it is fair. It is not always accurate and is not 100 percent foolproof. Innocent men and women are put to death and placed in prison for life. But it's the best system in the world to protect those who are innocent of a crime. There is no better system available. There are anomalies, of course. And people lie on the witness stand, no doubt, every single day. But juries are an incredibly resilient body of people and generally get things right inside a courtroom. I have looked at scores of trials, studied every nuance and every legal maneuver, and I find the system to work on all levels. Have prosecutors and lawyers and cops manipulated the system to their benefit? You bet your ass they have. Is it widespread? Not a chance.

Tracy continued. And forgive the redundancy of this next exchange, for you have seen some of it play out within my earlier narrative, but it bears repeating here.

"Investigators are not interested in finding evidence that supports the innocence of the accused," Tracy explained. "The case becomes a puzzle, but rather than the pieces fitting together as they should if the accused committed the crime, they try to put together pieces of a puzzle that don't actually fit. If it doesn't fit, force it. 'Stick to the plan,' get the conviction, make the evidence, lie if you have to."

My question to Tracy after these statements was simple: Why would these cops frame you over a sexual harassment case? One could argue that with the sexual harassment case still unresolved when Tracy was arrested for Doug's murder, the sheriff didn't want any trouble. Still, would a sheriff, I have to ask, risk everything he has, the men and women of his department, and a prosecutor risk all of the sheriff's prior cases that resulted in conviction, go ahead and murder a member of the community because of unemployment compensation and perhaps a monetary settlement? As it were, when you look at the facts, Tracy's sexual harassment suit was not that strong of a case. If something were going to be "fixed" or framed, wouldn't it have been easier to rig the system in the sexual harassment case? Why not have the good ol' boys club get together and lie about the sexual harassment suit?

Tracy responded: "I had audio tapes of the sheriff making lewd, sexual comments to me on the job. Doug notified the newspaper and made it public. This was highly embarrassing to the sheriff. He is a very proud man. He never took embarrassment well. ... I never considered the consequences or repercussions of filing the claim."

I pressed Tracy on this.

"It was after Doug's death and my arrest that I found out there was more to the story than I knew," she claimed. "(A source close to Doug) told me there was evidently a history between Doug and Ray Sanders. I believe it was (a friend of Doug's who told my source) that Doug wanted retribution for something that had happened between them (Sanders and Doug) in the past. I never found out what that was and wasn't aware that Doug knew Sanders prior. Whatever happened between them is what caused Doug to want retribution. There are just too many gaps that haven't been filled. Too many unanswered questions."

I never came across those gaps or unanswered questions. Further, I never came across any evidence to support such a statement about Ray Sanders.

Still, all that being said, I don't see how, if true, it could lead to a sheriff having Doug killed and then setting up his girlfriend for the murder. How could any of the evidence against Tracy—the concrete mix she bought, the paint from her truck, the paint in her garage, the note on Doug's truck and on and on—be known to the sheriff? How could the sheriff time everything to coincide with Tracy making those purchases? It just doesn't seem possible. If it is, it becomes one of the most elaborate and well-planned frame-ups in

American criminal history. And remember, all for a motive of a sexual harassment claim and a rift between a sheriff and Doug nobody else but a few are, allegedly, aware of.

I made several attempts to contact Key Witness, along with all of the major law enforcement players involved in this case. Incredibly, at least where law enforcement is concerned, none of them would respond.

A FEW DAYS AFTER that email exchange, Tracy wrote again. By now I had considered the idea that maybe she hadn't seen me on "Deadly Women," or she didn't care— that all she wanted was for someone to tell her story. But then I opened my email one morning and there it was: The questions about my comments on "Deadly Women" and how I had trashed Tracy as a convicted murderer.

I read the first few lines and thought: *Oh, boy* ...

62.

ON AUG. 13, 2001, TRACY appealed the verdict to the Superior Court of Madison County, Judge Lindsey Tise, the same court and judge who had overseen her trial. Her lawyers filed a motion for a new trial. It seems rather disingenuous to make an appeal, which often calls into question what went on inside a courtroom, to the same judge who supervised your trial and sentenced you, but there you have it: The American justice system at work. Tracy's fate fell into the hands of the same man who had sealed it.

Her main argument was that the court had failed to change the venue or sequester the jury and because of that reason, Tracy had not gotten a fair shot at proving her innocence. Clearly, Tracy was saying the judge did not do his job and had made an egregious error.

Months went by.

No word.

Tracy then amended her request for a new trial, adding to it a second argument that jury commissioners manipulated numbers in racial and gender groupings to, as she put it, "balance the box." Was Tracy claiming reverse racism? Was she trying to say that her conviction was based on the court not convicting enough white people?

It was clear that Tracy was trying to find any window in which to break through the system in order to get another crack at convincing a jury she had been framed.

Two more months went by.

Nothing.

In July 2002, Tracy filed a second amended request for a new trial, this time claiming ineffective assistance of counsel.

The court's decision took seven more months. In the end, Judge Tise denied Tracy's motions for a new trial.

"I was disappointed, of course," Tracy explained to me in May 2017. "But I soon realized that a motion for new trial is a formality, the first step in the appeal process. Unless there is new evidence that wasn't available at trial or an error from the trial that could have changed the outcome, the motion is always denied. The next step is the direct appeal. If I had known then what I know now, things would have been different. I've learned so much over the years."

What bothered Tracy "after all of these years," she said, was that "my lawyers never challenged the indictment. They just accepted it. That was the first mistake. The indictment, by law, must be perfect in form and each charge must have all elements of the alleged crime, including the exact date of the alleged crime, or narrowed down as close as it can be so the accused person can form a defense. No one could ever determine the date Doug was killed. The indictment said 'between the third and fourth day of June,' yet Doug's neighbors saw him on the third and fourth. I saw him on the fifth and Doug left a message on my voicemail on the sixth. So how can they say he was killed on the third or fourth? That never made sense. All they had to do was check Doug's phone records and pull the voicemail from my phone company."

Again, it's important to note that since none of that was done during the investigation (which is odd, by the way), we're left with Tracy's word regarding the voicemail.

With only one option left, Tracy and her team put all of their resources into one petition and, by March 2003, filed an appeal with the Supreme Court of Georgia.

It was longest of long shots, but, of course, Tracy's only chance at seeing a courtroom again and being able to fight for her innocence.

Tracy called home on Oct. 6, 2003. It was a casual, routine call. "Hello, mother."

As Tracy's mother began to talk, Tracy said later, she could "hear excitement in her voice" and knew "something had happened."

"Have you heard?" her mother asked excitedly. "Tracy, have you *heard*?"

"*Heard*? Heard what?"

"You won your appeal! You are coming home."

Tracy explained how she felt hearing those words: "My knees buckled beneath me as I stood against the wall on that prison phone. Tears burned my eyes and I couldn't see. It felt as if my breath had come out of my lungs. I cried, then laughed at the same time, and I could hear the elation in my mother's voice as she kept saying, 'You're coming home! You're coming home!' "

On Oct. 6, 2003, the Supreme Court of Georgia ruled in Tracy's favor. Incredibly, against all odds, "(W)e find that Fortson was denied the effective assistance of counsel when her attorney unnecessarily used a peremptory strike on a juror that had already been excused for cause by the trial court. We reverse and remand for a new trial."

Tracy read those words over and over.

She'd done it. Granted a second trial, Tracy was going back to court.

As far as going home, however, that wasn't going to happen.

"Since the day I was arrested," Tracy told me, "I have never returned home. After I won my appeal, the Georgia Department of Corrections had to call Madison County to make them come and get me. It was October when the decision came down, the day before Thanksgiving when they finally picked me up. The original bond, which was

$500,000 cash ($1 million in property), was reinstated. There was no way my family could make that bond. We didn't have the resources. So, I stayed in the county jail in Lincolnton, Georgia, until my second trial since Madison County did not house women."

63.

HONESTY IS SOMETHING I do not take for granted. Whenever I sit down for a television interview to talk about a murderer or serial killer, I stick to the facts as we know them. That's all we have, really. We expect (and rely on) our courts to carve out the facts of a case. The allegations made on a website dedicated to Tracy's innocence are, truly, contemptuous, unfortunate and, quite honestly, in my opinion, dubious.

"Deadly Women," like so many other (nonfiction) television series, is a straightforward, cookie-cutter true-crime show. There is no "investigating," as Tracy contends, going into making this type of programming. It's a series, like so many others on television today, based on the facts of a case. Nothing more. Definitely nothing less. Moreover, "Deadly Women" makes no claim to this side of "infotainment," which most nonfiction television can be defined as today.

That said, quite ignorant as to what goes into making a television series, Tracy ripped into me regarding my "Deadly Women" appearance about her case: "Mr. Phelps, I suppose I should have asked this prior to sending you any of my information, but frankly it didn't cross my mind until I saw you last night. I just happened to see an episode of 'Killer Women' on TLC and you were one of the consultants. (Not so sure about 'Killer Women,' never heard of an American series by that name and have never sat down for an interview with a series by that name, but anyway.) ... Don't take it personal, but I was disappointed. You were the typical, biased, 'heckler on the sidelines,' the one that hypes up the story. I guess that is what you do (?) I'm not sure what I expected you to be, but that wasn't the mental image I had. You just seemed so different from the person who wrote the letter, more critical and judgmental. And if you are that critical and judgmental, why me? What got you interested in my case? How did you find me?"

I might add here that those are the top two questions I get asked by convicted murderers after reaching out to them. Maybe not so much in Tracy's case, but it says a lot about who they are as human beings, I believe. For one, it tells me that their defenses are up. Two, it tells me they have something to hide—or they would not care about anything else but getting their story of innocence out.

I began my response this way: "In reply to your email about my work, life, 'Deadly Women,' etc. Look, Tracy, every convicted murderer I have ever interviewed or considered for a book/story has claimed to be innocent. As you know, there are a lot of 'innocent' people in the jails walking around, decrying how the system has railroaded them. That said, I do understand there are actually innocent people locked up. I'm not ignorant. Nor naive. I've written about one (Bobbie Jo Smith, my book about her is titled 'Bad Girls'). And I stand behind her to this day! I secured her a high-profile appellate attorney."

Tracy continued: "There is another show that creates dramatizations called 'Deadly Women.' As a matter of fact, Investigation Discovery aired a segment on 'Deadly Women' called 'Forever and a Day,' which just happened to be about my case. Were you affiliated with that? Although I never saw the show, I felt the effects of it. From what I've been told, the producers made me out to be a monster and never once contacted me to hear my side. Then there were those who evidently watched the show and decided to express their opinion of me by sending maliciously, cruel emails to my daughter. What about Doug's mom, Carol? I guess no one cared or even considered how it might affect her."

The producers made me out to be a monster, was what I focused on, putting aside for a moment the fact that I now knew she had no idea I had appeared on "Deadly Women" and commented on her case.

It is an interesting statement. The producers are mandated to stick to facts. All scripts need to be annotated—in other words, you write a line for a series and you need to source where you pulled the information from. Producers do not create monsters; crimes and convictions do.

Tracy forgets that she is a convicted murderer. Guilty or innocent, that is who she is in a court of law and the eyes of the public. There is no way to sugarcoat or get around this simple, inarguable fact.

I took my time responding to Tracy. I needed to think about how to answer her insults and accusations; that outward aggression in her last email was coming from a deep place of being repeatedly let down. She was incredibly defensive. Obviously, angry and bitter and, as I have learned in talking to convicted murderers, frustrated beyond belief by not being able to control what is going on in the outside world about her case.

"I go into every case I consider for a book with a slight bias, obviously, but also an open mind," I explained to Tracy some time later. "With regard to your story, someone I respect highly saw me on 'Deadly Women' talking about your case and handed me your case files to look at and told me that he/she believed you might be onto something and I would be stupid not to look into the idea that you were framed. … Moreover," I continued, ruffling my feathers, stepping high atop my soap box, "to answer one of your questions specifically: I am journalist. I don't have to explain to anyone why I do what I do for work. If you are not interested in my … investigative skills then I will gladly stop contacting you and look into doing the book without you. But I will never explain to you why I do what I do, nor do I have to prove my integrity to you. I am a well-respected journalist. You are a convicted murderer. The facts in your case as they are right now support your conviction. That's the end of that story. You need to prove to *me* you're innocent. I don't need to prove to you how or what process I go through to try to uncover it."

I felt a strong need to defend and explain myself to all of the Tracys of the world who have ever attacked me. We—the true-crime writing community and those who speak about true crime on television—do not need to rectify or justify our comments about convicted murderers.

Ever.

Backed into a corner, my fists up, I brought up "Deadly Women" again: "I have commented on about 80 'Deadly Women' cases over the past 12 years, including, as I said, yours. I have commented on about 200 TV cases overall. I don't 'hype' cases, as you say. That's a ridiculous statement. Again, for you to judge me on what I do on TV is your mistake. You don't 'get' TV—not many convicts would. Also, on TV we are strictly in the business of sticking to the facts as they are rendered by the court, and interpreting them. I am paid for my opinions based on the facts I have at the time. Period. You don't like what I say on television, that's tough shit. That's your issue. I don't have to prove *anything* to you about my TV work. I'm the crime analyst and expert; you are the suspect/perpetrator, until proven otherwise."

I mean, for shit's sake: *What am I* supposed *to say to this woman*? Take her word for granted that a sheriff's department, with the help of the GBI, framed her for a murder because of a sexual harassment case? Or that Doug Benton was murdered for turning in a drug dealer and then Tracy was framed for it? On face value alone it all sounds ridiculous, like some sort of Orson Welles Hollywood plot. Then, after the fact, there's this contention—without any proof whatsoever—that the murder victim had a history with the sheriff and *that* had something to do with his murder? Again, where is the damn evidence to support such wild, over-the-top claims?

The statement Tracy made about Doug's mother, Carol Benton, struck at the very core of what I do. I am a staunch victims' advocate. I pride myself and my work in telling the victims' stories on television and in books. I support families of crime victims. The idea that a woman who was supposed to uphold the law was convicted of a murder and is trying to school me on victims' advocacy, well, I found it beyond disingenuous, distasteful and insulting. Tracy had no idea what she was saying. She does not know me or my work. She was speaking from a self-centered pulpit—albeit, from the inside of a prison!

"I also know how to deal with victims' family members," I wrote. "I am very much known for my victims' advocacy work and portrayal of victims in the thirty-three books I have written. And yes, I know Carol supports you. Still, when, where and how I approach Carol Benton is my business. I don't allow convicted murderers to dictate to me how I go about working on my projects. I do that on my own. I promised you—in my letter—a voice; an avenue to tell your story alongside everyone else and prove to the world that you are innocent. You don't want that opportunity. Fine."

Tracy wrote back: "Thanks for reminding me that I am a convicted murderer."

She then asked me for a biography, outlining my career, which I had first offered to send, if she wanted.

"You want a bio," I said now, "have your daughter go on my website and send it to you."

A bully from behind bars.

Fuck that.

"So, to sum this up," I concluded to Tracy, "I don't need

to explain, nor will I ever, why I think you might have a good case, and I can maybe help to expose it, nor anything else about my choice of profession or my work on TV. I also will never allow someone to tell me how to operate my business. Finally, you asked: 'Does it actually matter to you that I have spent half of my daughter's life in prison for a crime that I did not commit?' "

There was the familiar guilt-trip. I had been waiting for it. I hear this all the time. Many convicts have written to me in a similar fashion. They try to call you out by making you feel as though all you care about is the story. The God's honest truth of the matter is, it does *not* matter to me that Tracy has spent 15 years in prison. All I have are the facts. I cannot take a side based on allegations, without any proof to support them. And so I explained this to her.

"Right now, all I have is a convicted murderer telling me she has been set up. I have no facts to support that argument. No proof. Only her opinions—and mine. Bottom line: Forget about the drama and judging: prove to me you are innocent. Show me. Talk is cheap. Being in prison, you understand that. If we don't speak again, good luck, Tracy."

I left it there. In truth, I expected to never hear from her again. Or, actually, I did expect a return email, because my experience tells me that convicts need to have the last word. Always. So I thought perhaps a nasty email would arrive in a day or two and that would be the end of our correspondence.

Tracy surprised me, however.

6 4 .

I WILL NOT BORE YOU, my trusted reader, with the tedious, redundant testimony of a second trial. Tracy's second trial started on March 22, 2004, and was moved to Effingham County, yet (remarkably!) Judge Lindsey Tise, from Madison County, sat on the bench again.

The witness list read like a facsimile of the first. Bob Lavender and Marsha Cole were at the helm for the state, with a new lawyer, Bill Crecelius, Jr., bringing 15 years' experience with him, sitting next to Tracy. Helping Bill out was his father, Bill Sr., adding an additional 20 years of courtroom practice to the team.

Over the course of several days, Lavender and company brought in the same set of witnesses, in nearly identical order to the first trial. There were no surprises here. If you're Bob Lavender, why try to reinvent the wheel. It worked once. Why wouldn't it work a second time? Evidence is evidence, right? It should never change. Interpretation and opinion of it might vary, but the evidence itself—like truth—should stand on its own.

Tracy had several problems throughout the second trial as DA Lavender paraded his witnesses into the courtroom and asked each the same set of questions he had three years prior.

"Look at Dr. Geoffrey Smith's testimony," Tracy

encouraged in an email. Smith, if you recall, was the medical examiner. "Go to where he is talking about the entrance wound of the bullet. He is talking about the fracturing of the skull and how much damage is done by the bullet. Now go on to where he says that the bullet recovered was small. The last sentence he says he would not have expected this much damage from a small caliber bullet."

Smith actually said, "So, for a small caliber bullet, I would not have expected to have seen this sort of damage that occurred to this individual."

I absolutely get how Tracy could hang her cap on this statement, or a similar discrepancy, but it doesn't change the fact, for me, that the bullet caused those fractures in Doug's skull. We can argue which gun fired the bullet, yet the injuries to Doug's skull remain unchanged.

Tracy went on, noting again that Bernadette Davy's testimony during the second trial was obviously questionable. Yet, once again, she is looking at Davy's testimony in the context of Davy having been disciplined and leaving her job for falsifying reports in the years hence. At the time of Tracy's second trial, Bernadette Davy was still considered to be a credible witness.

"Look at ... Bernadette Davy (during) the second trial," Tracy said. "She says she was 'unable to make a conclusion as to whether or not the bullet was fired from that particular rifle.' She was talking about the .22 rifle from my home. Now look (ahead). Davy says that her comparisons showed that the bullet recovered from Doug is consistent with a .22 CCI Stinger, which just happens to be one of the brands of bullets I had at my home. Yet she did not compare that bullet to actual bullets from my home. She used bullets on hand at the lab. Not the same."

Tracy is correct here. Her point valid.

When I took trial testimony from the first trial and matched it up to the second trial, there were a few anomalies and minor inconstancies (basic human error), but overall I found all of it to be pretty much a mirror image. Witnesses were sticking to their testimony from years before. Many had, likely, re-read (the transcripts) from what they had testified to during the first trial. In the end, the truth is absolute: one does not have to recall it; fundamentally speaking, it lives and breathes inside of them.[9]

The one major difference between the two trials was the fact that Tracy's new lawyer called his own set of witnesses. In fact, Bill Crecelius's first witness, Kelly Fite, a firearms examiner and former supervisor of ballistics at the GBI, having worked in the GBI Crime Lab for 31 years, stepped up and totally contradicted the DA's expert.

Fite had gone over to the GBI lab in February 2004 to compare the bullets with the firearms involved in the case.

"I test-fired bullets with the two rifles and compared the test bullets with the State's Exhibit 40," Fite explained after Crecelius asked.

And what did those tests reveal?

"The Remington rifle could *not* have fired State's Exhibit 40."

"So, far as State's Exhibit 28 and .22 rifle taken from Tracy Fortson's house, what was your finding in regard to that rifle?"

"I found that bullets from *this* rifle were similar to the class characteristics of State's Exhibit 40, *however*, there were no individual characteristics to say *that* rifle fired State's Exhibit 40."

What Fite meant was that the lands and grooves on the flattened bullet fragment taken from Doug's body did *not* match those on the bullets fired from Tracy's guns. Fite was challenging Bernadette Davy's testimony.

Jurors would have to decide who they believed.

Bill Crecelius called a document examiner next, W.A.

---

9   On this note, I will say that during my near year-long correspondence with Tracy, she wrote more than 70,000 words to me, none of which I could find to be an exaggeration or outright lie.

Robinson, a member of the National Association of Document Examiners, who boasted a specialty in fraudulent documents, certified through the Fraud Examiners Association.

Robinson had written on the subject and was also a certified peace (police) officer. He was more than qualified to testify as an expert in his field.

He first explained how a document examiner goes about studying a document. It was a meticulous science, actually. Took great patience and a jeweler's eye for detail.

The $64,000 question for Robinson was rather simple: Had he looked at the documents (Tracy and Doug's handwriting as compared to the note left on Doug's truck) and made a determination as to who wrote what.

Robinson took several minutes to explain how he had gone about studying all of the documents. How it wasn't just a matter of looking at one document and comparing it to the next. There was a process of tracing each common letter and not looking for similar characteristics but *exact* likenesses.

In the end, Robinson—no surprise—said there was no way Tracy could have been the author of the note. He compared the samples of writing by explaining that they were like looking at "apples and oranges," concluding, "There is no similarity *at* all."

During cross-examination, one new fact emerged. Lavender asked Robinson about the people involved in authorship of the documents and Robinson said who they were did not matter. He did not want to know anything about them so as to stay objective. For him, it was about the science alone.

"Did you know that any of them suffered from any particular learning problems?" Lavender followed up with.

"Well," Robinson said, nodding his head in agreement, "it is obvious that one person doing the writing has a learning problem simply because of the misspelled words in it."

"Dyslexia, are you familiar with that?" Lavender countered.

"I don't know about that, no, sir."

"That's all I have."

I ASKED TRACY TO explain her relationship with Doug at the time he was murdered. This was an important question, in the end. We've heard from Doug's "best" friends and what law enforcement uncovered: that Doug and Tracy were estranged, had been arguing all the time, and were not going to be getting back together. In the scope of a motive, that needs to be in place if you're the prosecution. If Tracy and Doug are blissfully in love, however, Tracy would not have a motive to kill him.

"One of the things that has always bothered me and continues to bother me to this day is when people referred to Doug and I as having a 'rocky relationship.' It's in most court documents relating to my case. That statement was attached to my case when Jeff Bennett was questioned by law enforcement at the very beginning. Jeff told investigators that we were always breaking up."

All of which—these statements as Tracy explains them—is true. But Tracy had also said her relationship with Doug was rocky, if we take those police reports from her early interviews to be fact.

"I would not consider my relationship with Doug as 'on again-off again,' " Tracy continued. "We had different opinions about certain things and we didn't always agree, but that didn't mean we broke up every time we disagreed. The things we disagreed on were most often a matter of right and wrong, borderline illegal activity, and flat-out criminal activity I refused to go along with. We were a very private couple. We didn't really hang out with other people. That is one reason, in my opinion, Jeff (Bennett) was so angry with

Doug.

"For anyone to say that they knew anything about our private lives or our relationship with each other, they were not telling the truth. Doug battled dyslexia; most people never knew that. This created a learning disability he had to deal with all of his life. It made it hard for him at school and it also made it hard for him when it came to getting a job, one reason for having his own business. He was not a social person, so we didn't do the party scene and rarely went anywhere with other people. Jeff and his ex-wife were the only couple we ever went anywhere with and even then, it wasn't often."

Tracy went on to say Doug's battle with dyslexia did not mean he was stupid. She called him "business-minded." A guy who was "always looking for a new way to make money." Those ideas, however, were not always "exactly legal," she alleged, which would always lead to a "disagreement" between them.

"I was sworn to uphold the law," Tracy explained. "I could not and would not participate in some of Doug's schemes to make money."

Tracy said it was a few weeks into dating Doug when she realized that he, as she put it, "Wasn't going to work every day like a normal person who owns his own welding business."

"How are you able to make a living without going to work every day?" Tracy asked Doug one morning.

"I worked so many hours during the summer months, I can afford to take off for a while," she claims Doug told her. "Besides, I have a guy on the job working under me. All I have to do is check on him every morning to make sure he is on the job."

To Tracy, this response sounded legit.

Tracy talked about several "deals" Doug was involved in with various people he had known most of his life, one of whom was "a sheriff." Tracy banged on about "corrupt behavior" going on here, most of which cannot be proven other than to say it would have been Doug's word against those involved. She also claims one of Doug's familiar "deals" was to file "fraudulent" claims against insurance companies. Tracy said she wasn't aware of the specifics, but knew it was going on.

Again, there is no evidence to support these claims other than, as of now, Tracy's word.

"So, as you can see, we didn't always see eye to eye," Tracy explained. "Our morals were different, to say the least. If Doug saw an opportunity to make money, he took it, right or wrong. I, on the other hand, was torn between my love for him and my conviction for doing the right thing. He didn't see anything wrong with what he was doing because he said that insurance companies were always ripping people off. The more I tried to get him to understand it was wrong, the more he defended his point."

This was one of the reasons, Tracy concluded, Doug always sat with his back to the wall, facing the door, like a cop.

"He always felt someone was after him."

In Tracy's view, when you talk about motive, why Doug was murdered, by whom, and how she could have been framed for it, "Well," she says, "someone was *always* after him."

AS TRACY'S SECOND TRIAL continued and her attorney called his next witness, in walked an unfamiliar face to most inside the courtroom: Tracy's now 18-year-old daughter, Elise Fortson, who stood with one hand up, taking the oath to tell the truth.

6 5.

TRACY SENT ME A one-word answer, responding to my previous email, in which I'd ripped into her insults and accusations.

"Agreed," was all she wrote.

This shocked me.

Then she continued to talk about her case.

In total, I received more than 132 singled-spaced pages of text from Tracy. She discussed her life, the "lies" told by law enforcement and the prosecution, and just about everything in between. In reading it all, I decided to allow Tracy to explain her "innocence" in her own words (which you've read throughout the text). It is the only way to get her voice into this book. It was not easy to keep up with the back and forth, all of the "discrepancies" Tracy found in her trials and the reports generated by her case. A lot of it, to be honest, is unprovable. It is speculation and, again, forgive the redundancy, opinionated accusation made by a woman who has been convicted of murder.

After that spat between us, I allowed some time to pass, after which I then decided to write to Tracy once more to see if she would continue with our correspondence. She answered right away. The past seemed to be behind us. She didn't mention our last exchange.

We carried on from there with an unspoken agreement

between us: She would fight for her innocence; I would ask questions and allow her to have a voice within the text. If nothing else, Tracy has stuck to the same narrative all these years: A steadfast belief that she was railroaded and framed for Doug's murder. Her tenacity in this regard has never wavered.

It is, as you have read, a hard concept to grasp without any tangible, hard evidence to back it up. Part of me wants to believe Tracy Fortson. But I just don't have the proof.

Tracy sent me names of Doug's friends. Names of people involved, either closely connected or on the periphery of the case. I made contact with some, others could not be found. No one wanted to delve into the past. We're talking almost 20 years ago. I've never run into such a shunning while writing a book.

"I got a letter from a guy in prison years ago that claimed he was friends with (someone close to Doug) and he told me that (this person) had gone into Doug's house after it was secured by police," Tracy told me in May 2017. "He went through the police tape. The guy's name (is *Stan*), but I never had a last name that I can remember. But if you ever have the chance to talk to (that person), it would be something I would like to know. Was he the person who went in the house in that timeframe after Doug's body was found that they thought was me?"

This is the sort of conjecture and disjointed "evidence" that is entirely impossible to track down. A guy in prison whose last name I don't have, a prison I don't know the name of, a family member going into Doug's house after the murder.

Tracy is hanging on the idea that it is all true.

Where is the letter?

She could not produce it.

DURING THE WINTER OF 2017, I sent Tracy those documents I uncovered regarding the investigation into

Bernadette Davy's career after Tracy's case had been adjudicated. She had never seen them, she said.

Not long after, she sent a simple email: "My jaw is on the floor."

The documents were part of a later court record in a case challenging Davy's expert testimony.

"I had a very hard time getting information from the GBI," Tracy told me after I sent her copies of the Davy documents. "It was as if they did not want me to have anything that would help me."

66.

ELISE FORTSON LOOKED A lot like her mother. A beautiful young woman with blond, shoulder-length hair, clear skin, penetrating blue eyes, a runner's build. Elise had been a loyal defender of her mother's innocence throughout the years. Sitting, testifying for her mother must have been difficult. Tracy had been behind bars since Elise was 15. Here Elise was, a legal adult, appearing in her mother's murder trial.

A student at the University of Georgia, Elise had lived with Tracy in Winterville at the time of Doug's murder. As she began to recall one of the main dates in question, Sunday, June 4, 2000, Elise said she remembered she and her mom heading out to the mall. It was near noon, just as all the stores were opening, when Elise and Tracy pulled into the mall parking lot. Elise was being dropped off to meet up with friends. Tracy pulled up, kissed her daughter on the cheek, said she'd see her in a few hours and left.

By 2:30 that afternoon, Tracy was back, in her black F-150 Ford pickup picking up Elise.

Leaving the mall, they drove to a nearby Walmart. It was around 3, Elise testified, when they arrived. They spent about an hour inside Walmart and drove home.

"Looking back on the weekend," Tracy's lawyer asked her daughter, "did your mother act unusual or out of the ordinary in any way during the course of that weekend?"

"No, sir."

Defense attorney Crecelius then asked if Elise recalled her mother acting strangely at all on that Monday or in the days after.

No. No. No.

Crecelius brought up the dog pen Tracy was in the process of fixing at their home and if they were doing the work during that critical time period when Doug was murdered.

"Yes," Elise said.

He asked about the changes Tracy was making to it.

"We were going to lay a concrete slab underneath."

Crecelius asked about a horse. Did her mother own a horse?

"Yes."

"Where was that horse kept?"

"Down the road from our house in a pasture."

Crecelius talked about a creek running through the pasture, which had dried up. Wasn't that was the reason why Tracy needed a watering trough?

Elise agreed.

It made sense: that is, Elise's testimony. I mean, why would Tracy bring her daughter to the Walmart to purchase items she was going to use in a murder plot later on? The fact that she purchased the watering trough and the creek bed had dried up seemed logical. However, for Tracy to have been set up and framed, it would mean that whoever was going to kill Doug and then frame her for the crime would have had to know *when* she purchased those items, thus opening up the opportunity to kill Doug and set the frame job into motion.

"Had she ever talked about putting a large watering trough in that pasture?" Crecelius wondered.

"Yes, sir."

Lavender objected. "Hearsay!"

"That is all I have," Crecelius concluded.

Lavender had very little. He asked a few questions about Elise's memory of that time and if Tracy had anything in the back of the pickup when she picked her up at the mall.

None of which Elise could recall.

After Elise was released, Crecelius and Tracy looked at each other. Talked a bit amongst themselves. Tracy shook her head in the affirmative.

"You ready?" Crecelius asked his client.

"I am."

Tracy walked up to the witness stand. There was only one way to tell this story: from her mouth to jurors' ears.

67.

TRACY FORTSON WAS 39 in 2004 as she stepped up to the witness stand to tell her story. This was going to be Tracy's chance—likely her last—to finally speak publicly about her case.

She looked tired, relaxed, confident.

Crecelius got right into it with the standard set-up questions, allowing Tracy to state on record that she did not kill Doug Benton.

"Did you shoot Doug Benton?"

"No, sir."

"Did you stab Doug Benton?"

"No, sir."

"Did you conceal the body?"

"No, sir. I did not."

Tracy came across poised, without sounding arrogant or unsympathetic. She wasn't crass in any way. She seemed rather resolute and steadfast in her belief that she had been wrongly accused.

They spoke about the relationship she and Doug had. Tracy agreed it was "rocky." Then talked about how she hunted in an area around Doug's property, before mentioning all the various items she'd transport in the back of her truck within the scope of a normal day during the course of a normal week.

How her truck—like most—had exterior scratches.

How the dent on her bumper did not occur when she was removing a horse-watering trough full of concrete and Doug's body, but when she'd "hit a deer."

How she had no idea there was any damage to the rear bumper of her truck.

How she'd cracked the back taillight on her truck not backing into a tree while dumping Doug's body, but by hitting a peach tree in her yard.

How she'd seen Doug on that weekend in question, June 3 and 4, and they'd gone out to eat.

Crecelius stopped her there, asking specifically about the evening of June 3, 2000.

Tracy said: "We watched a movie. First of all, we had to take care of the birds when we got there and then we watched a movie."

"And what movie was it?"

"Yes, sir," she testified: " 'An Officer and a Gentleman.' "

Tracy said she left Doug's on that night about midnight, returned about 1:30 a.m. They'd gotten into an argument during the movie, adding, "I got my feelings hurt and I went home."

Crecelius wanted to know why she would go back to Doug's house if they'd argued and Doug had hurt her.

According to Tracy, she "figured" after being back home for a time that Doug would be "more mad" if she didn't go back.

Tracy said she spent the night in Doug's bed. While Doug, as usual, slept on the couch. She claimed she left Doug's around 6 the following morning, June 4, Sunday. Drove home. Took Elise to the mall. Then stopped at that farm supply store to purchase the trough, a mineral block for her horse, and some concrete for a dog pen she had been working on. She described the entire trip into the store, why she needed those items, even recalling what she was wearing on that day: jeans and a T-shirt.

As she spoke, if I'm a juror, I am asking myself one question: *Why would a killer choose a store to buy supplies for a murder close to the scene and where she knew the clerk and could be easily identified?*

After a few more questions, Tracy explained how she unloaded all of the items she purchased at the farm supply store by jumping up on the back bed of her truck while it was backed up to her carport. Then she slid the bags of concrete mix off her truck and onto the floor of the carport, likely leaving concrete dust and residue in the bed of her truck and on the floor of the carport.

After dropping the mineral block for her horse off at the pasture up the road from her house, Tracy said she picked up Elise at the mall and headed over to the nearby Walmart.

She bought a shower curtain and other household items for her bathroom because she needed them. In fact, she added, after getting home, she replaced the shower curtain and placed the old one in the trash outside.

By then it was somewhere near 5 or 6 in the evening, which was when she got back into her truck and drove over to Doug's.

When she arrived, Doug was feeding his birds.

Tracy claimed she and Doug did not "fuss" about anything upon her return. She felt they were on good terms; the argument from the previous night forgotten. She stayed about two hours, left Doug's and drove home. She remained at home and never spoke to Doug again that night.

The next day, June 5, a Monday, Tracy had to go to court and testify in one of her cases from being employed by the sheriff's department.

"Was there anything unusual when you got home on the afternoon of June 5?" Crecelius asked.

"When I pulled up on the carport," Tracy said, "I noticed that the concrete I had bought and the trough I had bought were gone, and then I thought that was kind of odd—until I opened the storage room door to get my key to unlock the (front) door and I saw my boots and chaps and leather jacket, things I had left at Doug's."

Seeing those items she had left over Doug's now on her storage room floor, Tracy explained further, made her realize Doug had brought them over and dropped them off in a gesture to say they were finished. This was common behavior on Doug's part, she added. Doug would get angry after an argument and return all of her personal belongings in order to say it was over between them.

AS I WOUND DOWN my interviews with Tracy, she had an epiphany with regard to the watering trough and concrete. I'd never asked her about the idea—based on the premise that we believe her—of someone having to follow her around, know when she purchased the concrete and watering trough and other items in order to set in motion framing her. As it turns out, she answered this question without me asking.

"The trough and concrete went missing on Monday, June 5," Tracy contends. "It was gone when I got home from court and I just assumed Doug had taken it since my clothes had been left in the storage room. Yet, they wanted to know why I didn't report it stolen? It wasn't 'stolen' if Doug took it. I knew he would give it back eventually."

That's buyable. I can grasp this.

Then the question becomes, however: "Who would have known the concrete and trough were there inside her car port other than Doug?"

After all, there is no way Doug could have taken it.

"Well," Tracy said, "it just so happens that (a longtime deputy) … lived (not too far away from my house and) drove by my house twice a day. He hated me from day one, when I got hired, even though I've known him most of my life. He had told the sheriff that I would get him in trouble. I don't know what he was referring to, but I guess I fulfilled that prophesy."

Tracy maintains that this same man once said: "The 'Georgia state law stops at the Oglethorpe County line!' "

TRACY NEVER MENTIONED WHY Doug did not seem angry or upset while she was at his house the previous night for those two hours. It seemed that he'd gone from being angry with her to forgetting about the argument to now kicking her out of his life.

It was after she saw her personal belongings from Doug's in her storage room that the missing concrete and trough made sense, Tracy said. She figured in her mind that Doug had taken the items.

Tracy stopped over to Doug's that Monday night about 6. When she got there, she did not see any of the items she believed Doug had taken from her carport: the concrete mix, horse-watering trough.

Doug was home, tending to his birds when she pulled in.

"You need any help?" Tracy asked after getting out of her truck, walking over.

"No!" Doug snapped. He was pissed. Tracy was under the impression he wanted her to leave.

But she insisted on helping him.

"No," Doug said. He was adamant.

"So I went home," Tracy told jurors, having spent a total of 30 minutes at Doug's.

Had Tracy, the question became, asked Doug about the concrete mix or trough? She was there. She believed he had taken the items from her carport. Why not ask?

"He wasn't in a talkative mood at all," Tracy testified.

She couldn't get him to respond to her, she insisted.

The silent treatment.

She never spoke to or saw Doug again.

Tracy did, however, hear from him.

It was the next morning. Tuesday. Between 8 and 8:30 a.m., Tracy claimed. She was home. "I must have been outside" when Doug called. He left a voicemail—her old-school answering machine (the kind with the cassette tape) was not working, so her calls rolled over to voicemail.

Doug was firm, Tracy said. "Not to call him anymore, not to come over there anymore, that he didn't need a woman, and he just didn't want me back over there."

Tracy never bothered with Doug again after that, she said. It was nearly two weeks later, June 17, when a neighbor of Doug's, Lisa Watson, called Tracy and asked if she knew where Doug had run off to because neither she nor Larry (Bridges) had seen him in quite some time.

Tracy said no.

It was the first time, Tracy testified, she'd learned Doug was "missing," as she described it. She never mentioned a precedent: Like, for example, had she and Doug gone weeks without talking to each other in the past? Had they fought and not spoken for that amount of time ever before?

Next, Tracy said she knew the guy who owned the land where Doug's body had been found and also the guy who came across the trough while riding his ATV. She'd hunted on that land. But had not been out there for any reason since 1999.

Crecelius made a point to then ask about the gate into the property, which had been driven through and busted open, law enforcement believed, somewhere near the time when Doug's body had been dumped.

Tracy explained that she knew how to get onto the property without having to bust open a gate.

They talked about potting soil and grass seed Tracy had sitting around her house—common items most people have in their garage during summer months. The fact that Tracy owned a Stevens bolt action .22 rifle she kept in a spare bedroom and had never, "for any reason," kept in her bedroom. In fact, she could not recall the last time she had even fired that particular weapon.

Tracy admitted she bought all the paint they found at her house. The paint was actually for several birdcages she owned and needed to refinish, and for painting her mailbox, which had been painted that camouflage color a year before.

Then Crecelius asked about Painkiller, the so-called drug dealer Doug had been involved with.

"Do you know whether or not (Painkiller) went to prison?"

"I believe so."

"Did Doug have anything to do with him going to prison?"

"Yes, he did."

"What?"

"He gave evidence or assisted Madison County in the prosecution."

Crecelius asked if Doug feared Painkiller in any way after being part of the prosecution against him.

"Yes," she responded, without elaborating on context.

They discussed the note and Tracy said she did not write it. Then, after a lengthy back and forth regarding Tracy not being angry enough with Doug to kill him, Crecelius looked down at his notes and passed his witness.

DA Bob Lavender stood and began by asking Tracy for a timeline that weekend and where she went and if she and Doug had argued like that before.

"I believe you said it was a nine-month relationship that you and he had," Lavender asked at one point. "You all had had several break-ups like this, had you not?"

"We had had several spats, yes."

"And you all had gotten into several arguments, hadn't you?"

"Yes, sir."

Lavender's line of questioning felt directed all over the place and went nowhere, actually. The DA had a hard time getting to the point of it all.

As he continued, Lavender talked about Doug's residence and the doors into it, the back porch, the steps up to that back porch, where Doug slept, and what he wore when he slept. None of it made much sense in the scope of Tracy killing the man.

From there, Lavender asked about bullets and the weapon Tracy owned, if Doug was a hunter and if she knew Doug had weapons in his house.

She answered yes to most of everything.

But again, there was no punch line here—no "ah-ha," Perry Mason moment. Lavender's questioning offered nothing in the sense of adding to his case.

Then, abruptly, the DA said, "That's all I have."

No 11th-hour reveal.

No proof of Tracy's alleged anger.

No hard accusations.

No prior record of violence in Tracy's life.

Apparently, Lavender was under the impression that the evidence he had against Tracy Fortson spoke for itself.

68.

AFTER A STATE REBUTTAL witness, both sides rested. The judge then read a long, tedious charging document, likely putting half the courtroom to sleep.

With short closing arguments out of the way, Tracy's case—and her fate—was once again in the hands of a jury.

It was 3:45 p.m. on March 25, 2004, when jurors started deliberations—and just after 8:30 p.m. that same night when they emerged with a verdict.

Tracy was found guilty. On three counts.

Not guilty on Counts 3 and 4, both of which were the aggravated assault charges.

She bowed her head and shook it from side to side as each juror was polled, confirming his and her guilty vote. She'd fought, this time testifying on her own behalf, and lost for a second time.

It was unlikely there would be a third.

Tracy's mother was allowed to speak. Sharon Hodges looked broken. She had been through so much, twice watching her daughter convicted of the most deplorable crime on the books.

"I am Tracy's mother and I would like to ask for mercy. Tracy is my only child and has one daughter who misses her very much. She has changed in her heart." Sharon mentioned that Tracy had "found the Lord" and had been very active in prison conducting Bible studies, concluding, "For the sake of my family, her daughter's sake and everybody's sake, we just ask for mercy."

"Thank you, ma'am," was all the judge said.

With that out of the way, the judge showed no mercy by sentencing Tracy to life, plus 10 years.

Tracy Fortson was sent back to prison.

69.

"**SPEAKING OF CAROL BENTON,**" Tracy emailed me in late 2016, bringing Doug's mother back into our conversation, "I want you to speak to her ... she deserves to know what your intentions are. You do realize that she has been put through hell over the past 16 years. She was devastated and has never fully recovered. It's like an open wound that never heals, someone always reopens the wound."

This was the sort of direction, I'll call it, I did not appreciate. I don't need a convicted murderer telling me what to do, how to do it. Early on, Tracy was forever trying to dictate who I spoke to, what to ask and how I should treat them. It stank of control—which, of course, makes a guy in my position, looking for the truth—teetering on the fence with Tracy to begin with—wonder where the need for that control is rooted.

I let her have it again.

She wrote back.

"If you think I am judging you," Tracy said, "isn't that what you are doing to me? I don't have anything to compare. You may be a wonderful writer, journalist ... I'm not saying that you're not, I honestly don't know. I would really like to believe you are very passionate about your work and you strive to reveal the facts in your research."

Here is the bottom line: I can judge Tracy all day long. That is never an issue when dealing with a convicted murderer, or any subject for a book. We all judge one another. It's inherent in being human, for shit's sake. She had already been judged by jurors in a court of law. Twice. She never understood or accepted the fact that what I think or how I feel about her does not matter.

"I make observations, I have an opinion, I ask questions," Tracy continued. "Sometimes I piss people off and sometimes I get defensive when I get lumped in the same category with 'convicted murderers,' like you got defensive with me for saying whatever it was that you didn't like. But you're right, unlike you, I have to prove that I am not what the State says I am."

Lumped in the same category with convicted murderers?

I had to read it twice. Was this, actually, how she went about her life in prison? She had never been "lumped" into any convicted murderer category; she had been *convicted* of murder. That part of the argument ends there.

I continually asked Tracy for "factual" information about her case that might help prove her innocence—however big or small. Anything. Just something I could sink my investigative talons into and begin to clearly see what she has been screaming about all along. Much of what she pointed out never fell into either the black or white column we like to see in journalism. There was always that ambiguous, gray area.

"Let me say this," Tracy wrote not long after. "As of right now you say the state's evidence supports my conviction. Facts? Not even close. Let me know when you finish looking at the information (we) sent you. Then you let me know if you feel the same way. In the future ... I will try to refrain from being too critical and judgmental. Maybe I was the one not being fair."

That "information" one of her family members sent to me, again, was Tracy Fortson's interpretation of the facts.

It's explosive, of course. But the validity of it has to be questioned at face value—the key revelation within those documents cannot be backed up by signed affidavits or public court testimony under oath.

This new argument she was so anxious to get me to see consisted of two sources allegedly recanting their testimony at trial, and Tracy's alleged accusation of coercion by cops to keep both of these witnesses quiet and sticking to a carefully structured narrative to frame her from day one. More than that, in a new motion Tracy was now alleging that a key witness "was coerced to testify" against her. That new evidence Tracy presented? A nearly two-hour recording of a conversation between one of Tracy's family members and the same witness, in which she was now alleging that witness had been intimidated and influenced by the prosecution before her trial.

As she described it to me, "My long and weary battle, one that I will continue to fight," fell on what she called an *Extraordinary Motion for New Trial and a Motion for DNA Testing*, which Tracy, acting as her own lawyer, wrote and filed herself in September 2015. After that filing, Tracy was granted a hearing, which took place on July 7, 2016, overseen by Superior Court Judge Thomas Hodges. That late 2016 decision against her by the Supreme Court of Georgia for Discretionary Appeal was in response to the *Extraordinary Motion*.

"The District Attorney waited until the day of the hearing to file the state's response," Tracy told me.

I thought: *Why would you want to show your hand anytime sooner than at the last moment, especially if you have no legal reason to?*

The response by the State of Georgia to Tracy's *Extraordinary Motion* is a straightforward document, as these things go. The witness's name she alleges to have been "coerced" to testify is all over the state's response. I think it's inappropriate to use it here, simply because after several attempts to talk to this person, I got nowhere.

The opening paragraph references what is an alleged phone call between a family member of Tracy's and this witness. "The State," it turns out, "was not furnished with this recording until June 8, 2016," 18 months after the so-called recording had been made. Because that same witness never signed an affidavit claiming he or she was the other voice on that call, however, the state could not verify its authenticity.

Rightly so.

"(The witness) was not under oath at the time (he or she) allegedly made these allegations and was unlikely told the conversation was being recorded," the state wrote in its reply, going on to explain how Tracy's "assertions" are nothing more than "unsworn allegations."

This is true. Accusing someone of a crime—or, rather, several law enforcement officers—is not the same as proving it. Saying a witness was coerced and lied because he or she was scared for his or her life is not the same as that witness walking into a courtroom and testifying to those allegations under oath, putting the entire incident on record.

What's more, Tracy hangs her hopes, in many respects, on that same witness's testimony at trial, along with his or her conversations with police during the investigation into Doug's murder. Yet, as the state contended in its sarcastic response to that statement in the *Extraordinary Motion,* "(The witness's) trial testimony consisted of a whopping six pages."

Throughout his or her testimony, the witness does nothing more than discuss Doug's handwriting, several interactions with him, and how he or she had seen checks ($) Doug had written to Tracy.

In the *Extraordinary Motion,* Tracy alleges perjury by the witness and others during both of her trials. But as the state points out, "(The witness) has not been convicted of perjury, nor even charged."

Alleging perjury and proving perjury are, of course, two different things. Tracy's accusations might very well be 100 percent factual, but without any evidence to back her statements up, they fall flat.

"Along with his response to my motions," Tracy told me, speaking of the prosecutor's reply to the *Extraordinary Motion*, "he included an affidavit from the former Medical Examiner of the Georgia Bureau of Investigation, Dr. Kris Sperry. Dr. Sperry's affidavit contained false statements," Tracy alleged to me. "1. He claimed to be the medical examiner that performed the autopsy on Doug. He was not."

That's an unfair characterization of line #3 in Sperry's affidavit, of which Tracy is referring to here. In the hard copy of the affidavit Tracy sent me, somebody—presuming this was Tracy—highlighted with yellow marker line #3, in which, according to Tracy's read, Sperry erroneously and maliciously contends to being the medical examiner who performed the autopsy on Doug Benton.

Here is the unedited version of that complete line: "*I was the medical examiner for the Georgia Bureau of Investigation (GBI) who performed the autopsy of the decedent, later identified at Douglas Benton*," Dr. Kris Sperry writes in the affidavit.

Read that line again.

In it, Sperry, who admittedly takes on "hundreds of cases" as a paid forensic expert (many medical examiners, to the chagrin of many of their colleagues do this) all over the country, is stating for the record that he is the medical examiner for the GBI—*not* the pathologist who actually performed the autopsy.

What's missing in the affidavit is a very important comma after "(GBI)." The GBI, Sperry clearly states, is the civic body performing the autopsy, of which he is the Medical Examiner. Sperry, as Chief Medical Examiner, oversaw the duties of his pathologists. Sperry is in no way claiming to have done the actual work.

I mean, seriously: Why *would* he, after all? You look at the accompanying documentation from Tracy's trials, including the testimony of pathologist Jeffrey Smith, who physically performed the autopsy, and it clearly proves Sperry himself did not conduct Doug's autopsy. To believe Tracy, you'd have to consider that Sperry thought he could get away with lying on a public document, when all of the accompanying public information about that same autopsy proved otherwise.

That is ridiculous. It's beyond reaching.

This is a good example of what I mean when I say that Tracy argues her case to me, shows me a document, or points me to testimony, and the air begins to deflate out of her argument. I see what she is trying to say. I understand where she is coming from. Yet it does not mean what she is saying can be considered fact.

Place a comma where it belongs, I told Tracy, and then read the line again. Sperry is saying—quite clearly—he was the M.E. for the GBI, the body of government "who performed the autopsy." Medical Examiner is a title; pathologist is a job. The M.E. is the boss. He or she generally writes most of the affidavits (after the fact). Dr. Smith unmistakably states at trial he was the pathologist who conducted Doug's autopsy. Why would Sperry ever think he could say he performed the autopsy if there is a record of Smith doing it? Makes no sense. Also, every autopsy for any M.E.'s office is performed under the M.E.—the M.E., in other words, is responsible for each autopsy.

Moreover, many medical examiners testify in cases in which they have not performed the actual autopsy, but might have been present when one of the pathologists working under them has. Or they studied the documentation pertaining to the autopsy, maybe watched videos and/or listened to recorded notes from the pathologist. All part of the practice.

Tracy is trying to take what was written and make it

adhere to her case. She's trying to turn what is a grammatical error into a nefarious act of lying.

Another one of Tracy's core arguments was that some of the evidence was contaminated, "based upon the pathologist's report."

Here, she might have a case.

During the course of autopsying Doug's body, the pathologist (as Sperry states in his affidavit—once again excluding himself, by the way, from conducting the actual autopsy) was present when "an individual poured Clorox bleach over pieces of the shattered concrete due to the smell of decompositional fluid that had soaked into the concrete." In the following line, #6, Sperry states, emphatically, "To the best of my knowledge and belief, nothing of evidentiary value would have been affected by the action of pouring bleach over the concrete."

That is his *opinion*. We can argue his opinion, but he is the expert weighing in on this particular matter. To counter this, you would provide your own expert.

"He claimed that the action of pouring Clorox on the cement evidence would not have an effect on possible biological evidence that may have been present within the cement fragments," Tracy argued to me. "I have a letter from the GBI that verifies that Dr. Sperry had no part in my case. Dr. Geoffrey (sic: Jeffrey) Smith was the medical examiner (who) performed the autopsy which is reflected in the Medical Examiner's Report as well as in trial testimony."

Again, this is wrong and shows Tracy's ignorance.

Jeffrey Smith testified: "I am employed at the State Medical Examiner's office … I am a forensic pathologist," before saying, "Yes," he performed Doug's autopsy.

Again, there's only one Medical Examiner: the pathologist works under him or her.

Pouring bleach on evidence, well, that's another argument. Could it contaminate or destroy crucial evidence?

Hell, yeah, it could—and likely would.

Tracy needs her own expert to contend as much.

In reading her emails to me after I asked questions about missing commas and bleach and titles, I sensed an urgency, an anxiety she exuded in getting me to recognize her argument. As if I weren't getting it. Or, rather, I wasn't understanding what she was trying to say.

"Dr. Sperry lied when he said pouring Clorox on the cement would not have destroyed anything of evidentiary value. Anyone, including a lay person, would know that Clorox is caustic/corrosive and will destroy anything it comes into contact with, especially something like DNA. But, just to confirm it, (a family member of mine) contacted … a medical examiner from Oakland, California, and he said, 'Yes, pouring Clorox over that cement would have destroyed potential evidence such as DNA.' Whoever killed Doug and placed him in that container of concrete would have left some sort of DNA behind, but that would have been destroyed with no possible way to recover it once Clorox was poured on it."

I concur with part of this statement. But "lied"? That's quite a leap. Sperry is speaking his opinion from his professional position, however biased it might be. Moreover, what does Tracy's opinion about it prove? Incompetence? A frame-up?

In his affidavit, Dr. Sperry, after studying the case, gave his opinion that "the bleaching of certain pieces of concrete to remove the smell of putrefied discharge from the body of Doug Benton would not have destroyed anything of evidentiary value and was therefore not exculpatory."

It wasn't as if they doused the entire watering trough and Doug's body in bleach. "Certain pieces" of concrete only.

Big difference.

Was it not the smartest thing to do? Of course. But Sperry never lied, as Tracy suggests. That word is inserted into her argument to add power to what she is trying to sell. Sperry gave his expert *opinion* as a professional who had knowledge of the case. To call him a liar is beyond being uninformed.

Now, all that being said, I cannot imagine how frustrating it would be if I am Tracy and I know I have been framed. I sympathize with her in that respect. If she is telling the truth, I would certainly understand her attitude toward me and others erring on the side of the record.

Tracy then talked about how, in 2015, "Dr. Kris Sperry was investigated ... and resigned from the GBI because he was claiming hours for working at the Crime Lab when he wasn't there. He had his own independent forensic lab and was being paid to testify as an expert witness. In (an) *Atlanta Journal Constitution* article," Tracy went on, "Dr. Sperry was said to be a 'hired gun who tailored his testimony to suit his paying customers.' "

The article she references said a lot more than that. A feature by *Constitution* writer Alan Judd, it delved deeply into Sperry's work outside his job as Medical Examiner. He had made double his $184,000 state salary, according to Judd, testifying all over the country as an expert witness. Counterparts of professionals called Sperry "irreproachable" for being a paid expert who would say what his employer, whoever it might be, wanted him to.

In that same article, then GBI Director Vernon Keenan called Sperry "a doctor of national reputation and accomplishment ... (who) operates on an extremely high plane of expertise."

Keenan went on to note that talk from others was nothing more than banter, or common water-cooler "back and forth" from professionals in a chosen field who agree and disagree with what others in the same field.

I have seen and heard this myself.

Do some of these doctors stretch their opinions and take a side for a paycheck in a court of law? Absolutely. Do they get paid enormous sums of money for their often-biased opinions? Yes. Does it change the facts of a case?

Juries make that call.

Judd's in-depth article points to credibility issues with Dr. Sperry.[10] Yet, when I take into consideration what this information means in the scope of Tracy's case and the work—minimal as it was—Sperry did in her case, it means nothing. Sperry did not lie, as Tracy contends, to cover up for cohorts framing her. There's not any chance (and certainly no evidence) that accusation holds any weight whatsoever.

10   Read it here: http://www.myajc.com/news/special-reports/out-side-work-challenges-medical-examiner-credibility-judgment/OJXP-FLpsmGGq1CT4EY00CI/

70.

AS TRACY AND I spoke heatedly about her case through email in late 2016 and into 2017, I tried to explain that, regardless what she thought of me and what I do, I was giving her a chance to tell her story, in long form, once and for all. I wasn't going to censor what she had to say. I wasn't going to cut what she said to fit some sort of agenda. I wasn't going to use some of what she said and toss whatever didn't fit with what I wanted in the book. Although I could not obviously include every word she had written to me, I would get those core arguments for innocence she wanted into the public arena.

"I am just trying to speak in the facts," I explained. "Books and TV are different things. TV, as I said, pays me for my *opinions*; book work is about journalism and facts. Right now, on paper, you are a 'convicted murderer.' I can't change that. It's not a label; it's a fact generated by the court."

I should note here that those I did speak to about Tracy, friends and family, came at me with an attitude, as if I were part of the problem. It was as though I walked into this wanting to make sure Tracy remained guilty, just for the sake of writing a book. One person in particular, who probably had some rather cogent and important things to say about Tracy, attacked me personally and professionally right out of the gate, pointing a finger in my chest, calling me names, etc.

I can take it. Yet, as I told Tracy, there is no way I could ever allow this person a voice in my book.

As we exchanged email, I explained to Tracy that if she wanted to continue, she had my ear, but she needed to "prove to me that you are innocent. Your 'observations' and 'opinions' won't matter to my readers or to me. They (my readers) want undeniable proof. You need to share with me 'ah-ha' moments from your case. ... Saying that COP A set fire to (Doug's) house and COP B planted blood (not that you have) doesn't matter. Your *opinion* does not count in this. Showing me evidence where (your case) can be proven is what you need to do. Don't (be) defensive—stay offensive. Back up what you believe with the documents and point me in the direction of interviews that can support what you say."

Her response was to send me back to that *Extraordinary Motion*, an 85-page document, and the alleged cover-up a family member discovered during that recorded phone call with a witness long after her second trial.

The document is, as the title suggests, rather extraordinary with regard to accusation and speculation. Take, for example, this excerpt from page 9:

> *(One source) states in a recorded telephone conversation that he had been told, "We have who we want. Keep your mouth shut and stick to the plan." (This source) also stated that (he or she) had tried to obtain the original statement that (he or she) had given law enforcement during the investigation where (he or she) had stated "if anything happened to Doug(,) Ray Sanders did it," and found that the report had "disappeared. ..." (He or she) stated that both (he or she) and (another source) were coerced, intimidated and influenced by law enforcement officials prior to their testimony at trial.*

Those are serious allegations. The problem is, neither

source was willing to then back up his or her allegation with a signed affidavit (or go on record with me). For all we know, that recording could be somebody portraying the source.

Is it likely?

No.

Is it possible?

Yes.

We do not know because the source fails to acknowledge the call or sign a document stating it was him or her on the other end of the line.

Further along in her *Extraordinary Motion*, Tracy alleges how the same source "also stated that (he or she and the second source) were placed in an enclosed room with Oglethorpe County Sheriff Ray Sanders in an attempt to intimidate them, after they had told the District Attorney and Investigators that they believed Ray Sanders was responsible for Doug's death. Both (sources) were in fear for their (lives). It was implied to them that they both could end up like the victim, Doug Benton."

Thus, what Tracy is saying in her motion dispels the argument made by the prosecution that the source's trial testimony was of no consequence; what Tracy contends is that had both sources not been intimidated and "coerced," they could have testified "freely" and "openly" and given exculpatory evidence favoring Tracy's theory of a so-called frame-up.

"These people continue to lie even now," Tracy told me. "The current District Attorney … was not in office at the time of my trial and conviction, yet he continues to carry out the same kind of justice as the others."

I don't understand a statement like that. I mean, why wouldn't the DA strive to uphold a conviction by his predecessor?

Her next argument within the *Extraordinary Motion* is quite compelling—but again, only if it can be substantiated. Tracy focuses on ballistics, beginning her argument, once again, with those same two sources, noting their conversations with police early into the investigation led to the search of Tracy's house, where the weapon used to kill Doug was ultimately recovered. Tracy alleges a consistent cover-up chain of events taking place during this part of the investigation.

Both source interviews—early into the investigation—pushed law enforcement into searching Tracy's house. While there, they of course uncovered the murder weapon.

In Tracy's version, it all makes perfect sense—one piece of erroneous information leading to the next, which ultimately leads to her arrest and conviction.

In her *Extraordinary Motion*, Tracy writes, "Firearms examiner Bernadette Davy resigned from the Georgia Bureau of Investigation after admitting to falsifying a test report in an unrelated case."

That sets the previous allegation in motion. It is the basis from which she begins this argument that the bullet taken from Doug's body was part of the conspiracy. In support of that, Tracy's *Extraordinary Motion* goes on to say:

> *Bernadette Davy, of the Georgia Bureau of Investigation, testified for the state that she had examined the fatal bullet recovered from the victim, Douglas Benton, and determined that the bullet was a small caliber consistent with a .22. Upon further testimony, Davy stated the following: 1) the class characteristics on the bullet are identical to the class characteristics on the Stevens .22 rifle.*

This particular rifle was uncovered after that search of Tracy's home (the search based on what those two sources, according to Tracy, had to say), as the OCSD and GBI zeroed in on Tracy as a potential suspect in Doug's murder.

Comparison of State's exhibit 40, lead bullet from

Benton, to representative samples of ammunition of different manufacturer (from the crime lab), and the most consistent things that matched up were between a CCI Stinger .22 long rifle bullet. Davy's conclusion that the fatal bullet was consistent with a CCI Brand Stinger helped to seal the fate of Fortson since testimony of law enforcement officers that conducted the search of Fortson's residence stated that two types of 22 bullets were found, CCI Brand Stinger and .22 Long Rifle.

As Tracy's argument continues, she makes a case for, perhaps, even more shady business by law enforcement. In the initial report from the GBI's Crime Lab pathologist, Tracy points out, the "recovered bullet" from Doug's body was "too distorted to make an identification of the type of bullet or what type of gun it was fired from."

The problem with that argument is that it had been discussed already during both trials.

In April 2009, Tracy and her camp made an official open records request for "all information pertaining to the ballistic report by Davy."

That's a legit request, for sure. And might clear up what seemed to be some confusion.

Tracy's *Extraordinary Motion* continues:

(I) obtained the Official Chain of Custody Evidence Report from the Forensics Division of the GBI regarding all evidence received from the arresting county, Madison County Georgia. The Official Chain of Custody Evidence Report did not list bullets taken from Fortson's home—.22 CCI Stinger or otherwise. Therefore the testimony as to comparisons made by Davy with bullets taken from Fortson's home is not credible.

Tracy then asked for a report indicating the weight of the bullet in question.

GBI Special Agent Lisa Harris wrote back, saying the bullet itself had never been weighed.

This ballistics argument is interesting in that a report generated on Aug. 4, 2000, from the Division of Forensics Sciences, GBI, details all of this evidence: "On 6/27/00, the laboratory received the following evidence from the GBI ... Remington .22 rifle ... and .22 cartridge; on 7/11/00 ... sealed package labeled 'Douglas B. Benton...' containing .22 lead bullet."

As for the "results and conclusions," the document concluded, "the bullet ... was not fired from the weapon."

Who signed that document?

Bernadette Davy—cc'ing the GBI Medical Examiner, Madison County DA and the Oglethorpe County Coroner.

71.

SINCE HER SECOND CONVICTION in 2004, a lot has happened in Tracy's legal life (including the filing and dismissal of her *Extraordinary Motion*), yet none of it has had the effect Tracy has strived for since Day One. She is still in prison as of this writing. She is still fighting every day for her innocence. She is still sticking to the same story of being framed.

"I know you are skeptical," Tracy said in one of her more humbling moments. "I would be, too. There was a time when I believed that everyone in prison was guilty of whatever crime they were convicted of and no one could have convinced me otherwise. But now that it has happened to me, and I've seen how Georgia's justice system works from both sides, I'm not so quick to jump to conclusions. There was a time that I believed in the justice system. I believed that judges, lawyers and police officers were honest people. I don't believe that anymore. It's not about truth. It's about winning. It's about money. And everything is not what it appears to be."

For the record, I—like most people—do not believe everyone in prison is guilty of the crime in which they were convicted. That'd be naïve and ignorant. I would take it one step farther and say when speaking of females in prison, those numbers are far higher than when talking males. Lots of women are doing time for love and fear.

Tracy has a point here in what she says. Yet it's hard for me to come to the same conclusions she has. I don't see tangible evidence—that proof I like to see in cases where the wrongly convicted are sprung from prison. I still have a hard time believing so many law enforcement could be involved in a conspiracy to frame a fellow cop for a motive I don't see as being large enough in scope. I wish like hell those cops involved would have responded to my requests for interviews. The fact that across the board they did not raises a few red flags for me, but doesn't negate the investigation (as it stands), or the results it produced.

I could spend another 100 pages detailing more of Tracy's arguments and countering each with the facts in the case as they are. What I tried to do was take Tracy's core arguments and present them from her point of view and then share the facts of the case as they have been unearthed, and allow you—the all-important reader—to judge for yourself what happened and who is responsible. With the facts as they were presented in court, if I were a juror, honestly, I would have had to vote guilty. There was no other explanation offered, no other suspect, no counter argument—other than the frame-up theory—to some of the most damning evidence. You look at this case from the way in which it was presented in a court of law (twice) and Tracy Fortson appears to be guilty.

But then the question has to become: Does Tracy look *too* guilty?

Well, that's a position we cannot take. Sometimes, the evidence is overwhelming; other times, it is not.

What I will say is that the more I spoke to Tracy, the more I believe her. I hope someone can, at the least, take the case farther than I could and look into the notion that good ol' boy justice, of which we know exists in this country, served up the first and only female sheriff the county had seen up until then for reasons anyone outside that bubble cannot fathom.

IN 2015, WHEN SHE acted as her own lawyer and filed that extraordinary motion for a new trial, Tracy exhausted her final appeal. According to Northern Circuit District Attorney Parks White, Tracy's "case is finalized and closed." Tracy is serving her time at the Lee Arrendale State Prison in Alto, Georgia. She maintains that the murder charge against her was born from that sexual harassment claim she filed against former Oglethorpe Sheriff Ray Sanders, a suit she dropped after being arrested on the murder charge. One of the major problems Tracy faced was that she was unable to produce documentation that Doug was involved in Painkiller's conviction, which would have been the beginning of a basis for arguing someone else could have been responsible for Doug's murder.

In the years following Fortson's second conviction, former Oglethorpe County Sheriff Ray Sanders and his son-in-law faced assault charges for allegedly beating another man with a baseball bat at Sanders' daughter's home. Sanders, who was 71 at the time, and his son-in-law were charged with aggravated assault after a GBI investigation (with Mike Smith, Sanders' old buddy, the sheriff, recusing himself, allowing the GBI to take over). In 2009, a grand jury failed to indict Ray Sanders for the crime, though his son-in-law was charged.

"I'm just glad we had a good grand jury in there, and they saw fit to read through the lines," Ray Sanders told the *Florida Times-Union* in December 2009. "I didn't see no cause for me to be arrested in the first place, and if I hadn't been a political sheriff for such a long time, probably nothing would have come of it."

It was 2000 when Ray Sanders ended his 16-year term as sheriff after not running for re-election.

ON DEC. 8, 2016, Tracy wrote: "My application to the Supreme Court of Georgia for Discretionary Appeal was DENIED, all Justices concur. Not sure of any other option at this point."

I could sense her dread and disappointment and frustration.

Her legal battle was over. This, mind you, after 14 years. Save for an 11th-hour admission by a stranger, this left Tracy with no recourse whatsoever to pursue.

She has exhausted every appeal.

I asked Tracy to write a final appeal to you, the reader. Encouraging her to keep it sincere. All of her arguments were in the book itself. I wanted her to speak directly to you, person to person, convicted murderer to reader.

Here is what she sent:

I have tried my best to write a final plea to your readers, and yet I find myself at a loss for words. I suppose mere words cannot express how it feels to be locked away for a crime I did not commit. I mean, what can I tell them that has not been said already?

The truth is, I am a convict, an inmate, a prisoner of the State of Georgia, and yet, I am not a murderer.

I did not kill Doug Benton.

Still, I remain behind bars.

What else can I do to prove my innocence?

I can't hand you a piece of paper or tangible piece of evidence that proves it. I don't have a fearless hero willing to stand up against my accusers and tell the truth. All I can do is tell you my side of the story, show you the documents I have, and point out the untruths and errors in my case. It's up to you to decide what you believe.

As far as I know, there are no other legal options for me. So I will wait for the five members of Georgia's parole board to decide when, or if, I am ever set free.

I will wait, but I will never give up! For I know that, if God is willing, the sun will rise tomorrow and with the new day there is renewed hope and a new opportunity for things to change. And until that day comes, I will remain always hopeful, always vigilant and always ready.

If you would like to help, letters of support for my release are always welcome.

Georgia State Board of Pardons and Parole
2 Martin Luther King, Jr. Drive S.E.
Balcony Level, East Tower
Atlanta, Georgia 30334-4909

To write to Tracy in prison:
Tracy Fortson – GDC ID: 0000621875
Arrendale State Prison
2023 Gainesville Hwy.
Alto, GA 30510

ABOUT THE AUTHOR

Serial-killer expert, lecturer, and acclaimed investigative journalist **M. William Phelps** is the *New York Times* best-selling and award-winning author of 34 nonfiction books. Winner of 2008 New England Book Festival Award for *I'll Be Watching You,* and the Excellence in (Investigative) Journalism award from the Society of Professional Journalists (2013) for his *Connecticut Magazine* article "Blonde, Blue-eyed & Gone," Phelps has appeared on CBS's *Early Show,* The Discovery Channel, ABC's *Good Morning America,* NBC's *Today* show, *The View,* TLC, BIO, History Channel, Oxygen's *Snapped, Killer Couples,* and *Captured,* USA Radio Network, Catholic Radio, ABC News Radio, and Radio America, which calls him "the nation's leading authority on the mind of the female murderer."

Currently, he is associate producer, consultant and expert for Piers Morgan on his yet-to-be-titled serial-killer series for ITV in Great Britain.

Phelps has written for the *Providence Journal, Hartford Courant, Connecticut Magazine,* and the *New London Day.* He has been profiled in such noted publications as *Writer's Digest,* the *New York Daily News, Newsday, Albany Times-Union, Hartford Courant,* and the *New York Post.* He has also consulted for the Showtime cable television series *Dexter.* He is a member of the Multidisciplinary Collaborative on Sexual Crime and Violence (MCSCV), also known as the

Atypical Homicide Research Group (AHRG) at Northeastern University. He lives in a small Connecticut farming community and can be reached at his author website: www.mwilliamphelps.com.

Look for M. William Phelps on Investigation Discovery in reruns of his series, *Dark Minds,* focusing on his travels investigating unsolved serial-killer cases, and in his longtime recurring role as a leading crime expert on the long-running series *Deadly Women.* In addition, Phelps annually films about 20 different guest spots on various crime series all over the cable dial. You can write to him via his website or by snail mail at P.O. Box 3215, Vernon, CT, 06066.

OTHER BOOKS BY M. WILLIAM PHELPS

Perfect Poison

Lethal Guardian

Every Move You Make

Sleep in Heavenly Peace

Murder in the Heartland

Because You Loved Me

If Looks Could Kill

I'll Be Watching You

Deadly Secrets

Cruel Death

Death Trap

Kill For Me

Love Her to Death

Too Young to Kill

Never See Them Again

Kiss of the She-Devil

Bad Girls

Obsessed

The Killing Kind

She Survived: Melissa (e-book)

She Survived: Jane (e-book)

I'd Kill For You

To Love and To Kill

One Breath Away

If You Only Knew

Don't Tell a Soul

Dangerous Ground

For More News About M. William Phelps
Signup For Our Newsletter:

http://wbp.bz/newsletter

Word-of-mouth is critical to an author's long-term success. If you appreciated this book please leave a review on the Amazon sales page:

http://wbp.bz/targeteda

Another Great True Crime
Read From WildBlue Press

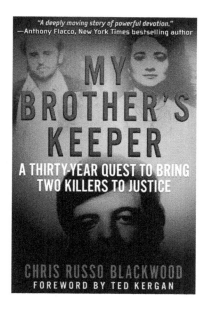

The moment he found out his brother was missing, Ted Kergan launched a relentless effort to bring two suspected killers—a teenaged-prostitute and her much older grifter boyfriend—to justice and find Gary Kergan's remains. Little did he know his quest would consume a fortune and take thirty years to reach a dramatic conclusion. MY BROTHER'S KEEPER is "a tremendous story of love and murder, faith and tenacity." (Steve Jackson, New York Times bestselling author of No Stone Unturned)

Read More: **http://wbp.bz/mbk**

Another Great True Crime
Read From WildBlue Press

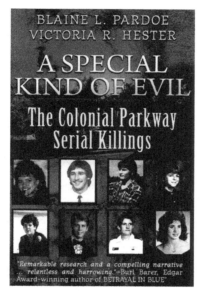

For four years in the 1980s, a killer, or killers, stalked Virginia's Tidewater region, carefully selecting victims, sending waves of terror into the local community. Now, father-daughter true crime authors Blaine Pardoe and Victoria Hester blow the dust off of these cases. Interviewing members of the families, friends, and members of law enforcement, they provide the first and most complete in-depth look at this string of horrific murders and disappearances. The author-investigators peel back the rumors and myths surrounding these crimes and provide new information never before revealed about the investigations.

Read More: **http://wbp.bz/aspecialkindofevil**

See even more at:
http://wbp.bz/tc

More True Crime You'll Love From WildBlue Press

RAW DEAL by Gil Valle

RAW DEAL: The Untold Story of the NYPD's "Cannibal Cop" is the memoir of Gil Valle, written with co-author Brian Whitney. It is part the controversial saga of a man who was imprisoned for "thought crimes," and a look into an online world of dark sexuality and violence that most people don't know exists, except maybe in their nightmares.

wbp.bz/rawdeal

BETRAYAL IN BLUE by Burl Barer & Frank C. Girardot Jr.

Adapted from Ken Eurell's shocking personal memoir, plus hundreds of hours of exclusive interviews with the major players, including former international drug lord, Adam Diaz, and Dori Eurell, revealing the truth behind what you won't see in the hit documentary THE SEVEN FIVE.

wbp.bz/bib

THE POLITICS OF MURDER by Margo Nash

"A chilling story about corruption, political power and a stacked judicial system in Massachusetts."–John Ferak, bestselling author of FAILURE OF JUSTICE.

wbp.bz/pom

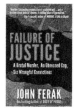

FAILURE OF JUSTICE by John Ferak

If the dubious efforts of law enforcement that led to the case behind MAKING A MURDERER made you cringe, your skin will crawl at the injustice portrayed in FAILURE OF JUSTICE: A Brutal Murder, An Obsessed Cop, Six Wrongful Convictions. Award-winning journalist and bestselling author John Ferak pursued the story of the Beatrice 6 who were wrongfully accused of the brutal, ritualistic rape and murder of an elderly widow in Beatrice, Nebraska, and then railroaded by law enforcement into prison for a crime they did not commit.

wbp.bz/foj

Made in the USA
Monee, IL
28 October 2020